Also by Barry Meisel:

Boss: The Mike Bossy Story (with Mike Bossy)

Losing the Edge

The Rise and Fall
of the Stanley Cup Champion
New York Rangers

Barry Meisel

Simon & Schuster

New York London Toronto Sydney Tokyo Singapore

SIMON & SCHUSTER
Rockefeller Center
1230 Avenue of the Americas
New York, NY 10020

Designed by Irving Perkins Associates

Manufactured in the United States of America

10   9   8   7   6   5   4   3   2   1

Library of Congress Cataloging-in-Publication Data

Meisel, Barry.
    Losing the edge : the rise and fall of the Stanley Cup champion
New York Rangers / Barry Meisel.
        p.   cm.
    1. New York Rangers (Hockey team)   I. Title.
GV848.N43M45   1995
796.96'264'097471—dc20   95-44892
                                                      CIP

ISBN 0-684-81519-2

Acknowledgments

Special thanks to my agents, David Black and Paul Chung, who bought the idea, sold the idea, and rode the roller coaster to New Jersey and back. And to Jeff Neuman and Frank Scatoni at Simon & Schuster and copy-editor Fred Chase, who nurtured and shaped the idea. And to Ira Checkla and John Hughes, who helped focus the idea.

Thanks to everyone on the Rangers' staff, all of whom helped in big ways: Jeanie Baumgartner, Frank Buonomo, Barbara Dand, John Gentile, Ann Marie Gilmartin, Kevin Kennedy, Rob Koch, Brad Kolodny, Matt Loughran, Kevin McDonald, John O'Sullivan, John Rosasco, Bill Short, Barry Watkins, Nicole Wetzold.

To the people who kindly contributed thoughts and words and deeds: Marv Albert, Glenn Anderson, Gary Bettman, Jeff Beukeboom, Brian Burke, Colin Campbell, Rob Campbell, Marg Cater, Bob Clarke, Pat Connolly, John Davidson, Mike Folga, Greg Gilbert, Adam Graves, Wayne Gretzky, Bob Gutkowski, Mike Hartman, Glenn Healy, Mike Hudson, Alexander Karpovtsev, Mike Keenan, Joe Kocur, Don Koharski, Alexei Kovalev, Nick Kypreos, Daniel Lacroix, Nathan LaFayette, Steve Larmer, Brian Leetch, Doug Lidster, Bruce Lifrieri, Kevin Lowe, Hal Macklin, Craig MacTavish, Stephane Matteau, Mike McCarthy, Mark Messier, Paul

Messier, Sal Messina, Joe Murphy, Mike Murphy, Bryan Murray, Petr Nedved, Sergei Nemchinov, Brian Noonan, Ed Olczyk, Mark Osborne, Benny Petrizzi, Arthur Pincus, Larry Pleau, Phil Pritchard, Jim Ramsay, Bernadette Ramsur, Mike Richter, Howie Rose, Sam Rosen, David Smith, Neil Smith, Esa Tikkanen, Dick Todd, Pat Verbeek, Jay Wells, Worldwide Pants, Sergei Zubov.

And to Jo Barefoot, Linda Cataffo, Dave Kaplan, Mike Lipack, Delores Thompson, Bill Turnbull, Barry Werner, and Kevin Whitmer inside the *New York Daily News;* Filip Bondy, Frank Brown, John Dellapina, John Giannone, and Colin Stephenson for their unparalleled playoff coverage in the *News;* Larry Brooks, Rich Chere, and Sherry Ross for keeping me sane. Also to Johnny Barounis, Mike Caruso, Mike Cohn, Debbie Cozeolino-Freed, Linda King, Mike Levine, Rick Minch, the team of Mike Oliveto and Rich Pike at All-Star Stats in Somers, New York, and Larry Sloman.

Finally, to Myron Shakter and all the long-suffering blue seaters in old Section 433 (may it R.I.P.), from the kid who did his high school journalism homework between periods in Row B, Seat 2, from 1973 to 1975.

Now we can live in peace.

A word about direct quotes:

In a vast majority of instances, the direct quotes from conversations for which the author was not present were obtained from one or more of the participants. In the remaining instances, the quotes were obtained from people who were told of the conversations by one or more of the participants.

For David and Jessica,
my Stanley Cup
champions, and Katy,
the coach of the team

Contents

Prologue

1

The celebration that had been fifty-four years in the making began at 10:59 P.M. Craig MacTavish knocked a faceoff into the corner, worked the final 1.6 seconds off the clock, and New York City erupted. On June 14, 1994, the Rangers lifted The Curse.

As the mob of players hugged and jigged near goalie Mike Richter's net, an eternally grateful constituency whose thunderous roar was once dubbed the Monster of Madison Square Garden rejoiced with equal measures of relief and delight. Grandfathers who were young boys when the Rangers last won a National Hockey League championship hugged granddaughters who see the world through the eyes of MTV. Businessmen in Armani suits, the ones who gladly paid as much as $2,500 for a ticket from some broker, high-fived the high school dropouts in backwards baseball caps, the kids who probably slipped some usher a twenty. They sang all their favorite songs: "Let's Go, Rangers" . . . "1994" . . . "1940" . . . "We Want the Cup."

"Now I Can Die In Peace," read one perfectly scripted cardboard message.

This scene lasted for seven minutes, and might have gone on all night if not for two men in navy blazers and white gloves who emerged from the center-ice runway underneath the WFAN radio perch at 11:06 P.M. These two guardians walked gingerly across the carpet that had been rolled onto the ice, carefully bearing the shiniest trophy the Garden had ever seen. The Stanley Cup had arrived. New York's perpetual wait was over.

Commissioner Gary Bettman grabbed the microphone. The team's captain, leader, and designated messiah, Mark Messier, broke out of a bearhug with MSG president Bob Gutkowski, the showman who had the guts and foresight to spend the night in a tuxedo. Bettman handed the grail to Messier, and the captain cradled the Cup as the Garden shook.

The Cup was passed by Messier to his best friend on the team, Kevin Lowe, who quickly handed it to Brian Leetch. Messier, who had won five Cups in Edmonton before the Rangers imported the superstar on October 4, 1991, with this night in mind, knew exactly how to orchestrate and milk the moment. Like a proud father at his child's graduation, he watched as his teammates took turns lifting the Cup. Once every Ranger had had a chance to fulfill his boyhood fantasy by bench-pressing the thirty-six-pound hardware overhead as he skated around the rink, Messier reclaimed the Cup and headed to the team's bench.

There, in front of the blue wall of New York City policemen unnecessarily bedecked in riot gear, Messier hoisted the Cup toward the arms of Mike Keenan, the embattled head coach who had been to the finals three times before and had lost each time, twice with Philadelphia to Messier's Edmonton Oilers, and once, in 1992 with Chicago, to Mario Lemieux's Pittsburgh Penguins. Keenan's broad smile stretched his mustache across his face as he turned and raised the Cup to the crowd, then handed it back to Messier. The captain had to take several strides along the ice to find the next honoree standing at the other end of the bench: Neil Smith, the president and general manager who needed only five years to help exorcise a city's fifty-four-year-old demon.

It surprised nobody that Keenan and Smith barely acknowledged each other that night. Although they had now accomplished everything they sought to achieve, their diametrically opposite personalities created an awkward working relationship even before training camp began. Keenan needed chaos and confrontation to thrive; he made demands and expected everyone around him—bosses and underlings—to satisfy him. He had no use for ceremony. Smith preferred order; he genuinely liked people, rarely played favorites, expected the loyalty he showed his employees to be returned, and was quite willing to stroke and be stroked to keep everyone happy. And Smith knew how to play the corporate game, although at times it drove him crazy.

Their relationship soured early in the regular season, the first time Keenan embarrassed Smith by ignoring protocol and going directly to Stanley Jaffe, the president of Paramount Communications, corporate owners of Madison Square Garden and the Rangers, to request a trade. Although he would eventually flaunt his disrespect for Smith's place in the corporate structure, Keenan wasn't being deliberately hostile by leapfrogging Smith and Gutkowski that time; he was simply heeding what he considered sage advice from the other powerful and highly successful coach in the corporation. When he first got the job, Keenan sought a few pointers from New York Knicks head coach Pat Riley. "Go to Jaffe," was how Riley suggested Keenan deal with any problem he needed addressed immediately.

Gutkowski and the Rangers' director of communications Barry Watkins spent most of the year holding the fractured Smith-Keenan relationship together and shielding it from public view. Gutkowski even got Keenan and Smith excited about each other for a short time before and after the March trading deadline, when he locked both men in his Penn Plaza office and instructed them to smooth over their differences and agree on a playoff plan. They did, and on March 21 the Rangers made three great trades to help solidify the roster that won the Cup. But the Smith-Keenan alliance deteriorated again late in the season and collapsed during the playoffs. It grew so bad they didn't speak during the finals.

The estrangement began during the grueling seven-game semifinal series against the cross-river rival New Jersey Devils, when Keenan's cold-blooded, combustible coaching style nearly destroyed the team and derailed the run toward the Cup. Unhappy with the way his key players were performing early in their Game 4 loss at New Jersey, Keenan inexplicably benched Messier and Leetch for most of the game, then concocted a preposterous story that the team's two best players and three others were badly injured.

Smith, who had regularly called Keenan "that madman" or "the pit bull" to his close friends and confidants almost from the moment he convinced Gutkowski and Jaffe that Keenan was worth hiring in April 1993, was furious. He knew that many of the players were incensed at their coach, too; they were so upset that Keenan hadn't given them a chance to win the game that it took a forty-five-minute closed-door meeting between Messier and Keenan at the Rangers' practice complex to quiet the turmoil. "I knew we just needed to win that series to win the Cup," Messier explained later. "It was important that he knew how close we were, and not to diminish our chances of winning by doing something crazy."

Exasperated as Smith was after the Rangers lost Game 5 to fall one game from elimination, he mellowed briefly when Messier guaranteed a victory in Game 6 and delivered a third-period hat trick to make good on it. And he damn near forgot about Keenan's gaffe after Game 7, when Stephane Matteau scored in double overtime to propel the Rangers to the finals.

But after the Rangers had won three of the first four games from the Vancouver Canucks to position themselves for the Cup, word leaked that Keenan was prepared to leave the Rangers to become the GM-coach of the Detroit Red Wings. Smith, who had once worked for Detroit and still knew many people in the organization, believed the story was true. So did a number of reputable people in and close to the Rangers' organization, people with extremely credible sources throughout the NHL. So did a handful of people around the league, people plugged into the network of very reliable information. They all had heard that Keenan's agent and attorney, Rob Campbell, had spoken to a Red Wings lawyer during the playoffs about Keenan becoming the club's GM-coach—whether the Rangers won the Cup or not.

Smith went berserk. Not because he didn't want his coach out; he did. He just couldn't believe that another Keenan controversy was threatening to derail the Rangers when the ultimate prize was just a win away. Over six agonizing days, as the Rangers lost the fifth game at home, and the sixth game at Vancouver, then finally won the agonizing and historic Game 7 by the slim margin of 3–2, Smith remained crazed with anger. He kept his comments off the record, but he made no attempt to hide his complete disgust with Keenan. It became common knowledge among the national and local media, even among Keenan's most loyal supporters, that Smith hated the man. This respected executive had become a petulant child crying to anyone who would listen.

Smith knew he couldn't fire Keenan after a Stanley Cup season, which further ignited his fury. Viacom Inc., the media conglomerate that had acquired the Rangers, the New York Knicks, the Garden, and the MSG Network earlier that season when it bought Paramount, was soliciting bids in excess of $1 billion for its sports package. The strict orders from above were simple: win or lose, the status quo must be maintained until a deal is done.

In his most immature moments, Smith vowed to friends that he would quit before he'd start another year with Keenan. He himself admitted he didn't know if he meant it, but he also admitted that his strained relationship with his coach sapped the fun out of running the Rangers. At such times, despite hollow public denials of the rift, Viacom's desire to keep its executive team intact, Gutkowski's futile attempt to play peacemaker, and New York City's brassy jubilance over the Rangers' success, it was obvious that either Smith or Keenan had to go.

Keenan, for his part, steadfastly and, to say the least, implausibly denied that he or his agent had talked to a representative of the Red Wings, or anybody, about a new job. He knew Smith despised him and wanted him out of the Rangers' lives, but he also knew Viacom intended to keep the front office in place. With four years left on his deal, a Cup on his résumé, and Detroit on his itinerary, he felt secure. He had no trouble telling reporters on the night of his greatest achievement that he intended to remain coach of the Rangers, "unless they fire me."

Twelve days later, with the afterglow of the triumph still lighting up New York, the architect of the city's sweetest championship season since the Miracle Mets of 1969 and the Knicks of 1970 sat anonymously in a first-class seat on American Airlines Flight 253, La Guardia to Toronto's Pearson International Airport, for a meeting that Keenan's lawyer had requested earlier that day.

Smith knew that Campbell wanted the same thing he did. After waiting a few days for the parties, celebrations, victory parades, and hangovers to end, the two men began struggling to concoct a way out of this sham marriage. Although he was furious at Campbell's client, Smith liked, respected, and trusted Campbell. And Campbell liked Smith, with whom he had negotiated before on behalf of Roger Neilson, whom Smith had hired as his first coach in 1989, and also Colin Campbell, Smith's longtime friend and coworker with the Red Wings, who left a job as an assistant coach in Detroit to join Neilson's staff in the summer of 1990.

As Smith silently rehearsed his plan to get Keenan out of his contract, the GM's thoughts kept drifting back to the champagne-drenched locker room, the wild postgame party at the Garden's Play-by-Play Club that lasted until 3 A.M., and the victory parade from Battery Park up Broadway's Canyon of Heroes to City Hall in front of 1.1 million New Yorkers.

For five years on the job, Smith, a Toronto native who became a New Yorker the day he was hired, dreamed of how wonderful life would be if the Rangers ever won the Stanley Cup. Twelve days after they had, on a summer Sunday, he couldn't stop asking himself the same three questions:

Did Rob summon me because he has a new, clever plan? If he doesn't, how can I get Keenan out? If I can't, how am I ever going to make it through another year with that madman?

The Pit Bull Arrives

2

He ordered a portrait of the Stanley Cup tacked to the wall as soon as he arrived. Handsomely framed and singularly illuminated under a bright track light, the picture of the grail was mounted over a walkway through which every Ranger had to pass every day on his way to the practice ice. There was to be no mistaking what was important in 1993–94. There was to be no forgetting. That reminder was one of a thousand little touches that not only emphasized Mike Keenan's attention to detail, but his vision of the task he inherited when he signed a five-year contract worth $5,110,875 on April 15, 1993.

From the day he was hired until the day he quit, Keenan believed that Smith had been reluctant to hire him, but was instructed to do so by Jaffe and Gutkowski. The truth is, Jaffe wanted Scotty Bowman, who was coaching in Pittsburgh but had let it be known he didn't plan to return.

Bowman had nearly become Smith's boss in the summer of 1989. That was when Smith, Detroit's director of scouting, was initially offered the GM's job by former MSG president Jack Diller after Phil Esposito was fired, but a few days before his official signing Diller asked him to let Bowman temporarily act as his mentor while he learned on the job. Smith, who had little choice, said yes; but Bowman, after meeting with Diller and Smith and listening to the Rangers' plan, said no.

Although four years had passed since the Rangers nearly blew the opportunity to grab one of the NHL's bright young executives, Smith knew he wouldn't be comfortable with Bowman as his coach. He believed there was one better choice on the open market, one experienced leader who could whip the talented, underachieving, unfocused club he knew he had into a Stanley Cup champion.

Smith convinced Gutkowski it had to be Keenan.

He did it during one long conversation in Smith's fourth-floor Garden office, on Thursday, April 14, two days before the end of the 1992–93 regular season, while interim head coach Ron Smith floundered through a season-ending seven-game losing streak. Gutkowski wasn't sure whom he preferred, Jaffe's first choice or Smith's. All three men knew it had to be one or the other.

They knew they needed a Pat Riley, someone strong enough to carry the emotional baggage of fifty-three years without a Cup, someone unwilling to hide from The Curse. Although they were about to miss the playoffs, they knew they had a championship-caliber team. They just needed a championship-caliber coach. Smith reminded Gutkowski of Keenan's immediate success in Philadelphia and Chicago. He explained how Keenan's iron-fisted style was perfectly suited for a team that had spent nearly four cozy seasons under the fatherly Roger Neilson, and hadn't gotten past the second round of the playoffs in 1990 (despite finishing first in the Patrick Division), 1991, or 1992 (when they won the Presidents' Trophy for the best regular-season record in the league).

Neither Smith nor Gutkowski was particularly concerned with the fact that Keenan's teams burnt out and flopped the year after they reached the Stanley Cup finals. They didn't care that Keenan only lasted from 1984–88 with Philadelphia and from 1988–92 with Chicago. They were more worried about how he fought with and eventually divorced himself from management in both places because of his inability to work constructively with and respect his superiors.

The Rangers knew, for example, that in the midst of a wild brawl at the end of the pregame warm-up before Game 4 of the 1987 Stanley Cup semifinals between the Flyers and Canadiens, Flyers owner Ed Snider had raced toward Keenan, who was standing in the tunnel near the visitor's dressing room and looking onto the ice while his players, some of whom had returned to the ice in various stages of undress, wrestled with their opponents in a horrifying scene.

"Mike, you've got to get out there and stop it," Snider said.

"Shut up and get out of here," Keenan shouted at the Flyers' founder.

They knew, too, about his insatiable desire for power. They knew that

Keenan was fired by Chicago in November 1992 for insisting that senior vice president Bob Pulford be fired. Pulford was the GM when Keenan was hired as head coach in June 1988, but was delicately reassigned by owner Bill Wirtz in June 1990 to make good on a promise to Keenan that he would become GM-coach. Two years later, after Keenan had agreed to concentrate solely on general managerial duties, it wasn't enough that he had a four-year contract and the authority to run the entire hockey operation. He told a club attorney he wanted his job description in writing. "And I want Pully out," he demanded.

"Mike, if you're saying it's Pully or you, you're out," he was told.

But for all the legitimate reasons not to hire him—including the fact that he was sure to ask for a staggering contract—Smith kept returning to the fact that the Rangers were good enough to win the Cup if they had the right coach leading them. And he knew that if he didn't hire the right coach, if the Rangers failed again in 1993–94, the team would lose the prestige and credibility it had built the previous few years, and he'd probably lose his job. "Mike Keenan gives us our best chance," he finally said.

"Are you sure, Neil?" Gutkowski asked. "He's like a hurricane. When he hits shore, the damage occurs."

"I can deal with the devil," Smith said, "as long as he wins."

Gutkowski leaned over, looked Smith in the eye and replied, "You may have to. But now let's go see if we can get him."

Gutkowski called Jaffe, reported that Smith had targeted Keenan as his first choice, and said they were planning to fly to Toronto to quickly close the deal. Jaffe approved. Smith called Keenan's attorney, Rob Campbell, and made arrangements for the four men to meet the next day in Toronto.

Campbell set the ground rules. Keenan was flying to Germany that weekend to coach Team Canada in the World Championships, and he planned to leave with an NHL contract in hand, so a deal had to be finalized immediately. He told the Rangers that Keenan was already weighing other possibilities. The Detroit Red Wings, who had actually signed Keenan to a future contract the previous winter but voided it with Keenan's permission after owner Mike Ilitch encountered resistance from within and changed his mind, were interested again. The expansion Mighty Ducks of Anaheim had asked him to consider becoming their first GM-coach. And the Flyers had already offered a five-year, $5 million contract that Keenan showed the Rangers. After not making the playoffs since 1989, Snider's painful memory of Keenan's incorrigibility was overshadowed by the team's unsatisfactory bottom line.

Gutkowski and Smith arrived armed. After a round of handshakes and a few brief pleasantries at Campbell's downtown Toronto office, they had lunch at a nearby hotel. Then they returned to Campbell's office.

Neither side danced. Gutkowski addressed his biggest fear, that there existed the potential for disaster, since Keenan had been the GM-coach in Chicago, liked the power that came with the dual role, and had earned his reputation for being unwilling to work smoothly with superiors.

"You're not going to be the GM here," Gutkowski said. "Can you be just a coach again? Can you work with Neil?"

Keenan said he was positive he could. He said he was struggling with the long periods away from his fourteen-year-old daughter, Gayla, and wanted the freedom to spend summers with her at his cottage on Georgian Bay in Ontario. He insisted he no longer wanted the twelve-month, twenty-four-hour-a-day hockey life that was sapping time from his family.

"I don't want to be a GM," he said. "I just want to coach. I enjoy that more than anything. I know I can work with Neil."

"You know, Mike, we're not here because we think you can make us competitive again," Gutkowski replied. "We think you can make us win the Stanley Cup. That's why we're in Toronto today and that's why we're not leaving until we find out if you really want the job."

Keenan began selling himself to the Rangers. He said he hungered for the challenge of winning the Cup in New York, of ending the drought that had overwhelmed so many players and coaches before him. He said not only didn't it scare him, it exhilarated him.

What he didn't say was that his marriage was in trouble, that his wife of twenty-one years, Rita, was not going with him no matter where he went. He didn't say that the Rangers were his first choice because he had already done Philly, he wasn't sure he wanted to spend five years building an expansion team in Anaheim, and the challenge of winning in Detroit didn't compare with the challenge of winning in a vast metropolis where he could lose himself in his job. The discussions lasted all day. Finally, Gutkowski and Smith huddled privately in Campbell's office. Both men knew they wanted him. Both men knew they were going to have to match the Flyers' five-year, $5 million offer to get Keenan to say yes immediately, and they wanted an immediate answer as badly as Keenan did. So the Rangers presented Campbell with this offer, an unbelievable contract for a coach who had been fired twice in five years:

$660,875 signing bonus payable immediately, of which $160,875 was considered salary for April 15 through June 30, 1993.
$750,000 for the 1993–94 season.

$850,000 for the 1994–95 season.

$900,000 for the 1995–96 season.

$950,000 for the 1996–97 season.

$1,000,000 for the 1997–98 season.

$50,000 bonus for any season in which the Rangers finished first over-all; $25,00 if they finished second overall.

$40,000 bonus for any season in which the Rangers finished first in the Eastern Conference.

$25,000 bonus for any season in which the Rangers finished first in their division.

$50,000 bonus for any season in which the Rangers won their first play-off round.

$75,000 bonus for any season in which the Rangers won their second playoff round.

$100,000 bonus for any season in which the Rangers won their third playoff round.

$200,000 bonus for any season in which the Rangers won the Stanley Cup.

$25,000 bonus for any season in which Keenan won the Jack Adams Award as coach of the year; $12,500 if he finished second in the voting, $7,500 if he finished third.

- An annuity that pays $50,000 per year from October 21, 2004, the day Keenan turns fifty-five, until his death.
- A maximum of $5,000 per year, for five years, for the purchase of a life insurance policy of Keenan's choice.
- A car phone, a computer with printer, a fax machine, and a satellite dish for his home.
- The club's choice of a fully insured automobile, or an $850 per month automobile allowance.
- A maximum of $50,000 moving allowance to cover the cost of his transfer from Chicago.
- All closing costs on the sale of his Chicago home and the purchase of a home in New York.
- A $975,000 personal loan for the purchase of a $1.3 million home in Greenwich, Connecticut, payable within five years at a rate of 5 percent.
- All employee stock option and/or stock ownership plans, 401(k) matching contribution plans, medical, dental, group life, disability, and accidental death and dismemberment insurance that were cus-

tomarily made available to the management of Madison Square Garden Center, Inc.

The guaranteed value landed a few bucks over $5.11 million. The bonus package was worth a potential $3 million if the Rangers won five straight Cups, and realistically figured to net Keenan another $500,000 to $1 million if the unthinkable happened and he lasted all five years, or if they won just one Cup.

Keenan said yes. Suddenly, he was rich.

Three days later he was sick, flat on his back in a Munich hospital.

On the morning of the happy Garden press conference in which Smith handed Keenan a black leather Ranger jacket and then hugged him after Keenan put it on, Keenan cut himself shaving. It wouldn't have mattered, except that Keenan was then driven by limousine from the Garden to ABC-TV's Manhattan studio for an interview to be aired the following day between periods of the network's playoff coverage. He was rushed directly from the studio by limousine to Kennedy Airport for his flight to Germany, and he was in such a hurry that he forgot to remove the heavy blush that was applied to his neck and face to dull the bright TV lights. Hours later, on the plane, he began feeling queasy. He noticed that his neck and chest had swelled grotesquely. He was suffering from an infection.

Still, he coached Team Canada, a collection of NHL players from teams that had missed the playoffs. Eric Lindros of the Philadelphia Flyers was one of his top players. So were two Rangers, Adam Graves and Mike Gartner, who were still smarting from the Rangers' inexplicably bad season.

Barry Watkins, the Rangers' director of communications, flew to Germany with Smith a few days after Keenan to begin preparing the new coach for the overwhelming public relations aspect of the job. Watkins knew that Keenan's image and reputation with the media were not sterling. He wanted to prep Keenan on ways to enhance his relationship with the press and the public, so he prepared a two-hundred-page manual, an introduction to the New York media.

Watkins wrote biographies on every columnist and hockey beat writer in town. He explained how the seven newspapers that most closely cover the team—*Daily News, Post, Times, Newsday,* Gannett's Westchester-Rockland papers, *Newark Star-Ledger,* and *Bergen Record*—went about their business. He described WFAN, the city's twenty-four-hour, all-sports radio station that carried the Rangers' games, but covered the team with an independent and critical eye. He explained the unique relationship with cable TV station MSG Network, an arm of the Garden that also treated the Rangers as news, and was definitely not a house organ.

He wrote chapters and clipped stories that detailed some recent media–head coach sagas in New York, like Ray Handley's forgettable two years feuding with the media that covered the Giants, and Bud Harrelson's constant PR problems as manager of the Mets. He also showed Keenan how Pat Riley of the New York Knicks and Buck Showalter of the Yankees maintained pristine images that enabled them to better do the jobs they were hired to do.

Watkins never got his head start, because Keenan was too busy shuttling between the hospital by day and Team Canada's bench by night. He did get some time alone with him at their hotel, but that only served to underscore how incoherent Keenan was from the illness, the medication, and coaching stress.

Watkins was awakened one morning when his phone rang at 9 A.M. "Barry, Mike Keenan," the caller said, using his first and last names to identify himself, something he did over the phone with Watkins even to the day he quit, although they had become good friends and this impersonal intro had become a running joke. "I want you to come to my room. And would you bring Kevin with you?"

Kevin was Kevin McDonald, the Rangers' assistant PR director. McDonald was in Germany on behalf of the NHL. The two arrived at Keenan's suite a few minutes later, settled into the sitting area, and noticed how serious Keenan looked.

"I want to talk to you about something personal," Keenan began somberly. "I know we're going to be working together closely, I know your reputations, you're the best. So I want you to hear this from me. I'm going to get divorced from my wife."

The men were stunned. Stunned not only at the news, but surprised that Keenan was sharing this with them. Watkins asked if Keenan's acceptance of the job in New York played a role in the breakup.

"No, no, no. It has nothing to do with it. We've had some problems for a while. It's been a real tough process of long distance, no time. It's going to become public, and I'm going to want you to tell me how to handle it."

Watkins recommended that Keenan discuss it openly with the media, because it would make him a more likable figure, an average Joe rather than the Napoleonic Iron Mike. As he spoke, Keenan's eyes reddened. He was groggy from the drugs, his guard was down, and he was genuinely sad. This poignant conversation had gone on for twenty minutes when Don Beauchamp, Team Canada's PR director, knocked on the door.

"Mike, I'm sorry, I need to go over a few things for a few minutes," Beauchamp said. Keenan apologized, excused himself into another room with Beauchamp, and left Watkins and McDonald waiting.

Twenty minutes later, he returned. Beauchamp left.

"I asked you guys to come in here because there's something serious to talk about," Keenan began again. "I want you to know it from me first. I'm getting divorced from my wife."

McDonald looked at Watkins, who gazed back at McDonald and then Keenan in disbelief. Was he joking? Was this some kind of a gag or stunt? They didn't know what to say. So Watkins went along, repeating his first question about whether the breakup had anything to do with his coming to New York.

"No, no, no," Keenan recited again. For the next twenty minutes he convinced the two PR guys he wasn't goofing because he told the exact same story, grew emotional at the exact same times, asked the exact same questions, listened to the exact same advice. He was out of it. That's how sick he was. Watkins and McDonald got very little accomplished. Smith, who was in Germany primarily to scout but had hoped to start assessing the roster and brainstorming the season's plans in Keenan's spare time, got nothing accomplished.

Germany was a waste of time.

The roster that Neil Smith gave Keenan on April 17, 1993, was not good enough to win the Stanley Cup. That would have been a polite, professional way of stating Keenan's opinion in late July, when Smith and assistant GM for player development Larry Pleau held their first organizational meeting with the new coaching staff—Keenan, associate coach Colin Campbell, and recently hired assistant coach Dick Todd—in Rye.

Keenan expressed this view more directly. In front of his bosses, his assistant coaches, and his trusted attorney, Rob Campbell, he ripped the team. He didn't think it had enough toughness or grit. He didn't think it was big enough. He had enough fancy players to succeed in the 84-game regular season, but he didn't think he had enough warriors to withstand the grueling, two-month Stanley Cup playoff marathon. He wanted more players whose names were already etched on the Cup, or had reached the finals, and knew how much rougher and meaner those games were. He wanted more players who had played for him, and had proven they were willing to do anything once the playoffs began.

The difference between hockey's regular season and playoffs is much bigger than that between the regular seasons and postseasons in football, baseball, and basketball. Although the intensity grows with the rising stakes in all four sports, only in hockey does the game's basic cadence and strategy change.

Since only twelve of the NFL's thirty teams make the playoffs, a single-elimination tournament over a month of Sundays that leads to the Super Bowl, regular season games are critical. Teams plot playoff game plans no differently than they do regular-season strategy.

Only eight of major-league baseball's twenty-eight teams make the playoffs, and only four made them from 1969 to 1993. The 162-game schedule is a true test of a team. The Championship Series and World Series pair two teams in best-of-seven series that belie the better regular-season team's superiority as often as they demonstrate it.

The NBA's regular-season and playoff schedules most resemble the NHL's, but basketball relies almost exclusively on individual matchups all year long. And its championship trophy, named after former commissioner Walter Kennedy, lacks the legendary history of a Cup that existed for twenty-four years before the NHL was born in 1917–18.

Since sixteen of twenty-six teams make the NHL playoffs, all a top team does for six months is meander across North America playing a game every two or three days. It rarely sees even its closest rival more than once a month. Individual matchups are uncommon, and those that do occur can rarely be preplanned for more than a day or two; they last only sixty minutes, and then it's off to another game in another city, against another team with another style.

The playoffs, on the other hand, condense seven games against the same foe into a twelve-day span. The threat of elimination in two weeks from a tournament for which they've spent six months preparing turns ordinary checkers into robust bangers. Total goals decrease as teams concentrate more on defense. Players too timid to block slap shots for eighty-four games regularly begin sliding face-first toward enemy stick blades. Superstars who found opportunities to coast during the regular season do nothing but eat, sleep, and think hockey.

That's why Keenan loved Mark Messier as his captain, leader, and number one center. He had coached Messier twice before, with Team Canada at the 1987 and 1991 Canada Cup Tournaments, and he knew that Messier's appetite for winning was as insatiable as his own. But Keenan wasn't sure Brian Leetch was mentally or physically tough enough to be his team's top defenseman. He wanted left wing Adam Graves as a power forward, but he didn't want Mike Gartner as his scoring right wing because he felt Gartner lacked the indomitable commitment to success he was going to demand. And there were plenty of goaltenders around the NHL, he believed, who were more skilled and more reliable than Mike Richter.

Keenan liked the towering and muscular defenseman Jeff Beukeboom, who had won Cups with Edmonton in 1987, 1988, and 1990, but he had no use for James Patrick, a skilled and speedy defenseman who had been a Ranger since 1984, but who had failed to achieve the stardom most had predicted for him a decade ago. Irritating left wing–center Esa Tikkanen, another Oiler import who had arrived with four rings on his fingers, was far more integral a piece to Keenan's puzzle than crafty center Darren Turcotte, who scored his 25 to 30 goals but was far too passive for Keenan.

The new head coach hadn't met most of his players as of this late July powwow, but that day he would have gladly traded Leetch for his number one defenseman from Chicago, Chris Chelios, if he could have. He would have traded Richter for his number one goalie from Chicago, Ed Belfour. He turned the tables on Smith by asking him, "Do you think the team, as is, could win the Stanley Cup?"

"I think we have the nucleus," Smith replied.

Smith and Keenan left Rye that day pointed in different directions. Keenan incorrectly believed Smith wanted the status quo, and that incensed him. Smith didn't know what Keenan wanted. He drove back to his Garden office humbled, depressed, and confused. He was puzzled by Keenan's detached yet confrontational approach because a month earlier, at the NHL expansion draft, they had worked together so smoothly.

Because teams could only protect one goaltender before Anaheim and Florida stocked their new franchises, the Rangers knew they were going to lose John Vanbiesbrouck. Smith wanted to get something in return for the talented goalie, so he shopped him around the league all year. The problem was, any team that took him would have to expose another of its own goaltenders to the expansion teams, so nobody bit—until minutes before the trade deadline before the draft.

Smith convinced Vancouver GM Pat Quinn to take Vanbiesbrouck and expose him along with Kay Whitmore, a young goalie the Canucks wanted behind their number one goalie, Kirk McLean. Smith was certain that Florida coach Roger Neilson was going to reunite himself with Vanbiesbrouck; since teams could only lose one goalie to expansion, he told Quinn this was the Canucks' only way of holding on to Whitmore.

Smith explained that he also had a deal arranged with Winnipeg, so he proposed the following to Quinn: if the Canucks still lost Whitmore, Smith would send Quinn a third-round draft pick, Quinn would send Vanbiesbrouck to Winnipeg, and the Jets would send goalie Bob Essensa to New York. If the Canucks kept Whitmore, the Rangers would get Doug Lidster, a useful thirty-three-year-old defenseman from Vancouver to help beef up the team's depth. Winnipeg would be left out.

Florida took Vanbiesbrouck, as Smith predicted. With him gone, Keenan needed an experienced backup to play the 20 or 25 games he didn't give his number one goalie. He liked veteran Glenn Healy, whom the Islanders had left unprotected. So Smith worked a deal with Tampa Bay GM Phil Esposito. The Lightning, a second-year franchise eligible to draft a goalie from Anaheim or Florida in Phase II of the expansion draft, drafted Healy and traded him to the Rangers for the third-round draft pick Smith didn't have to give the Canucks.

It was an excellent example of what Gutkowski expected from his two top hockey people, of how he imagined Smith's and Keenan's talents could blend without strife. Keenan told Smith what he needed, and Smith got it without paying too high a price. It happened again on July 29, a few days after the Rye meeting, when at Keenan's urging Smith signed free agent Greg Gilbert, a dependable checking left wing who had won a Cup with the Islanders in 1983 and played three years under Keenan in Chicago.

But Smith quickly saw that to Keenan, loyalty and the team concept were not reciprocal. The preseason began with two games in London, England, against the Toronto Maple Leafs. The Rangers won both games at the end of a whirlwind five days of practices and public appearances on behalf of the mustard company sponsoring the event. There was virtually no time for Keenan to huddle with Smith until after the 5–3 and 3–1 victories, when the Rangers flew home by commercial jet.

Flights home from road games are when all NHL staffs huddle to assess their recent game or strings of games. With their thoughts fresh and hours of dead time ahead, it's a constructive way to break the monotony of travel. That's what Smith was thinking when he left his wife, Katia, and headed over to where Rob Campbell, Colin Campbell, and Dick Todd were seated together. All the Rangers' coaches and executives were in business class, adequately separated from the players in coach. But as Smith looked around, he couldn't find Keenan.

"Rob, where's Mike sitting?" Smith asked Campbell.

"Oh, Mike's not on the plane," the attorney replied. "He went right to Chicago. Didn't he tell you that?"

Since the London contingent wasn't due on the ice until two days later in Glens Falls, New York, the village in the Adirondack Mountains near Lake George where the rookies had opened their camp, Keenan planned to spend a day with his daughter and estranged wife. Not only hadn't he asked Smith permission to do this, he didn't tell the GM of his plans, nor did he instruct anyone to do so.

"That's when I knew the guy didn't respect the chain of command and the way people have to work together at this level," Smith said. "He didn't even bother to talk to me, to tell me where he was going."

A week later, Smith and Keenan sat in the press box atop the Glens Falls Civic Center watching a scrimmage with Pleau, Colin Campbell, and Todd, when Keenan began discussing the team's defense.

"Leetch is your number one defenseman," Keenan said to the GM. "Who's your number two?"

"Well, Mike, I don't really do it that way," Smith replied.

"You have to do it that way."

"Okay, then our number two has always been Patrick, but I hope this year it's Zubov."

Muscovite Sergei Zubov was a talented, erratic defenseman whose perpetual five-o'clock shadow made him look far older than twenty-three. He was a fifth-round pick in 1990 who played four seasons for the Red Army team and was a member of the Commonwealth of Independent States' gold-medal-winning team at the 1992 Olympics.

Zubov arrived for the 1992–93 season, but split time between New York and the Rangers' minor-league affiliate in Binghamton, New York. He displayed offensive promise, but lacked the defensive seasoning necessary to play regularly in the NHL. Worse, he had already fallen into Keenan's doghouse before the London junket because his aerobic capacity was among the worst on the team when the players were tested during precamp physicals.

Keenan scowled when Smith mentioned his name.

"Would you trade Zubov for Grimson?" he asked the GM.

Stu Grimson was Keenan's goon in Chicago. "Grim Reaper" was the left wing's nickname. He was twenty-eight years old, 6-5 and 227 pounds.

"I certainly wouldn't want to," Smith replied.

"But you'd do it if it'd win you a Cup, right?"

"Mike, I'd do anything to win us a Cup."

Keenan dropped the subject, and never again suggested so preposterous a deal. Throughout the preseason, though, Keenan continued to demand that Smith make the moves he had urged in July. Impatiently, with no knowledge of the state of Smith's negotiations with Beukeboom's agent, Keenan pushed Smith to sign Beukeboom, a training camp holdout asking for an exorbitant contract.

Keenan rarely confronted Smith directly. Instead he sent messages. Some were subtle suggestions to the PR staff, others were outbursts to the media. The first one was the worst. It happened on September 23 at Nassau Coliseum, after the Rangers lost 4–2 to the Islanders. With Smith standing twenty-five feet away in the narrow hallway outside the visitor's dressing room, Keenan loudly blamed the GM for the team's makeup, one he said was too physically weak for the championship run. When asked if he was going to make changes, he said, "That's up to the general manager, not me."

When asked if he had told Smith he needed more rugged players, the coach replied, "I've suggested we need more physical players, yes."

Finally, out of reporters' earshot, he flung one final salvo when he said with disgust, "I'm working for a guy who thinks this team is good enough to win the Cup."

Keenan's mouth betrayed him again before Opening Night, although this time he only embarrassed himself. During the London trip, he had agreed to wear a wireless microphone for MSG Network's telecast. It offered viewers a terrific new perspective. When executive producer Mike McCarthy and producer Joe Whelan asked the coach a few weeks later in the preseason if he'd wear one again, Keenan agreed.

Keenan must have forgotten about the mike, though, because near the end of the game he cursed at the officials, a profane little tirade captured wonderfully by modern technology and broadcast into thousands of metropolitan area homes. Keenan didn't realize this until he was asked in the postgame press conference if he thought live profanity over the air was part of the image he intended to project this season.

At first he was confused. He looked at Watkins.

"What are you talking about?" he asked.

Told that he had cursed on air, Keenan went berserk. He finished his press conference in a huff, then started screaming to Watkins about the two producers, claiming they had failed to activate a seven-second delay that would have censored his expletives. Watkins wanted to avoid a confrontation, so he tried accepting blame for the snafu. Keenan shrugged him aside.

"Don't you try to be a good guy, Barry. It's not your fuckin' fault. It's their fault. They fucked me. They fucked me. Get me McCarthy and Whelan. Now."

The game hadn't been over thirty minutes, so the producers were still busy. They weren't about to drop what they were doing simply because they were summoned by Keenan. The coach waited about ten minutes, seething, and then decided to leave. He was headed for the fifth-floor elevator in the runway behind the dressing rooms when he coincidentally met up with McCarthy and Whelan, who had just left the MSG studio on the fourth floor.

"You fuckin' cocksuckers. You fucked me," Keenan spewed, his furrowed brow and curled mustache inches from their faces. "You could have hit the button. You fucked me. You could have hit the button."

Whelan, who always wore a smile, was surprised to be treated this way, especially by a guy who a month earlier had needed a big favor from him. Keenan wanted to open training camp by showing his players a video history of famous parades down Broadway's Canyon of Heroes, so he asked Whelan to create one. The producer spent a lot of time and effort on the project, and he delivered a wonderfully edited, stirring depiction of famous New York City celebrations like the ticker-tape parade for the 1969 Mets.

As Keenan bellowed, Whelan silently wondered how this could be the same man he had just helped out.

McCarthy, like Whelan a good-natured professional whom Keenan couldn't intimidate, calmly explained that there was no delay button, that such a device didn't exist on this live TV telecast, and that there never was any discussion of a delay button. He let Keenan vent, continued to politely defend the network's intentions, and explained that the episode was embarrassing for all concerned.

And that was that.

Everyone employed by the Rangers, from Smith to the players to the part-time assistant water boy, quickly learned that Keenan was most comfortable in an environment of fear and intimidation. Those were the working conditions he established. Watkins was one of the very few people whom Keenan let know it was an act.

"Murph, Murph," Keenan screamed at equipment trainer Joe Murphy before one meaningless preseason game. "What the fuck is a garbage can doing here? This is a professional locker room." Keenan grabbed the small plastic can that might have been one foot from where it should have been and fired it down the hallway.

Ridiculous incidents like that happened all the time. Keenan would get stick boys running around in a panic because a picture frame was cracked or off-center. As he watched people scurry he'd invariably wink at Watkins. "I got those guys going," he would say with a sardonic smile.

Keenan created hysteria inadvertently as well. Two hours before the season opener, at home on October 5 against Boston, ten to fifteen people were eating their pregame meals at circular tables in a tiny room across the hall from the Rangers' dressing room. The Rangers set up this small convenient buffet of salads, cold cuts, and drinks for the coaches, doctors, trainers, and equipment staff to grab before games. A few people were helping themselves at the buffet table and others were already eating when Keenan quietly walked in with Watkins. Keenan grabbed a plate, looked around and innocently said, "There doesn't seem to be any more rolls."

"No," replied Watkins, who was busy handling pregame media requests and didn't stop to eat. "It looks like they ran out."

"Anybody know where they keep the rolls?" Keenan asked nobody in particular.

While Keenan sat down to eat his salad and cold cuts, Watkins returned to the hallway. He couldn't believe what happened next. In ten minutes he counted twelve people—including trainer Dave Smith, physical therapist Howie Wenger, team psychologist Cal Botterill, and stick boy Tommy Horvath—who asked him if he knew where the rolls were or the person to call to get more rolls. This was without Keenan screaming, without him uttering anything more than an offhanded, "Did anybody see the rolls?" This was the environment he had created. He had everybody on edge. And he loved it.

The Rangers split the first two games of the Keenan Regime at home, then practiced at Rye before flying to Pittsburgh for their road opener. Before they left, Keenan summoned Ed Olczyk to his office for a role meeting, something he liked to do with players he was hardly using.

Olczyk (pronounced OLE-check) was a twenty-seven-year-old center and left wing who had been acquired midway through the previous season. He was a speedy 1984 U.S. Olympian who at the age of eighteen saw a dream come true when his hometown Chicago Blackhawks made him the third overall pick in the 1984 draft.

He played three seasons in Chicago, then was traded to Toronto, where he became a star. He scored a career-high 42 goals in 1987–88 and a career-high 90 points the following season. Toronto sent him to Winnipeg in 1990, and Smith got him two years later for ruffians Kris King and Tie Domi.

Olczyk wasn't Keenan's type of forward. He was a stylist, not a banger, and he hadn't played on a team that lasted more than one playoff round since 1985. Keenan buried him without giving him a chance. He hardly played Olczyk in the preseason and he scratched the forward from the first two games at home, the 4–3 loss to Boston and the 5–4 win over Tampa Bay.

Keenan was behind his desk when Olczyk entered for his role meeting.

Campbell and Todd were seated on the couch next to the desk. Olczyk sat in the chair facing Keenan's desk, folded one leg over his other knee, and listened.

"Eddie, we haven't given you a chance and I don't know if we're gonna," Keenan said. "But tell me something. What can you do for me?"

"I can tell you everything I can do for you," Olczyk replied. "But it's not what I say, it's what I do. I'm a player. I want to play. When you weren't coaching, Mike, you wanted to coach. I can tell you I can score for you, I can tell you I'll check, I can bust my ass for you in practice. But I have to be able to show you what I can do on the ice, in games."

Olczyk made sure he made occasional eye contact with the assistants listening intently on the couch. But after what seemed like five minutes, he turned back to Keenan and noticed the head coach gazing out his office window, looking bored. Finally, Keenan looked back at Olczyk and down at his shoes.

"Are those really alligator shoes?" Keenan asked.

Olczyk paused, not knowing if his coach was serious, "Yeah," he finally said.

"Oh. Okay. Thanks," Keenan said. Then he looked away from the player and shuffled a few papers to signal the end of the conversation. Silently, Olczyk rose and walked out.

"He was just testing me," Olczyk told himself. "To see how I'd react."

The Rangers visited Pittsburgh the following night, the beginning of the end of James Patrick's Ranger career. During a second period in which Keenan said the most tenured Ranger "let his teammates down and did not play competitively," he benched the defenseman. He was, however, forced to insert him back onto his defensive rotation in the third period, after Kevin Lowe bruised his foot and Jay Wells and Doug Lidster took penalties.

The Penguins' Martin Straka broke a 2–2 tie on a power play with six minutes left. Although Patrick was on the ice, he was not directly at fault for the goal. Still, Keenan seethed after the 3–2 loss. Smith walked down from the press box intending to discuss the game with his coach in an office adjacent to the visitor's dressing room, as GMs always do with coaches after games on the road. But when Smith arrived, he found Keenan pacing outside the office in the hallway where he had just met the media.

Without a nod, a word, or even a grumbling "goddamn it, we lost," the coach strode over to Smith as soon as he saw him approaching, stuck his nose in the GM's face, and blamed the loss on the defenseman he wanted immediately off the team.

"You can trade that fuckin' Patrick or do whatever you want," Keenan hissed. "He'll never wear the uniform again."

"Mike, I'm not his father," Smith said. "I'll get rid of anybody you want. This isn't personal."

It wasn't long before players, management, and support staffers all learned that Keenan could be tolerable or even charming after victories, but would be a nightmare to be around after losses, always looking to blame someone to keep the onus from falling on his shoulders. Unlike coaches who reserve their wrath for their best players, making an example to the team of those who can best take the heat, Keenan would often single out those in the most insecure positions.

Mike Hartman was the last man on the team, a twenty-six-year-old left wing born and raised in Detroit who played five years in Buffalo before bouncing from Winnipeg to Tampa Bay to the Rangers. He was a fighter, a plugger, an insurance policy. Hartman fell even further down the depth chart when the Rangers claimed center Mike Hudson off Chicago's roster in the October waiver draft. Hartman was of little use to Keenan, who didn't think he had enough NHL talent to rate a regular spot on the roster. That's what Keenan told him at their role meeting when Hartman insisted he could play regularly in the NHL as he had since 1988.

"Difficult things happen in life," Keenan told Hartman. "Sometimes you get a raw deal. Life isn't fair, Mike. Life isn't fair. It's just not fair."

Hartman realized he was going to be a season-long whipping boy as early as the first period of the Rangers' fifth game. The Rangers were already down 2–0 in the first period to Quebec when Hartman got a shift with Adam Graves at center and Joey Kocur, the team's fighter and one of the league's most feared punchers, at right wing. This grinding line was instructed to dump the puck deep into the Nordiques' zone and forecheck their defense. When Hartman got the puck, however, he failed to drive it deep enough, committing a turnover.

Play carried back up ice, flowing back and forth for twenty to thirty seconds, and then Quebec scored to make it 3–0. His head bowed, Hartman glided back to the bench with his linemates. Keenan awaited.

"You just cost me a goal," Keenan barked. "You cost the team the game. You'll never play for me again. Now just sit down."

The game continued. Healy replaced Richter in goal after the first period. The Rangers mounted a comeback. At one point, Keenan shouted, "Kocur . . . Hudson, next up," deliberately leaving out the left wing on the fourth line, which was supposed to be Hartman. When Hartman rose, Keenan grabbed the back of his collar and yanked him back onto the bench. He stayed there most of the game, even when Keenan in the second period called for "Kocur . . . Hudson . . . Mike Gartman, you're up next."

Hartman looked at Mike Gartner, who looked back.

"You or me?" Hartman asked.

"I don't know," said Gartner, who took the shift.

The Rangers' special teams staged a furious rally in this ragged, dirty game. Referee Dave Jackson called every stick infraction he saw. But while the Rangers killed Quebec's eight power plays, the Rangers went 6-for-7 on theirs. The 3–0 deficit became a 6–3 lead after Alexander Karpovtsev and Messier scored in the third period. With about two minutes left, Keenan said, "Kocur . . . Hudson, you're up."

Hartman remained planted.

The two forwards replaced the three Rangers who changed lines. It left the team one left wing short for an instant before Keenan erupted.

"Get out there, Hartman," he screamed. "What the fuck are you doing?"

The Rangers won three straight from October 11 to 15, then dropped a 4–3 decision at Philadelphia. With three days before the next game, at home against the expansion Mighty Ducks of Anaheim, Keenan was able to put the team through two full days of on-ice drills and off-ice workouts at Rye.

Keenan's practices were remarkable for their brevity and intensity. Players loved them because they were short, hated them because they were rigorous. Most NHL coaches run practices that last for sixty to ninety minutes, but rarely work a player for more than ten to twenty. For every two-on-two drill that takes fifteen seconds, twenty other guys stand around and watch and chat.

Nobody joked at Keenan's practices. Nobody had time to flick a water bottle in a teammate's direction or lean over the glass to chat with somebody hanging around the rink. Two seconds after four players charged two-on-two down ice, the next foursome was expected to be en route. Virtually every misplaced pass prompted a whistle signaling the drill had to be rerun.

A Keenan practice was skated at game tempo. If his players were sharp, it lasted as little as thirty minutes. If his players screwed around, he screamed and they started over. There were no brilliant exercises, no novel drills. He never once practiced the power play. He simply insisted that all the fundamentals be done the way they had to be done in games.

Forwards sprinting down the ice were not permitted to make sweeping circles as they finished their two-hundred-foot jaunts, because forwards sprinting down ice in games made short stops if they got near the front of the net. Defensemen who didn't earn their money stickhandling out of their zone against forechecking forwards were not permitted to stickhandle past teammates in practice, either.

Keenan constantly dangled carrots: Practice correctly, you're out of here in no time. Fool around, I'll keep you here all night and skate you up and down the ice until you vomit. Off the ice, his rules were no different. Each Ranger had to complete his twelve-station weight training a few times each week early in the year, before the grind of the season required the coach to let up.

Most significantly, Keenan required his players to ride the stationary bike after games. That concept flabbergasted most of the players until they realized they felt better the morning after games. It was easily explained: an athlete's recovery time is related to the amount of lactic acid that builds up in his muscles after strenuous activity. The quicker the lactic acid dissipates, the quicker the athlete recovers. Most hockey players eat, drink, and rest after games, allowing the lactic acid to work itself out of the system overnight. Keenan wanted the players riding and stretching, a low level of activity that accelerates the dissipation.

And the players who didn't play much worked out much more strenuously, to maintain their level of conditioning.

"From early on in the year, there was no question in my mind. We were the best-conditioned team in the league," Olczyk said.

Physically, perhaps. Mentally, no. At the Garden against the expansion Ducks, the Rangers performed miserably, their worst game all season. Keenan seized the opportunity to stamp the evening as unacceptable. Midway through the first period, he benched Leetch. Midway through the second, after Terry Yake made it 2–0, he ordered his players to the bench during a TV timeout.

"Excuse me," he said.

"Excuse me," he screamed.

"If anyone wants to fuckin' play, please stand up."

Heads turned left and right. Nobody knew what to do. Finally, Olczyk stood up. And then every Ranger stood up. Graves, Olczyk, and Gartner finally hopped over the boards and onto the ice in front of Keenan's icy stare. Tony Amonte made it 2–1 off a Leetch assist. But after Yake, an anonymous forward plucked from Hartford's system, made it 3–1 at 14:37 of the second, Keenan followed his players into the dressing room for the second intermission.

"You're no fuckin' Chelios," Keenan screamed at Leetch in front of the entire team. "Everybody in this organization thinks you're so great. You're not that fuckin' good. You're not as good as anyone tells you you are." He called the Rangers uncaring unprofessionals who lacked desire and total commitment. "That's why we always wanted to play you guys in the Canada Cup," he yelled at the three Russians in the lineup.

The Rangers controlled the third period, but Leetch's power-play goal at 7:23 was the only one of their 18 shots to get past goalie Guy Hebert. With about ten minutes left, Olczyk stood up and exhorted his teammates from the end of the bench, "Let's go guys, let's get it going."

"Sit down and shut up," Keenan ordered.

When Yake scored a power-play goal to complete his hat trick with 6:21 remaining, Keenan had had enough. He told his players his night's work was done. "You guys quit on me, so why should I bother with you? You haven't played, so why should I coach?"

With players barking out their own positions and trying to keep their lines and defense combinations in order, the Rangers completed a 4–2 loss in fire-drill fashion. Olczyk and Mike Hartman, fourth-liners who had hardly played, made sure they took a shift. Keenan didn't say much in the dressing room afterwards, but his night's work wasn't done; he had one more message to send.

"Let's be mindful of the fact that this team didn't make the playoffs a year ago," he told the media when he was again asked if he had the type of team he needed to win. "You draw your own conclusions. It's not up to me to evaluate. My only responsibility here is to play and work the bench as well as I can during the course of a game. I think this is a great opportunity to see what we have to work with. Better that we find out what we've got here now, than wait until springtime—a lesson learned, hopefully, a year ago."

The next day's practice was the most exhausting the Rangers suffered through all year. It might not have been had the players reported for work sufficiently humbled by their previous night's effort. With a game at Tampa Bay two days later, this was supposed to be a practice in which the players worked lightly on the ice and heavily off it to maintain their physical conditioning. But after a few bad passes, a few sloppy line rushes, and a general malaise, Keenan abruptly blew his whistle. He swung his stick over his head like a lumberjack with an axe, and took a two-handed chop at the crossbar that splintered his stick into a million pieces.

"Everybody get the fuck off the ice."

One by one the players trudged back to the dressing room, sat in their stalls, and waited. When Keenan entered, he told the players they were embarrassing the organization. "You've been stealing money for years," he told Patrick. Keenan concluded by reminding the Rangers of where they had finished the year before, and where they were headed if they didn't shape up.

"You're losers," he taunted them several times. "Losers."

And then they went back to work. Silently, briskly, they drilled. And then they put the pucks away and skated. Up and back. Up and back. Up and back. Players doubled over in pain as they completed their rink-long sprints by digging their blades into the ice and spraying blankets of snow at the boards to stop. Nobody dared coast to a halt at the end of a lap.

This went on for twenty minutes, until Keenan ordered his players into the workout area to complete the weight and exercise-bike workouts that had been plotted by the training staff before practice turned so grueling.

"I feel sick," Colin Campbell said late that afternoon, after the players finally crawled home to their beds. "And I wasn't even on the ice."

The NHL's 1993–94 regular season had begun differently than the previous eleven seasons, because it started without Steve Larmer. After playing 884 consecutive games for the Chicago Blackhawks, every game for eleven straight seasons since he joined Chicago to stay as a rookie in 1982, the quiet, workmanlike right wing who had averaged 37 goals a year while earning a deserved reputation as one of the smartest defensive forwards in hockey, opted to leave the Blackhawks.

Larmer was tired of playing for a team that didn't get better, tired of living and working in the same environment, tired of wallowing in mediocrity. So he held out, voluntarily ending his ironman streak 80 games from the all-time record, and insisted on being traded. When the Blackhawks started shopping him around the league, Keenan told Smith he wanted him. Keenan loved Larmer's dependability, work ethic, and stoicism. He loved the thought of another ex-Blackhawk on the roster, because Keenan wanted as many players as possible who had bought into his programs elsewhere. Larmer wasn't a complainer, and Keenan believed he had a better chance of selling his impersonal method to the Richters and Leetches if he had allies in the dressing room, veterans who had lived through Keenan's approach and could explain it when it inevitably reached its greatest levels of insanity. Keenan knew that at some point in the year, for some dramatic effect, he'd do something as stupid as kicking a player off the ice at practice for wearing the wrong color tape on his socks, as he did to Kocur one day. When that player cursed Keenan under his breath for being a nonsensical lunatic as he returned to the dressing room to redress, Keenan wanted a Larmer around to describe the bigger picture.

Keenan's bigger picture was the same as Smith's: a Stanley Cup outfit. They just went about it as differently as any two respected hockey people could while residing on the same planet. Smith told Keenan he wanted Larmer, too, provided Chicago GM Bob Pulford's price wasn't too high. He told Keenan that to pull this deal off, he had to work carefully and not tip his hand. He was willing to deal Turcotte or Patrick for Larmer, but not both. He told Keenan to lie low, say little, and stay patient.

This was, of course, impossible.

When Smith encountered resistance from Pulford, Keenan concluded that Pulford's hatred of Keenan had to be the reason he didn't want the Rangers to land Larmer. Smith tried to explain that Chicago's asking price was right wing Tony Amonte, a speedy winger from Boston who was a potential 40-goal scorer and who had blended well in 1992–93 with Messier and Graves. Pulford needed to infuse his aging roster—the one Keenan left him the year before—with young talent, and kept pressing for Amonte, a boyhood friend of the Hawks' star center, Jeremy Roenick.

"I'm not giving them Amonte for Larmer," Smith said.

Almost every day for several weeks after the regular season began, Keenan asked Smith for a Larmer update.

"I'm trying," Smith told him one afternoon.

"I know you are," Keenan replied, feigning support.

On October 28, after a 3–3 Garden tie with Montreal left the Rangers perched at a mediocre 5-5-1, Keenan stormed off the bench at the final buzzer, made a sharp right turn under the stands, and looked for Watkins.

"Get me Jaffe," Keenan barked, loud enough for everyone in the runway to hear.

Watkins didn't dare summon the Paramount president. Instead he phoned Suite 200, the Garden's executive lounge, and told Gutkowski what Keenan had asked. Gutkowski, who regularly insisted that his employees respect the chain of command, was annoyed at Keenan for contemplating a breach of protocol. He was disappointed, but not shocked. He told Watkins that night he'd talk to Keenan, but before he could, the next day he got a call from Jaffe.

Jaffe told Gutkowski that Keenan had called him about acquiring Larmer. He told Gutkowski he wanted to see him, Keenan, and Smith in his office. Gutkowski called Keenan.

"Mike, that's not the way it works here," Gutkowski said angrily. "We hired you because we want you, we value your input. Your voice should be heard when it comes to trades. But Neil's the GM. You want to do something you think will improve our team, you talk to Neil and work it out with Neil. Don't do it this way again."

Keenan said he understood, but turned the conversation back to Larmer as quickly as he could. "You'll get more mileage for your money if you go and get this guy," he told Gutkowski. "I can't get anywhere with Neil on this. It's your choice. If you want to do something with Jaffe, it's your choice."

Keenan wanted this meeting with Jaffe as yet another forum to push his request for Larmer, as well as to impress the boss he mistakenly thought had instructed Smith to hire him. He seized the opportunity to repeat his July performance in Rye for Jaffe's and Gutkowski's ears: not enough toughness, not enough size, not enough players battle-scarred by the play-offs. He didn't like Leetch, Richter, or Alexei Kovalev, the enigmatic, marvelously talented, very immature twenty-year-old Russian right wing whom Smith had selected in the first round of the 1991 draft. As far as Keenan was concerned, Leetch was too soft, Richter lacked mental toughness, and Kovalev was a flaky foreigner not to be relied upon. In this meeting with his three direct superiors, he questioned the commitment of all three players, their willingness to sacrifice themselves and push themselves beyond the level of success they had already reached.

The more Gutkowski listened, the more certain he became that Keenan should never be the Rangers' general manager, and would have a problem becoming a GM with any team. His need to so bluntly criticize so many players so early in his tenure—in front of the president of the company that owned the team—showed Gutkowski a stunning lack of judgment and perspective. His desire to trade three marvelously talented young players with box-office appeal after coaching them for only eleven games proved he was too impulsive.

"Mike, we're not going to trade everybody," Gutkowski said. "We hired you to make these guys better, that's why you're here, that's your responsibility. That's why we're paying you the money we're paying you."

"We're not going to trade Brian Leetch," Jaffe added. "We're not turning the Rangers into the New York Blackhawks because, to be honest about it, Mike, what have they ever won?"

Jaffe and Gutkowski told Smith and Keenan to exchange ideas, trade opinions, and work together. They tried to end the ninety-minute meeting on an upbeat note. Depression didn't set in until the meeting adjourned and Gutkowski rode back to the Garden. Gutkowski had thought the Rangers were a contender when he walked into the room, but he trudged out with one bleak picture in his head.

"I've got the worst team on earth," he told himself.

Smith stewed silently through most of the meeting. He didn't agree with Keenan's take on the team. He knew Keenan was capable of exaggeration and oversimplification, and he was sure the coach would do anything to make himself look better to the big bosses at Smith's expense. But the GM left the meeting upbeat, believing that the chain of command had been reestablished. He took Keenan into a back office and got Pulford on the phone. Again, Pulford asked for Amonte. Again, Smith said no. He tried to get Chelios for Amonte, which only elicited a growl from the grumpy GM. The two men left Paramount an hour later empty-handed.

Smith was annoyed at how Keenan wanted the public to believe that Larmer would already be a Ranger if Smith had acted decisively. The man who traded for Messier in 1991, who traded Tomas Sandstrom and Tony Granato to the Los Angeles Kings for Bernie Nicholls in 1990, and who stole Adam Graves from Edmonton via the old free-agent rules of 1991, knew how to be decisive; what he didn't know was how to silence a coach who couldn't distinguish between decisive and precipitous action. And he needed to, because other options were opening.

A day after the Jaffe meeting, Hartford GM Paul Holmgren called Smith and told him he was interested in Patrick and Turcotte, two players who had already found themselves chained to Keenan's doghouse. And the Whalers had expendable young players who could fill Chicago's needs.

"What would you give me for Larmer if I could get him?" Holmgren asked.

"Turcotte," Smith said.

"But I need Turcotte and Patrick."

"Well, then you've got to give more than Larmer."

"Okay, I'll give you Nick Kypreos, too," Holmgren said, referring to the twenty-seven-year-old rugged left wing who was more a fighter than a skilled forward.

"No, I'm not taking Kypreos for Patrick."

The GMs tabled the discussion for a few days, then picked it up again on November 2. Holmgren told Smith he could acquire Larmer and defenseman Bryan Marchment for left wing Patrick Poulin and defenseman Eric Weinrich. He told Smith he'd do it and trade Larmer to the Rangers.

Smith got excited. It wasn't often a general manager had the opportunity to trade for a 30-goal scorer who could check, who was a solid citizen, who didn't get hurt, and at thirty-two was still in phenomenal shape. It was rare for a player of Larmer's caliber to be on the open market, sitting out, forcing Pulford's hand. And since Keenan wanted Patrick and Turcotte out, Smith hoped this would placate his coach.

He agreed to Holmgren's three-way deal, provided Holmgren upped the ante for Turcotte and Patrick.

"Okay," Holmgren said. "I'll make it Larmer, Kypreos, Barry Richter, and a sixth-round pick in 1994."

It was a stunningly good deal for the Rangers. They added an impact player to their nucleus, the best player in the deal. Besides getting Larmer for Keenan, Smith responded to another of the coach's complaints by adding a little toughness in Kypreos. And he pleased the scouting director in him by getting a pick and a legitimate defensive prospect in Richter to replace on the organizational depth chart the two players he lost.

Smith also knew that, for at least a few days, he had shut Keenan up—not just by getting Larmer, but by responding to Keenan's desire to rid the roster of Patrick and Turcotte. It was the theme Keenan carried throughout the season, one that paid huge dividends at the trade deadline:

Addition by subtraction.

"Life Isn't Fair"

3

Mike Keenan based his method on his mandate. He was hired to win a Stanley Cup. Nothing less would do.

Professional sports is an abnormal environment, Keenan once said. Millionaire businessmen with huge egos join a private club called a league, and play with expensive toys called teams. They buy and sell a select group of healthy, young athletes. They throw hundreds of thousands—sometimes millions—of dollars at them long before they're mature enough to handle the fame and fortune. But because they pay, they buy the right to slap a city's name on the players' chests, and demand that these athletes represent a rabid band of fanatics by playing a game we've played all our lives. In front of fifteen thousand people every night, the athletes are expected to win. They are expected to endure the fear and mask the pain of losing, while ignoring the intense pressure of intramural competition for these highly coveted jobs.

Michael Edward Keenan learned how to mask pain before he was five years old. The first of Thelma and Theodore Keenan's four children was born October 21, 1949, in Toronto. Mike was a young child when the Keenans moved to Whitby, Ontario, just outside of Oshawa, where Ted worked on the assembly line of the local General Motors plant. Ted was a fun-loving, easy-going Irishman. Thelma was the family's compass, a hard-driving woman who raised the kids and clerked at the local Eaton's.

When Mike was four, his baby brother Patrick died of pneumonia.

"I still remember his funeral," Keenan said.

His parents bickered for as long as he can remember, too. School was a refuge from the arguments and fistfights that pierced the silence of his Irish Catholic upbringing. His teachers noticed right from the first grade that Mike was a leader, so he was entrusted with responsibility. In church, he was an altar boy. In class, he was an officer. In sports, he was the hockey team's captain. At Dennis O'Connor High School in Whitby, he was the ninth grade's Athlete of the Year in 1965. That honor and the offer of a hockey scholarship to St. Lawrence University in the fall of 1968 were the adolescent highlights of his life—before a mutual friend introduced him to Rita Haas, a smart and pretty Canadian farmer's daughter whose grandfather was a victim of the Holocaust.

He spent four years at St. Lawrence as a grinding, hardworking forward without a lot of natural talent, but with a passion for hitting. He organized a bunch of his teammates and formed a band named Nik and the Nice Guys. Keenan didn't play an instrument, so he grabbed the microphone and appointed himself lead singer, although he couldn't sing.

Mike and Rita were married in 1972, after his parents were divorced. He earned his BS in physical education, then enrolled at the University of Toronto, where he earned his master's in education and played for the 1972–73 Canadian collegiate champion hockey team. After being cut by the NHL rival World Hockey Association's Vancouver Blazers in training camp, he played the following season for the Southern Hockey League's Roanoke Valley Rebels.

He and Rita settled in Oshawa in 1975. She taught math. He got a job at Forest Hill Collegiate Institute in Toronto, where he taught phys ed and coached the girls' swim team and the boys' hockey team. In 1977, he began a two-year stint with the Junior B Oshawa Legionnaires. In 1979, he landed his big break: general manager and head coach of the Junior A Peterborough Petes.

After he guided the Ontario Hockey League champion Petes to the Memorial Cup, he drew the attention of his idol, Scotty Bowman, who was GM-coach of the Buffalo Sabres. Bowman hired Keenan to coach the Sabres' American Hockey League farm team in Rochester, New York. In his third season at Rochester, his Americans won the Calder Cup. When Bowman didn't step aside and promote him to coach the Sabres, Keenan quit and spent a year coaching at the University of Toronto. He won another Canadian collegiate championship, and was quickly ushered into the

NHL by the Flyers in May 1984, nine days after the team's legendary captain, Bobby Clarke, ended a fifteen-year career and was elevated to general manager.

Keenan was hired to replace Bob McCammon, whose 98-point team had been beaten in the first round of the playoffs for the third straight year. Keenan whipped the Flyers into a 113-point unit that finished first overall in the NHL and stormed to the Finals, where they were overwhelmed in five games by the vastly superior Oilers. For that he was named Coach of the Year.

The Flyers won their second and third consecutive Patrick Division titles the next two years, finishing second overall in the league both times. Keenan became the first coach to win at least 40 games in each of his first three NHL seasons. He recorded his 150th win on March 22, 1987, reaching that plateau faster than any coach in NHL history.

The Rangers knocked the Flyers out of the first round of the 1986 playoffs, but Philadelphia regrouped the next year and returned to the Finals. Behind a rookie goalie named Ron Hextall, they battled back from a three-games-to-one deficit against Edmonton, forced a seventh game, and lost 3–1 to the Oilers. Hextall won the Conn Smythe Trophy in defeat.

Despite this success, Keenan developed a reputation for tormenting his players. He inherited a skilled, mild-mannered Swedish defenseman named Thomas Eriksson, who had made the NHL's rookie team in 1983–84 and played for Sweden's Canada Cup team in 1984. Two weeks into his first season as coach, Keenan verbally abused the sensitive Eriksson so badly that the defenseman ran to Clarke's office, crying.

"I want to go back to Sweden," Eriksson told the rookie GM. "I hate it here. Keenan's going to kill me."

"Thomas, at least finish out the season," Clarke told him.

Eriksson played two years under Keenan, then quit and returned to play in Sweden.

"He was a good young defenseman, but Mike finished him," Clarke recalled. "By the time Mike was through with him, the kid couldn't even play for us in the minors. He just verbally abused him so bad."

The Flyers drafted Ron Sutter in the first round of the 1982 draft and traded for his identical twin, Rich, two years later. Ron was the superior player, which created an awkward situation since the two were so close. "You'd better start playing better," Keenan once warned Ron, "or I'm going to bench your brother."

Keenan constantly criticized the gentle manner of two graceful and professional superstars, defenseman Mark Howe and left wing Tim Kerr.

Howe was a sleek defenseman whose mild nature belied the genes of his fearless and intimidating father, Hall of Famer Gordie Howe. Kerr was a 6-3, 225-pound teddy bear of a forward who loved to plant himself in front of the net and swat rebounds past goalies while defensemen bounced off his tree trunk of a torso.

By Keenan's fourth year, his players rebelled. Even his staunchest supporters, center Peter Zezel and right wing Rick Tocchet, two mentally tough players who thrived when he challenged their manhood, lost the desire to perform for a man who did not know how to pocket his whip.

Clarke blew up at Keenan in their final year together after injuries forced the recall of their first-round draft pick, center Glen Seabrooke, from their AHL farm club in Hershey, Pennsylvania. Clarke and Keenan had discussed their options before settling on Seabrooke as the best choice for the moment. The Flyers dressed the twenty-year-old, but, curiously, Keenan did not use him at all. Afterward, Clarke asked Keenan why they had bothered recalling a young prospect rather than a veteran from the minors if the coach didn't plan on using him.

"I sent [assistant coach E. J. McGuire] to Hershey to watch him the other night," Keenan said. "E.J. said he was horseshit."

"Mike, why the fuck would you do that after we talked about bringing him up? And why send E.J. down to watch him? At least make your own judgment."

In the summer of 1987 Keenan led Team Canada to a dramatic finals victory over the Soviet Union in the Canada Cup. But the Flyers in 1987–88 fell from first to third in the Patrick Division. Several weeks after they blew a three-games-to-one lead and were eliminated by Washington in the first round of the 1988 playoffs, captain Dave Poulin, Brian Propp, Kerr, and Howe met with Clarke and pleaded with the GM to fire the coach. "The only thing Mike Keenan taught me, Bob," Poulin told Clarke, "was how not to treat people."

Clarke fired him, although he also knew the vulnerable side of Keenan, the man who sat with Clarke's kids every Christmas and sang carols at the GM's piano. He saw the man who kept the Flyers together as a family in November 1985 in the wake of the death of goalie Pelle Lindbergh, who crashed his Porsche while driving drunk one day not far from the team's Voorhees, New Jersey, practice rink.

"Mike was a desperate man in those early days," said Clarke, who left the Flyers in 1990 and returned in 1994. "He partied with a sense of desperation, he coached with a sense of desperation. Everything in his life was done with a sense of desperation. He thought the owner, the GM, everybody, worked for him."

Early in Keenan's second year with the Flyers, he asked owner Ed Snider, vice president Keith Allen, and Clarke for a meeting with the coaching staff. They agreed. Keenan arrived in a dark suit and tie, with pages of neatly organized notes. In front of his bosses, and assistant coaches E. J. McGuire, Paul Holmgren, and Bill Barber, he began demanding organizational changes. Recalled Clarke: "He told Mr. Snider, 'This is what I need, this is what we have to do.' And Mr. Snider said, 'Mike, Clarke's the GM of this team, not you.' Mike was trying to take right over."

At Chicago, Blackhawks owner Bill Wirtz and GM Bob Pulford quickly hired Keenan to replace Bob Murdoch, who in his only year went 30-41-9 and failed to prevent the Blackhawks from a quick first-round playoff elimination. Keenan made sure this time he would take over; early in his tenure, he persuaded Wirtz to agree to elevate him to the dual job of GM-coach beginning in 1990–91.

After a first regular season in which the Blackhawks went 27-41-12 and struggled to make the playoffs, they reached the Stanley Cup semifinals in 1989 and 1990. Keenan spent two years publicly belittling the team's beloved superstar, center Denis Savard. Then, two weeks after the 1990 draft, the rookie GM engineered a fabulous trade in which he sent Savard to Montreal for defenseman Chris Chelios and a second-round draft pick, elevating Jeremy Roenick into Savard's spot as the team's leader.

The Blackhawks finished first overall in the NHL in 1990–91, but lost to Minnesota in six first-round games. Keenan rebounded during the summer of 1991, when he led Team Canada to its second straight Canada Cup triumph. Chicago then rebounded in 1991–92 by marching to the Stanley Cup finals, where they were swept by the Pittsburgh Penguins. Keenan pushed Roenick just as he had pushed Savard, as he had pushed Howe, as he had pushed Kerr. It came as a relief to the Hawks when he stepped aside and hired longtime Blackhawk Darryl Sutter as head coach. But one month into his first season as an executive without a bench to stand behind, he issued Wirtz his Pulford-or-me ultimatum and was out.

The Hockey Hall of Fame's reference library is littered with biographies of players, coaches, and managers who failed for entire careers to win the Cup. Still, New York's fifty-three-year drought had become legendary, and had intensified the pressure on every Ranger team that dared attempt a legitimate playoff run. From his unsuccessful trips to the finals with Philadelphia and Chicago, Keenan knew how exhaustingly difficult it was to win it all, no matter how good a team was. He knew it would take discipline, tough love, and all of his motivational powers and leadership skills to get the Rangers hungry enough to win. He decided the day he took the job that he would have to know which Rangers could be counted upon when the situation looked bleakest.

As he saw it, he had 84 games to find the twenty players who could best win. He didn't want a pretty collection of skaters who knew how to breeze through a regular season; he wanted a gritty band of warriors who knew how to cope with the playoffs in April, May, and June. He didn't want Brian Leetch or Mike Richter playing hard for him; he wanted them playing hard for each other. He wanted Mike Gartner sacrificing for Alexei Kovalev, who was sacrificing for Adam Graves, who was sacrificing for Kevin Lowe.

"Life isn't fair," he said one day early in training camp, pushing aside the notion that coaches should treat all players alike. "What's good for the goose isn't necessarily what's good for the gander. That's just the way it is. If you have a problem with that . . ."

The unfairness of life had been impressed upon Keenan at an early age. Sadly, this was a truth known as well by Neil Smith; it was one of the few parts of their world views the two had in common.

Three of the five people in the Smith household died before Neil's nineteenth birthday. "It gave me reason to worry," he recalled. "I worried that my family wouldn't stay alive."

Neil Smith was born in Toronto on January 9, 1954. His mother, Marg, was an extroverted woman who grew up in Manitoba and played defense from 1934–39 for the Winnipeg Olympics of the only women's hockey league in Western Canada. She was a saleswoman for a children's clothing store. His father, Sid, was the general manager of a television supply company that installed antennas and other TV equipment. He moonlighted playing piano and organ in a local dance band.

At the age of four, Neil awoke at home to the sobs of his grandmother, mother, father, and older sister. When he asked why everyone was crying, he was told his grandfather was dead.

Six years later, Sid Smith was bothered by a bout of indigestion. He checked himself into a Toronto hospital. One day later, exactly thirty years before the Rangers' Stanley Cup parade, he suffered a massive heart attack and died. He was fifty.

"I still see my grandmother, Margaret Topp, who lived with us and helped raise me. She's consoling my mother, who's crying. I come around the corner, out of my room, in my pajamas. I still hear what she's saying: 'They called me and now he's dead.'"

Although he was only ten, a boy still fantasizing about one day skating for his beloved Maple Leafs, Neil became more protective of his seventeen-year-old sister, Pat, and his mother, just as they became more protective of him.

Neil's grandmother died in front of his eyes in 1972. Although she was ill with cancer, it surprised him to find her gasping unconsciously when he paid her a visit in the hospital one afternoon by himself. Frantic, Neil raced to find a nurse.

"Help her, help her," he screamed.

The nurse asked Neil to step aside, then examined Mrs. Topp. An instant later, the nurse called for Neil. "I think your grandmother has just died," she said. "Does the family want us to try and keep her alive?"

He was eighteen, forced to make an instant decision nobody that young should ever have to make alone.

"Well, yeah," he replied.

The medical efforts failed. Stoically, Neil left the hospital. Before he went to tell his mother, he called a family friend. He still hadn't shed a tear. He was planning and worrying.

"Mrs. King, I think my grandmother just died. I have to tell my mom. Could you go to the store and be there when I get there? She might be in the store alone and if she needs to leave, someone will have to watch the store."

Neil walked into the store. His mother was waiting on a customer. He saw her and burst into tears. Twenty-three years later, as he told the story, he cried like a boy.

That same year, his mother met Jim Cater. Neil rebelled against the man who a year later became his stepfather. "Mom doesn't need me anymore," he told himself.

Hockey was his refuge. When he was in grade school, his mother and sister constantly harped on his unwillingness to open a textbook. He was extremely intelligent, his teachers told his mother, but he barely passed his elementary courses.

"Why get an 80 when 50 passes?" he'd say.

Instead, he spent his time playing hockey, watching hockey, talking hockey. When he was eleven, he knew the numbers of every member of the 1964–65 Leafs. He hung pictures of his favorite player, Chicago's Stan Mikita, on the walls of the family's rec room.

Smith was a gangly defenseman who could skate and stickhandle. He played Junior A hockey for the Brockville, Ontario, Braves from 1972–74. He easily graduated from Don Mills Collegiate High School and earned a hockey scholarship to Western Michigan University. His mother insisted that he first attend Grade 13. "This way if you don't like college in the States, you can go to the University of Toronto like Pat," she said.

He loved college in the States, especially since he had enrolled as an NHL draft pick. At Brockville in 1974 he was eyed by a young New York Islander scout named Jim Devellano. The Islanders drafted Smith in the twelfth round of the 1974 draft.

Smith taught at the Islanders' Long Island Hockey School in the summer of 1976. He graduated from Western Michigan with a degree in communications and a minor in business in December 1977. He took a few graduate courses to maintain his NCAA eligibility while he completed his fourth year on the team.

The International Hockey League's Kalamazoo Wings signed him for two playoff games in 1978. He attended the Islanders' training camp in September 1978, got cut, and was reassigned by the Isles to the camp of the WHA's Indianapolis Racers, where he skated briefly against a seventeen-year-old rookie named Gretzky. He was cut again. He signed with the IHL's Saginaw Gears, where he played one season. In 1979–80 he played with the IHL Dayton Gems and the Hampton Aces of the East Coast Hockey League.

Enough was enough.

In 1980 he moved to Long Island and lived with Nick Amodio, a friend he met at the hockey school. He got a job selling women's giftware for a company in Manhattan. He hated commuting by train into the city every day, but he loved watching the Islanders at the Coliseum or the Rangers at the Garden. One night when the Islanders were in the Garden, the blue seaters spat on assistant coach Lorne Henning up in the auxiliary press box. (Although they're lavender now, the mezzanine seats at the top of the Garden once were as blue as the language from the mouths of the Rangers' most loyal fans. This cult made evenings miserable for anybody associating with the opposition.) Smith, who was sitting nearby as Devellano's guest, had an idea.

"Jimmy, nobody affiliated with the Islanders can go up there without being recognized and spat on, but I can. I can watch the games at the Garden without anyone knowing I'm working for the Islanders. I'll do anything. Can I?"

Devellano agreed to ask Islander coach Al Arbour. A few days later, Arbour called Smith and agreed to let him prescout Ranger home games whenever a team playing the Rangers was due to visit the Coliseum next. His salary? A press pass and the night's expenses.

Arbour sent Smith a handful of scouting forms. He must have liked

Smith's work, because by the end of the regular season the Isles were as-signing him to games in Hartford, Boston, and Washington. The Islanders won their second straight Cup that year, but Smith got nothing: no ring, no party invites, no nothing.

He did run the team's hockey school in the summer of 1981. When it was over, he asked to be made a full-time advance scout. He was offered the same $10,000 he was making selling women's purse mirrors. He ac-cepted.

In 1981–82 he scouted 150 NHL games. The Islanders won another Cup. Smith didn't get to go to Vancouver for the Cup clincher and he re-ceived no bonus, but this time he got a ring.

Devellano became general manager of the Red Wings that summer, and he brought Smith with him to Detroit. He paid him $22,000 to be one of the team's pro scouts. A year later Smith became the director of the Wings' farm system. Two years after that, in 1985–86, he became the team's direc-tor of scouting, and general manager and governor of the Wings' AHL team in Glens Falls, New York. The Adirondack Red Wings won the 1986 Calder Cup in Smith's first season as a minor-league GM, and under his direction the Wings used a second-round pick to select Adam Graves.

Despite bare drafts by Detroit in 1987 and 1988, Smith's stock rose be-cause Adirondack was a financial and hockey success. When the AHL Red Wings won another Calder Cup in 1989 six weeks after the Rangers fired general manager Phil Esposito, Smith's name began circulating as one the Rangers needed to consider.

At 3 A.M. on June 18, 1989, after a night toasting themselves for their draft picks the day before, Smith walked the streets of downtown Min-neapolis with his good friend, Ken Holland, the Red Wings' Western Canada scout, telling how he planned to handle the interview that had been scheduled for later in the month.

"I'm going to tell them they have to rebuild their farm system, their scouting staff, the way they delegate authority. I'm going to explain that if they seriously want to win the Cup, they're going to have to let a guy build from the foundation up, the draft picks, and spend five or six years doing it. If they think they don't have to do that, I'll point to the fifty years they've been waiting.

"But I'm gong to have plans. I'm going to be able to tell them who I plan to interview to become coach, who I want as assistant GM, how I need a director of scouting, how I need to fire a bunch of the old scouts and bring in better ones. I'm going to be so prepared, they're going to have to take me seriously."

A month later, the job was his.

• • •

Mike Richter had inherited the number one goaltender's job on Keenan's team by default at the age of twenty-seven. The expansion rules had forced Smith to select between Richter and Vanbiesbrouck, something Roger Neilson and Ron Smith couldn't do. Neither he nor John Vanbiesbrouck flourished playing as a tandem, because both felt they were good enough to play the majority of the games. Neither wanted to sit behind the other on the depth chart, both hungered to play in every big game, and both believed that a team had to go with one goalie in the playoffs. Neither wanted to be left out.

Richter played four seasons with the Rangers before Keenan arrived. He was the fourth goalie selected in the 1985 draft, a second-round pick made by Craig Patrick, the Ranger GM who was fired and replaced by Phil Esposito in 1986. Richter grew up in Abington, Pennsylvania, a Philadelphia suburb. He dominated the Philly-area youth leagues, then elected to play a high school year at Northwood Prep in Lake Placid, New York. He impressed NHL scouts with his quick glove hand and incredibly strong lateral movement. He played two years at the University of Wisconsin after the Rangers drafted him, spent a year with the U.S. National Team, played in the 1988 Olympics, and turned pro in the spring of that year.

He played the equivalent of two full years over three seasons in the minors before establishing himself as a bona fide NHL goalie midway through the 1989–90 season, Neil Smith's first year. Like almost every Ranger, Richter slumped in 1992–93, badly enough to earn a brief midseason demotion to Binghamton.

Teammates liked him immediately because he unselfishly accepted blame, something Vanbiesbrouck occasionally forgot to do. Coaches liked him because he was smart, he listened, and he understood he had more to learn. And the media loved him because one question generated a thousand words.

"It's a really interesting part of the game," he said of the media's role. "You're going to help yourself out, and help the press out, and help the game out if you handle it well. You can't hide from it. If I decide not to talk to the press, they're still going to write. So I might as well fill in with the way I think the story's going to go. But then a reporter can get into dangerous waters, too. Pat Riley in his book said, 'Everything I've ever said to the press was a message for my players.' So it makes a writer wonder why he should talk to a guy, what he's going to get, and if that answer is honest. I don't think it's fair to lie to the press."

Richter knew how to protect his privacy, too. When he didn't want to talk, he took his seat toward the front of the bus and buried his head in a book. At home, he rarely answered his telephone and hardly ever returned a message left on his answering machine. He, Leetch, and Messier were three single guys living on Manhattan's Upper West Side. At times they car-pooled to practice, a forty-five-minute drive to Rye Playland, the Westchester County amusement park and home of the Ice Casino, the antiquated public rink that the Rangers refurbished when they built their practice complex in 1980.

Often, though, Leetch and Messier rode without the goalie, a last-minute guy who regularly scrambled to make practice on time, who liked to dawdle on the ice after practice, and who often dawdled in the locker room blabbing with reporters.

By NHL goaltending standards, he was remarkably normal. He didn't throw up before games like Glenn Hall used to in the 1950s and 1960s. He didn't strip naked and then re-dress in the exact order he had undressed before every period of every game in which he played, like Gary "Suitcase" Smith did in his fourteen NHL seasons for eight different clubs. He didn't talk to his goalposts like Patrick Roy in Montreal, nor wildly bang them with his stick like Ron Hextall did in Philadelphia.

Richter certainly didn't know much about Chuck Rayner, who played goal in front of some weak Ranger teams in the late 1940s. Rayner was once asked what he would do if his son decided he wanted to be a goalie. "I'd grab the stick out of his hand and hit him over the head with it," Rayner declared. That was something Bill Smith of the Islanders thought about doing whenever an opposing forward came near his crease.

Richter didn't study racehorses like two great goalies of the 1970s. Gilles Villemure of the Rangers trained and rode trotters at Long Island's Roosevelt Raceway during the off-season. The Bruins' Gerry Cheevers often put his money where his hunch was. Richter grew up handicapping another great goalie of the 1970s, Bernie Parent, who led the Flyers to Stanley Cups in 1974 and 1975. Fortunately, he avoided Parent's eccentricities, which included a month of missed action resulting from his decision to undergo a circumcision at age twenty-seven.

Two years short of his college degree when he turned pro, Richter took courses one summer at Cornell University and the next summer at Columbia. Keenan didn't bring a goalie coach with him to New York, because he believed that no coach should tinker with a goalie's style. Richter possessed the physical tools necessary to become a workhorse number one goalie. What Richter lacked, Keenan believed, was mental toughness.

The coach rode the goalie relentlessly. He taught Richter to respect every shift, every move he made in his crease and around the net. Keenan was more imposing than any NHL shooter Richter faced; the goalie never felt his coach's quest for excellence wane. It couldn't, for Keenan knew he was going to need Richter to deliver two dozen world-class efforts over a two-month springtime span, a game every other night. Keenan pulled Richter from nine of his career-high 67 starts, once after he allowed two goals on six shots over the first 5:50 of a midseason game at Detroit, even though he was 16-0-3 in his previous 19 decisions.

"Ultimately," Richter said long after Keenan had departed, "he never asked from me more than I asked from myself."

Richter and Leetch were good friends, neighbors, and the only two 1994 Rangers whom Neil Smith had not acquired. Leetch was Craig Patrick's final gift to the organization, the ninth player chosen in the first round of the 1986 draft. He was a speedy little offensive-minded defenseman from Cheshire, Connecticut, not far from Hartford. From the blue line he scored 70 goals in 54 games over two seasons at Avon Old Farms High School. He was headed to Boston College, where the Rangers got to see how he played against premier NCAA competition.

The pick was unpopular when it was made because the Rangers needed size, and Patrick drew snickers when he said his scouts predicted Leetch would grow and fill out by the time he finished his college career. Two years later, Patrick looked prescient.

No, Leetch didn't grow. He was still 5-11 and 185 pounds when he finished a year with BC and a year with the 1988 U.S. National Team. But when the 1988 Olympics ended and Leetch joined the Rangers for the final 17 games of the 1987–88 season, it was obvious that this polite, quiet twenty-year-old kid with the strawberry blond hair was special.

He played big. Although he was new to the NHL, he carried the puck with an air of supreme confidence and stepped up in critical moments as if he had been in the league ten years. His skating was magnificent, his hands were phenomenal, his reflexes and ability to see the ice and make plays made him seem clairvoyant. From the moment he slipped the No. 2 jersey that Brad Park wore in the 1970s over his head, it was obvious that this American-born player had a good chance to be the Rangers' Park of the 1990s.

Two years later, he was. Four years later, he eclipsed Park's legacy by becoming the first Ranger to win the Norris Trophy as the NHL's best defenseman since Harry Howell in 1966–67. Just as Park had Boston's Bobby Orr blocking his Norris hopes, Leetch had Boston's Ray Bourque, but in this one season Leetch scored 22 goals and 80 assists for a phenomenal 102 points, ninth in the league. He blossomed from star to superstar.

Not coincidentally, it was Messier's first season as a Ranger. As soon as he arrived in October of 1991, Messier befriended Leetch. He knew how good Leetch already was, but he also believed that this unassuming lad could become even greater. Although Messier was seven years older, they became close confidants on and off the ice.

The 1992–93 season was disastrous for Leetch. He missed 34 midseason games with a neck injury that compressed the nerve running toward his left shoulder. He returned at less than full strength on March 10, but nine days later slipped on a patch of ice while stepping out of a cab in front of his Manhattan apartment building, fracturing his right ankle.

The embarrassing fracture—Leetch denied unproven rumors that he injured himself because he was drunk—ended his year and punctuated the Rangers' embarrassing season. He privately vowed to spend the summer of 1993 rehabilitating his shoulder, rehabilitating his ankle, and building his adequately toned body into one that better complemented the phenomenal talent he was.

And that was before Keenan got ahold of him.

Leetch enjoyed hanging out on Cape Cod with his college buddies during the off-season, and in the first few years of his NHL career he didn't mind having to melt a beer belly off his fleshy body at training camp. His hands, feet, and eyes were his most cherished body parts. His reflexive skills were going to carry him, not his brawn. He was never going to be a chiseled specimen, anyway.

He was an American-born player who grew up in the right place at the right time, in New England in the 1970s, a few years after Bobby Orr changed the way defensemen had to play. He grew up in an era when Canada had begun to lose its viselike grip on its national sport.

In 1967–68, when the league expanded from six to twelve teams, crossed the Mississippi River, and put teams in Los Angeles, Oakland, Minneapolis, St. Louis, Pittsburgh, and Philadelphia, 95 percent of the NHL was Canadian-born, 3 percent was American and 2 percent were Europeans. In the decade that followed, U.S.-born players shattered the stereotype that Canadians were meaner, tougher, and more dedicated to the game that was their religion.

Twelve years later, when the NHL absorbed the four WHA teams, who had drawn from the untapped Scandinavian pools of talent, Americans made up 11 percent of the player pool, and now it was North Americans—U.S.- and Canadian-born players alike—who believed their style of play on their cozy two-hundred-foot by eighty-five-foot ice surfaces was superior to the European style played on two-hundred-foot by one-hundred-foot sheets.

By the time Leetch broke into the league, Americans made up nearly 20 percent of the player pool, Europeans more than 10 percent. And Canadians, who once disparagingly called the blue line "a Swedish speed bump" because of the typical European player's reluctance to cross it and take his lumps, lusted after the new breed of Swede, players like Sandstrom of the Rangers, who dished out as much punishment—usually with his stick—as he absorbed. Keenan did not have a prejudiced bone in his body; he didn't care if a player was born in Finland or Flin Flon, Manitoba, so long as the player was willing to do anything to win. Keenan believed Leetch had world-class skills; he just didn't think Leetch had enough desire to realize his vast potential.

On what basis he formed that quick judgment, he never told the defenseman. At one their first talks in training camp, he did politely ask Leetch how good he wanted to be. Keenan told Leetch he believed that, as dominant as Leetch was offensively, the team needed him to be as dominant in the defensive zone. He wanted Leetch to curtail his individual rushes, rethink his attempts at creating offense, and jump only on the prime opportunities rather than at every opportunity.

A few games into the regular season, before the outburst between periods of the Anaheim game, Keenan dispensed with diplomacy.

"You're no Chris Chelios the way you're playing," he bluntly told Leetch during a one-on-one chat in his office at Rye. "If you're going to be a leader on this team, you've got to accept the responsibility of playing like one."

The unflappable superstar digested the frank criticism, shrugged, and kept reminding himself of his determination to make up for his dismal 1992–93 season. He kept riding the exercise bike after practices and after games, as Keenan demanded. He kept applying himself to the Rangers' rigorous weight-training program, as Keenan demanded. He kept reminding himself early in the season that although Chelios was one phone call away, Keenan didn't know *him* yet.

But Leetch did know that Keenan cared. Midway through the season, Leetch broke up with his longtime girlfriend. Keenan called him at home one night to ask how he was. As well as keeping his intense practices short, Keenan reminded the players to spend time with their families. He gave the Rangers a liberal number of days off—when they won. But the punishment when they lost outweighed the rewards. And for some players, there were no rewards to balance the scales.

• • •

No Ranger was mistreated more than Mike Gartner, a respectful, chari-table, religious man who reported to training camp at the age of thirty-four in as fine physical shape as he did when he played with the Washington Capitals at the age of twenty-four. Gartner was a right wing who had scored 30 or more goals in each of his eleven NHL seasons before he came to the Rangers at the 1990 trading deadline from Minnesota for right wing Ulf Dahlen.

Gartner scored 40 or more in each of his three full seasons in New York before Keenan arrived. He was one of the NHL's fastest skaters, a future Hall of Famer who scored his 600th goal on December 26, 1993, passed Chicago Blackhawks great Bobby Hull on the all-time list on March 9, 1994, and ended his fifteenth NHL season with 617 goals, fifth-best in history.

He didn't finish the season as a Ranger.

The Ottawa, Ontario native, who was president of the NHL Players' As-sociation, had the terrible misfortune of being one of the few players in the league never to reach the Stanley Cup semifinals. Many of his Washington teams weren't good enough, but some were, and since he was one of their offensive leaders he was rightly held accountable. Gartner was one of those players who produced wonderfully during the regular season, but regularly failed to equal his output in the playoffs, when the games grew more fierce, the checking grew tougher, and the stakes grew higher.

Keenan had coached Gartner with Team Canada at the 1987 Canada Cup, and he didn't think the winger had enough guts to survive the post-season war he knew the Rangers would have to endure. Although Gartner was the team's number two right wing most of the year, and although he was effective on the power play and a good penalty-killer, Keenan did not see Gartner playing a major role in the Rangers' Stanley Cup run. "If you want that responsibility," Keenan said, "then that commitment has to be demonstrated on the battlefield." He asked Smith to trade Gartner early in the year, pestered him to trade Gartner midway through the year, and begged him to trade him late in the year.

On October 28, in the dressing room after the 3–3 tie with Montreal that prompted his demand for a meeting with Jaffe, Keenan looked Gart-ner in the eye and told him, "You're fuckin' embarrassing yourself." When Gartner scored his 600th NHL goal, his name was discussed with the five men ahead of him on the charts: Howe, Gretzky, Marcel Dionne, Phil Es-posito, and Bobby Hull.

"The people you mentioned," Keenan said, "are legends." The person who had just joined them, he implied silently, was not.

On January 19, Gartner underwent arthroscopic surgery to remove bone chips from his right elbow, an injury that had bothered him most of the season. Gartner waited until the All-Star break so he wouldn't have to miss many games. The medical staff estimated Gartner would miss two weeks and six or seven games. He returned to the lineup in seven days, missing one game. Keenan never said a word in praise.

On February 21 at the Garden, throughout most of the Rangers' 4–3 overtime win over the Penguins, Keenan kept Gartner on the bench. He didn't explain why.

On February 26 at Dallas, after a 3–1 loss, Keenan stormed into the room after the players and yelled, "Mike Gartner. What have you ever done in your life?"

"Excuse me?" Gartner said.

"You were embarrassing out there," Keenan charged. "You just embarrassed yourself."

"What are you talking about? Explain yourself."

"I don't have to. Just ask the two million people who just watched you in New York."

On March 9 in Halifax, Nova Scotia, Gartner scored his 611th goal and passed Hull for fifth place during the Rangers' 7–5 neutral-site victory over the Capitals. But with the trade deadline twelve days away and Keenan's contempt for him obvious to every writer covering the club, he was widely rumored to be on the verge of being dealt. The questions about his Ranger future marred his milestone goal.

"I will not speculate on anything," he said. "I will not speculate on speculation."

Keenan was willing to let Gartner remain a Ranger if Gartner was willing to accept a third- or fourth-line role, but Gartner's intense pride did not allow him to accept such relegation. Between periods of a 3–2 loss in Montreal on January 8, Keenan asked Gartner in front of his teammates if he had "ever gotten the shit beaten out of him by the Montreal Canadiens, and if so, is that why you're playing so scared?"

"No I haven't, Michael," Gartner replied, coining a retort the Rangers used behind Keenan's back all year.

Keenan justified his treatment of Gartner by preaching loyalty: loyalty to the group. Loyalty to the players who were sacrificing more than he felt Gartner was, or ever would.

This is how Keenan described the loyalty he wanted from his players: "I want you to sit in this room and look up across the locker room and see a teammate and be able to say, 'You can depend on me. To do whatever you're asking me to do. It doesn't matter what the coach thinks.'"

Nobody was more loyal than Mike Hartman, who would have fought every heavyweight in the league if Keenan asked, but was lucky to get one or two shifts in the one or two games he played a week. Hartman didn't miss a practice, always stayed out late after morning skates, and never said an unkind word publicly about his precarious predicament as the last man on the team.

Yet on February 14 in Quebec, with the Rangers ahead 4–2 in the third period of a game they won by that score, Keenan needlessly embarrassed Hartman and deprived him of a chance to play. He had called for Hartman to take a rare shift at right wing with Graves and Messier during a TV timeout, and Hartman had a few seconds to stretch the legs that had grown cold sitting on the bench for two periods. During the seventy-second delay, the PA system at Le Colisée broadcast a loud, lively tune to the strumming of a banjo.

"What's that?" Nick Kypreos yelled out. "Hey, Harty, are those your hamstrings?"

Hartman laughed at Kypreos's quip, just as his teammates laughed. Keenan didn't think it was funny.

"What are you laughing at?" Keenan said, staring into the player's face. "Sit down, Harty. You're not going out. You're through."

When something like that happened, Hartman sought the sympathy of the Black Aces. Olczyk, who coined the team's one-for-all phrase "Heave Ho" early in the year and won the team vote as "the player's player" for his positive outlook during a personally miserable year, anchored the Black Aces. They were the band of seldom-used Rangers who named themselves after the color of the practice jersey worn by the guys who couldn't crack the lineup.

Olczyk, Hartman, backup goalie Glenn Healy, defensemen Doug Lidster and Peter Andersson, and swingman Phil Bourque were the Aces, united by their mutual misery. Like their more important teammates, they endured the worst of Keenan; unlike their teammates, they rarely got a chance to contribute to a winning team.

Whenever one of the Aces emerged from a Keenan role meeting, or finished a game in which he dressed but did not play, he'd seek the support of the Aces, who would regularly sing Keenan's familiar refrain:

"Life isn't fair, Eddie . . . Oh, life isn't fair."

"Yes, life isn't fair, Dougie . . . Life isn't fair."

Healy, the chatty backup goalie, had difficulty adjusting to a role in which he played once every two weeks after a season in which he led the Islanders to the semifinals. He hated Keenan's demeaning manipulation of goalies, the way the coach yanked one for the other twelve times in the 84-

game season because of the way the goalie or team was playing—at least twice as often as most other coaches.

Midway through the season, Keenan summoned Healy into his office. On his desk was a copy of a story in which the goalie compared Keenan to Al Arbour, the second-winningest coach in NHL history, behind Scotty Bowman. "Go ahead, tell me, tell me, what's the difference between me and Arbour. Tell me, Glenn."

Healy looked at his coach.

"Four Cups," he said simply.

"Get the fuck out of my office," was Keenan's reply.

Their combustible relationship came to a head on March 5 at Nassau Coliseum. When Richter yielded a goal to Pierre Turgeon at 0:45 of the second period to give the Islanders a 3–2 lead, Keenan yanked him. But at 11:56 of the period, after Healy had made three saves and the Rangers had tied it 3–3 on a Kovalev goal, Healy gave the puck away and the turnover led to a goal.

Keenan yanked him.

Healy plodded back to the bench. He threw his stick into the corner of the bench and took a few steps toward his coach. "Are you fuckin' taking me out for that?" he asked.

Keenan did not reply.

"You cocksucker," Healy hissed.

"That's why there's a five-day waiting period on guns," Richter said later.

The Black Aces used to laugh about their nonstatus. Olczyk, Kypreos (an Ace soon after his arrival in the Larmer trade, though he eventually matriculated to full-time status), Healy, and full-timer Kevin Lowe were hanging around in the players' lounge before practice one morning at Rye when Keenan walked by toward the medical room. All four Rangers were inches from the coach when he strode past.

"Hi, Kevin," Keenan said. And he kept walking.

Players bitched all year about Keenan's treatment. They bitched behind his back to each other, allowed an occasional anonymous quote to sneak into a trusted beat writer's notebook, and ripped him off the record all year long. Yet Keenan got away with his behavior—not because he was a head coach with a five-year contract, and not because the Rangers won virtually all season long.

He got away with it because he had one very key ally. He had Messier.

Mark Douglas Messier was born into hockey on January 18, 1961. His father, Doug, was a rugged minor-league defenseman who played from

1960–70 for Seattle, Edmonton, and Portland of the old Western Hockey League. Doug coached Mark and Mark's older brother, Paul, in the suburban Edmonton youth leagues as soon as they were old enough to skate. During Mark's formative years as a dominant NHL power forward with the Oilers, the elder Messier from 1982–84 served as the acid-tongued general manager–coach of the Moncton Alpines, Edmonton's American Hockey League farm club.

Doug never let Mark win, not at cribbage, bridge, arm wrestling, golf, or hockey. Instead, he taught his son to win by making it so important around the house. Doug had a teaching degree from the University of Alberta, but he put it to best use training Mark how to be a pro.

Mark played his first professional game at the age of seventeen. He signed a five-game tryout contract with the Indianapolis Racers of the World Hockey Association in November 1978. He was signed out of the Western Junior Hockey League to replace another seventeen-year-old, a skinny, pimply-faced kid named Wayne Gretzky, who was sold by Indianapolis to Edmonton. The Racers didn't like what they saw in this raw left wing with the square jaw and the mean streak. But the Cincinnati Stingers signed Messier in January, where he played on a line with another unproven youngster, Mike Gartner.

The WHA died after that season, a voluntary demise brokered by NHL president John A. Ziegler when the established league accepted four franchises—Edmonton Oilers, New England Whalers, Quebec Nordiques, and Winnipeg Jets—and called them expansion teams. Edmonton GM Glen Sather and chief scout Barry Fraser retained the rights to Gretzky, used their first NHL draft pick ever on defenseman Kevin Lowe, and took Messier with their second choice, a third-rounder, the forty-eighth selection in the 1979 draft.

It was easily one of the best choices in hockey history. The Oilers won five Cups, one of them in 1989–90 after Gretzky was traded to Los Angeles and Messier was promoted to team captain. Messier made the successful switch from left wing, where he was a first- or second-team All-Star from 1981–84, to center, where he was a first-team All-Star in 1989–90. He won the Conn Smythe Trophy as playoff MVP in 1984 and the Hart Trophy as regular-season MVP in 1989–90.

Over his twelve years with Edmonton he learned the value of tough love from Glen Sather, who single-handedly ran the team owned by Peter Pocklington. Sather the president and general manager kept salaries laughably low, although the Gretzky–Messier–Paul Coffey–Grant Fuhr Oilers were one of the best teams ever built and were a terrific draw at home and on the road. Sather the coach belittled his players when he needed to, befriended them when he wanted to. Sather the friend was shrewd enough to keep Messier in his confidence and on his side, for he knew Messier was as much a conduit to the locker room as any assistant coach. He was far more influential among teammates, far more important internally, and far more popular publicly.

Mike Keenan knew the same things.

He and Messier never sat down privately to discuss their unique relationship. They didn't have to. Both men were wise and experienced enough to recognize the situation. Messier allowed Keenan a filtered glimpse into the locker room. In exchange, Keenan allowed Messier a voice that no other Ranger had.

Messier was loyal to Keenan in front of his teammates, on and off the ice. He listened to their gripes and remained quiet during the many bitch sessions. Keenan was extremely respectful of Messier, on and off the ice; no veteran was excused more often from practices and morning skates, no player was complimented more often.

To reiterate a point in front of the team, Keenan would say, "Isn't that right, Mark?" To communicate the players' views, Messier would walk into Keenan's office and close the door before he spoke.

Only the imports—former Keenan Blackhawks Larmer and Gilbert, and ex-Oilers Messier, Lowe, Graves, Beukeboom, and Esa Tikkanen—knew from experience how to tolerate a coach like Keenan. Messier had to help educate the rest, and still find time to stand as the Rangers' lightning rod against The Curse of 1940.

The Rangers were New York City's star-crossed franchise because of their half-century of Stanley Cup ineptitude. They maintained a special love-hate relationship with their strong and intensely loyal fans, who spat upon any opposing fan who dared visit the Garden to degrade their Blueshirts, but could shower abuse themselves on the players for one bad pass on a power play early in October. Constantly derided by the suburban devotees on Long Island, whose Islanders won in only their seventh year of existence and reeled off four straight Cups from 1980–83, Ranger fans simply bought more tickets to the games at Nassau Coliseum and outbellowed the bellowers.

They accepted their role as the butt of jokes across the NHL landscape by reminding themselves of the popular New York notion that it was simply a pitiful reaction by fans suffering from our continent's inferiority complex against anything from the Big Apple. This was the arena in which Messier had to work. He relished the opportunity. It was no different, he said, than the fishbowl in Edmonton, where Albertans demanded continued success after the Oilers stopped the Islanders' Drive for Five in 1984.

Beginning in September 1991, after a season in which the Rangers succumbed weakly to the Washington Capitals in six first-round games, Neil Smith began stockpiling the Oilers whom Sather could no longer afford or was unwilling to pay once Edmonton's string of championships ended. Smith first pilfered Adam Graves, a twenty-three-year-old left wing from Toronto whom he had drafted in 1986 for Detroit. The Red Wings had the first pick overall that year and chose Joe Murphy, but they also rated Graves a high first-rounder. When nobody selected the rock-solid young man whose father was a cop and whose mother raised a flock of foster kids in a home filled with love and compassion, the giddy Wings grabbed him and privately labeled him the steal of the draft.

In November 1989, before Graves had become the dominant two-way forward Smith predicted he would one day be, Detroit peddled him to Edmonton. When Graves played out his option following the 1990–91 season to become a free agent requiring arbitrated compensation, Smith signed him. He won the arbitration hearing by having to surrender only Troy Mallette, like Graves a strong young forward, but unlike Graves one who had yet to become more than a borderline NHLer.

On October 4, 1991, Sather and Smith negotiated a more pleasant trade, the Messier blockbuster. For $1.5 million that Pocklington to this day denies he received, center Bernie Nicholls, future considerations, and the two prospects Sather had wanted for Graves (left wing Louie DeBrusk and right wing Steven Rice), Messier became a Ranger.

The future considerations? Another trade a month later, one Smith insisted upon in exchange for the cash, that further strengthened the Rangers' nucleus and enhanced their Stanley Cup chances. The Rangers sent mediocre veteran defenseman David Shaw to Edmonton for Beukeboom, 6-5 and 225 pounds, the intimidating and dangerous body-checker every defense needs.

Lowe arrived next, on December 11, 1992. After playing thirteen years on Pocklington's payroll and watching Gretzky and Messier traded before they took their proper places atop the NHL's salary structure, Lowe held out for his fair share. Sather let him sit for 30 games before trading him to New York for a prospect, Roman Oksyuta, and a third-round pick in the 1993 draft.

Tikkanen, soon due his big payday after playing eight years in Edmonton, was a late-season pickup for center Doug Weight on March 17, 1993. Smith and Sather made the deal on the day the teams were to play at the Garden; when the two players reported for work that night, they were pointed to opposite locker rooms. The unflappable Finn simply shrugged and went to work for his new bosses.

Tikkanen shadowed Gretzky better than anybody in the league, played center or left wing, irritated most of the NHL's big scorers with his non-stop mouth, and frightened them with his stick work. Tikkanen was a valuable asset for another reason, too: he was a kook, a practical joker whose gibberish blend of English and Finnish served to ease the tension of the 84-game grind.

Nobody laughed, however, when the Rangers collapsed after the deadline and missed the playoffs. Critics pointed to the aging imports who had already won their championship rings and labeled the Rangers past-their-prime fossils with too many ex-Oilers.

"Who should I get?" Smith replied with exasperation, "Sharks and Senators?"

He acquired Russians, too. What looked to be a minor preseason swap of defensemen turned into a shrewd steal of a deal from Quebec for Smith and his scouting staff. He sent rookie Mike Hurlbut to the Nordiques for Alexander Karpovtsev, a twenty-three-year-old Muscovite who played four seasons with the Dynamo Moscow team of the Soviet Elite League and had just arrived in North America. Karpovtsev lacked NHL knowledge, and his 6-1, 200-pound body lacked sufficient muscle, but he showed poise with the puck and was unafraid in the corners. Keenan liked him, and he quickly unseated Doug Lidster as the team's sixth defenseman.

Karpovtsev joined Alexei Kovalev, Sergei Zubov, and Sergei Nemchinov as the Rangers' Russian bloc. Kovalev was the most talented of the group, a gifted twenty-year-old right wing with relentless strength, a hard and accurate shot, and incomparable stickhandling moves that infuriated every Ranger coach since his arrival in October 1992. Kovalev was the fifteenth pick of the 1991 draft, the first Russian ever taken in the first round. Christer Rockstrom, the Rangers' crack European scout, considered this enigmatic kid the most talented player available that year. Kovalev seemed to be able to do whatever he wanted with the puck; his only problem was a stubborn desire to display his talents every time he touched it. It wasn't enough to join a rush and finish an attack. He had to skate around all five opponents and fire a perfect shot past the enemy goalie. He was a selfish and immature forward who didn't know when to pass, when to leave the ice at the end of a shift, how to play in his half of the rink, or what the NHL's two-way game was about.

Nemchinov was a throwaway twelfth-round pick in 1990, drafted at the age of twenty-six after nine solid and unremarkable years for the Central Red Army and Soviet Wings. The Rangers hoped they were getting a defensive center when they signed him prior to the 1991–92 season. He exceeded expectations by scoring 30 goals, including 28 at even strength and five that were game-winners, while still displaying dependable checking skills. Better yet, he was mature, durable, and feisty. Few outsiders knew he spoke fine English, because he rarely talked. He was dubbed Sarge, and respected for his professionalism.

Kovalev, who kept a silly purple and yellow troll in his locker, looked and acted younger than twenty. He stood in stark contrast to Nemchinov and Zubov, who handled a very brief demotion professionally. After not dressing for the first two games of the season, he was shipped to Binghamton, but twenty-four hours later he was back when Lowe suffered a minor injury and Patrick was involuntarily checked into Keenan's doghouse.

The 1993–94 Rangers built by Smith and entrusted to Keenan took shape in November. Beukeboom ended his holdout by signing a three-year, $2.3 million contract on November 4, two days after the Larmer trade. Zubov and Karpovtsev solidified their roles as regulars on defense. After their 5-5-1 start, the Rangers reeled off seven straight victories and took possession of first place for good on November 13 with a depth chart that looked like this:

Left wing: Graves, Larmer, Gilbert, Kypreos, Hartman, Bourque.
Center: Messier, Tikkanen, Nemchinov, Olczyk, Hudson.
Right wing: Amonte, Kovalev, Gartner, Kocur.
Left defense: Leetch, Lowe, Karpovtsev, Andersson.
Right defense: Beukeboom, Zubov, Wells, Lidster.
Goal: Richter, Healy.

Richter, who started 0-4 with a 4.11 goals-against average, didn't lose a game for nearly two months. He went 17-0-3 from October 24 to December 19, breaking a team record held since 1940 by Davey Kerr. The team went 12-0-2 from October 24 to November 24, their longest unbeaten streak in twenty-one years. They went 13-0-3 at the Garden from October 24 to January 5, their longest home unbeaten streak in twenty-two years.

Keenan solidified his lines by moving Larmer to right wing with Graves and Messier, and putting Kovalev at center with Tikkanen and Amonte. He got the most out of his top six forwards by cleverly taking full advantage of a new regulation installed at the start of the season. To accommodate sixty-second TV commercials that wouldn't normally fit into the game's flow, the league required the insertion of four seventy-second stoppages, at the first whistle after 17:00, 13:00, 9:00, and 5:00 remained in each period, as long as neither team was on a power play. Keenan made sure he got the Graves-Messier-Larmer line on the ice with Leetch and Beukeboom whenever the game was close to a TV timeout. After a seventy-second break, which was nearly twice as long as the time between most whistles and subsequent faceoff, he would throw the Tikkanen-Kovalev-Amonte line on with Zubov and Lowe. Then he'd come back with his well-rested number one unit. It wasn't uncommon for the Rangers' third line of Gilbert-Nemchinov-Gartner to get little ice time in a game. The fourth line, Kypreos-Olczyk or Hudson-Kocur, hardly played at all.

Through a phenomenal 17-1-2 streak from October 24 through December 15, it wasn't so much the Rangers against their on-ice foes as it was the Rangers against Keenan's image of what the Rangers needed to be when the playoffs began on April 17. Over the first three months of the regular season Keenan rarely mentioned an opponent's strengths and weaknesses, and he almost never matched lines for a strategic advantage. The regular season was basic training, because the war was still months away.

Despite Richter's hot streak, Keenan stayed on top of the goalie and made sure he treated every practice like it was the third period of Game 7 of the finals. "Fuck, you can't handle the stick as well as Eddie Belfour can," he yelled at Richter one day at Rye. "What the fuck is your problem? Are you sure you've been playing this game? You're fuckin' up drills in practice, you're worse than you were the day before."

"You'd walk out saying, 'I'll fuckin' show him,'" Richter explained. "Either way, someone's hitting you in the head, going 'boink' and making you go out there and play harder. One way or the other. It's a skill. It's a skill for a player to be able to do it to himself. It's a skill for a player to be able to hear a criticism or any kind of input from a coach and respond in a positive way."

The formula worked. The Rangers won a majority of their games and kept Keenan relatively sane. The Rangers were 30-12-3 at the All-Star break, first in the Atlantic Division with 63 points and first overall in the NHL.

The Garden was the site of the NHL's forty-fifth All-Star Game on January 22, and the Rangers dominated the spotlight. They donated a league-high four players to the Eastern conference squad: Graves, Leetch, Messier, and Richter. Messier scored a goal and an assist in the East's 9–8 triumph. Graves had two assists and Richter stopped 19 of 21 second-period shots, including four breakaways by Vancouver ace Pavel Bure, to win a new truck as the game's MVP.

"I put the truck in his garage," Bure said.

• • •

The second half of the season began with a three-game, six-day trip to California. Like most GMs, Smith accompanied his team on a majority of its road trips. Getting away from the office gave Smith the chance to watch his team practice, something he wouldn't have time to do at home even if he worked out of an office at Rye rather than the Garden. It gave him a chance to assess the other teams by watching their practices live, and it gave him an opportunity to network with agents and hockey people who didn't come to New York.

Unlike most GMs, Smith rarely saw his coach on the road. The brief postgame powwows that were traditional between GM and coach after games were awkward—when they happened at all. Smith barely made the team's flight to San Francisco because he was so ill, sick with the flu, and sick of how Keenan kept complaining about him. The coach didn't like the GM making every road trip because he didn't like the way Smith hobnobbed with the players at breakfast in the hotel, picking up the checks. Smith acted as much like a buddy as like a boss, which Keenan believed undermined his ability to play bad cop.

He didn't tell Smith this. He complained to his PR guy, Barry Watkins, who found himself just as uncomfortably in the middle whenever Smith complained to him that Keenan was acting like a jerk.

"Talk to each other," Watkins implored both men. "You wouldn't need me."

Smith grew tired of Keenan's disrespectful treatment of everyone. Keenan treated Watkins like a brother, but would not even say hello to Watkins's assistants, Kevin McDonald and John Rosasco. One day at Rye, Keenan walked out of his office toward the coaches' dressing area wearing only a towel. To get from his office to the dressing area he had to pass through a hallway where McDonald and Rosasco happened to be standing. There was barely enough room to get by without bumping into the men, yet Keenan walked past two of his employees without saying hello or even nodding. He just ignored them.

Keenan constantly asked Matthew Loughran, the director of team services, who coordinated the team's travel, to juggle flight arrangements and practice times with very little notice. When he did speak to the capable and well-liked McDonald, it was usually to have him run some trivial errand. Interns and secretaries were ignored, unless he needed something done immediately.

Even Watkins was bitten by the pit bull. It happened one day in early February, due to a scheduling mix-up. The Rangers had a game in Ottawa on February 12, a game two nights later at Quebec, and three days off before a game at the Garden. Keenan wanted to stay in Quebec and take the team to the Laurentian Mountains for three days.

Keenan had planned this retreat in his mind for over a month, but was told by Watkins three weeks before that they had to return to New York immediately after the Quebec game. They had two mandatory charity events on their schedule for the fifteenth and sixteenth. The PR department had confirmed these commitments with Keenan months ago, but he didn't have them logged in his ledger, they totally slipped his mind when he came up with the idea of staying in the Laurentians, and he hadn't been reminded of them by Watkins because they were still three weeks away.

Keenan went ballistic. He summoned Watkins to Rye and bawled him out so severely, Watkins returned to the Garden looking like he had lost a prizefight. Watkins didn't bother pointing out Keenan's culpability, because he felt it was futile applying logic to the rantings of a madman. He took the punches, walked away, and reminded himself that Keenan had to take a bite out of someone every once in a while to absolve himself of blame. Watkins quickly forgot about it, since it was the only time in a year of intense day-to-day dealings that the coach took anything out on him.

Keenan had more problems with Kovalev, who was suspended for a total of eight games for three stick incidents over the first 55 games. Keenan threatened to bench him. He threatened to trade him. In a 6–3 loss to Boston at home on February 23, a game in which Kovalev scored his first goal in 10 games and only his ninth of the season, Keenan put him on the ice early in the third period and let him take a shift that seemed to never end.

Kovalev kept skating over to the bench to change on the fly, and Keenan kept waving him back out. So he stayed out. And out. And out. Keenan did it to shame Kovalev for his tendency to overstay shifts, but the young forward thought he was being rewarded with extra ice time. Talk about losing something in translation.

Keenan finally got through to Kovalev a few games later, when he shifted him from right wing to center. The open ice in the middle of the rink and the added responsibility of taking faceoffs and defending the slot woke the Russian up. He responded to Keenan's shrewd move by scoring 14 goals in his final 25 games.

On March 14 at Florida, the Rangers' fourth game in six nights after a tie at Boston and a loss at Pittsburgh, Keenan for the second time in the season refused to coach the team. The Rangers were playing poorly in a game they eventually lost 2–1, and at one point Keenan sarcastically asked if anyone was going to play. "I don't care who goes out," he said. Again, the Rangers started changing lines themselves. Players screamed, "I'm the next left wing," "I'm up at center."

It was another eight-minute span of chaos.

Keenan considered Smith's insecure personality a serious weakness. He respected Smith's ability to scout talent, but he believed he had a far keener eye for creating a winner than his boss did. He was a gambler, and he despised what he considered Smith's aversion to risk. He contemptuously labeled the GM a wimp who avoided confrontations.

Ironically, Keenan rarely confronted the GM with his complaints. He insulted him behind his back and embarrassed him by ignoring him in front of other employees. Smith couldn't understand why.

"What did I do?" the GM asked Watkins midway through the year. "He asked for players, I gave them to him. He asked to have the dressing room redone, I gave it to him. I've given him every tool to work with. Why doesn't he like me?"

The answer was simple. Keenan could not or would not distinguish between the personal and professional aspects of the relationship. The mandate was win a Cup, not make a friend. Keenan wanted everybody on edge, even his boss. But as the Rangers cruised toward the Presidents' Trophy and a first seed in the playoffs, Smith grew more miserable by the day.

Keenan and Smith's sour relationship reached its regular-season nadir (not to be confused with the even greater depths of their playoff divorce) on March 18, three days before the trading deadline. A 7–3 Garden loss to Chicago left the Rangers 1-3-1 in their last five games. They were still atop the East, but the rival New Jersey Devils had crept to within two points. Messier was out a few days with a bruised thigh. Lowe's back was bothering him. And the Rangers' next five games were on the road over eight days beginning in Calgary the day after the deadline.

Gutkowski took a call from Rob Campbell, Keenan's agent, who voiced many of the same complaints Keenan had voiced at the Rye powwow in July and at the Jaffe meeting in October: the team wasn't gritty enough; it wasn't going to withstand the two-month playoff marathon; Keenan was frustrated by Smith's inability to make a deal.

Protocol had been breached again, but Gutkowski didn't have time to wallow in formality. He knew his GM and coach hadn't been communicating well. He knew from his informal conversations with Keenan that the coach didn't have the team he wanted.

"You're gonna get seduced like you were two years ago," Keenan warned him several times, referring to the quarterfinal loss to Pittsburgh in 1992, a year the Rangers won the Presidents' Trophy and believed they were going to win the Cup. "You hit the marathon, all of a sudden you're in the second round, and you don't have enough."

Gutkowski agreed with Keenan that the team's mix wasn't quite right, but he wasn't getting paid to make the hockey decisions. Instead, he called Keenan and Smith to his office at 10 A.M. the following day, March 19. Smith balked. He did not think he'd have any luck communicating productively with Keenan. For his part, Keenan welcomed the opportunity to speak his piece again.

The meeting began promptly in the conference room adjacent to Gutkowski's Penn Plaza office. "I've got real concerns," he told his fractured tandem. "I've got concerns about the team, but I have concerns about this relationship. You guys may be talking, but you're not communicating. I don't care how much you guys hate each other, if you hate each other. We're going to sit here until we get everything out in the open. If you guys have got problems with each other, you have to be honest with each other, look him right in the face and tell him why you don't like each other, why you do, what are the problems you have. We're not leaving here today until we figure out what we have to do."

Keenan spoke first. "Neil, you think I want your goddamned job and I don't," he said. "We're not good enough. You think we are good enough, and I don't think you're going out and making trades that have to be made."

The coach did not get nasty or personal. He did not question Smith's work ethic. He limited his criticism to what he considered the GM's flawed opinion of the Rangers' Stanley Cup chances, and Smith's insecure belief that Keenan wanted his job.

"I don't think you're out to get my job," Smith said.

"Look, Neil," Gutkowski interrupted. "You can say that, but I've gotta be honest with you. If I read in the papers that somebody's after my job, that's gotta bother me. If that bothers you, get it out in the open, let's talk about it."

"No, it really doesn't bother me," Smith insisted. "I'm here to do the best to get Mike what he wants. But, Mike, sometimes you don't say what you want. You want things done, but you're not specific."

"Neil, you're very analytical," Keenan said. "You have an analytical hockey mind. I'm more of a touchy-feely guy. I know if I'm making stew, when I lick the spoon I'll know if it needs a little more salt."

"Mike, that's a good point," Gutkowski interjected. "But if you think you need salt, but you don't tell Neil it needs salt, how the hell is Neil gonna go get you salt?"

"I don't know," Keenan conceded sheepishly.

"You're gonna sit there in the dark because you're not telling him what you want," Gutkowski said. "That's the rap I hear on you, Mike. So if you think you gotta have salt, then tell Neil. And you know what? Neil's pretty good at going to get salt."

Smith was energized by the analogy. The constructive dialogue relaxed him. "Mike, you gotta let me know, I'll do what you want, tell me what you want."

For ninety minutes they talked. Gartner's name came up. Keenan said he believed Smith did not want to trade away Gartner because he had traded for him, and because Gartner was such a popular Ranger with the fans. The truth is, Smith had tried to comply with Keenan's request in January, but had difficulty finding a team willing to surrender anything of value for a thirty-four-year-old right wing making $1.2 million who had never enjoyed playoff success.

When the GM and coach stopped identifying each other's flaws, they started brainstorming the team's playoff needs. They agreed that the corps of forwards needed to get bigger and grittier. They agreed that they needed more depth up front. When Gutkowski heard the meeting headed in this direction, he stood up, walked out the door, and headed back to his office.

"You guys tell me when you're done," he said.

Two hours later they emerged, smiling. Later that afternoon, Smith called Gutkowski and thanked him for the meeting. "It was a really good meeting. I never thought it would work out that way."

Keenan called and said, "It was very positive. I hope we can do something now."

For the first time in weeks, Gutkowski was confident they would. He liked knowing that whether the Rangers traded half the team away two days later or stood pat, Smith and Keenan were going to decide from a Calgary hotel room without killing each other.

"At the end of that meeting I walked down to see Monie Begley [the Garden's director of public relations]," Gutkowski recalled. "I said, 'Monie, if we win the Stanley Cup, it'll be because of that meeting.' It turned out to be the final piece."

Gutkowski's meeting ignited the events of March 21, 1994, trade deadline day, the most productive day in the Smith-Keenan relationship and one of the most impressive days of Smith's executive career. With assistant GM Larry Pleau, Keenan, and assistants Campbell and Todd piled into his

Calgary hotel suite, Smith worked his two phone lines all day and acquired the final pieces of the outfit Keenan eagerly planned to take to war.

Smith pulled off five trades that drastically improved the Rangers' depth at forward, added Stanley Cup experience, rid the team of two disgruntled spares, and addressed Keenan's oft-stated desire for additional grit, toughness, and size. He acquired two more ex-Oilers and two ex-Blackhawks. He added by adding and he added by subtracting.

Gartner was traded to the Toronto Maple Leafs for Glenn Anderson, Messier's longtime right wing and a five-time Cup winner. Amonte was traded to Chicago for right wing Brian Noonan and left wing Stephane Matteau, two forwards Keenan had coveted all year. Center Todd Marchant, a prospect who signed with the Rangers after finishing his year with the 1994 U.S. Olympic Team that competed at Lillehammer, Norway, was dealt to Edmonton for center Craig MacTavish. Peter Andersson was sent to Florida for a draft pick. Bourque was exiled to Ottawa for nothing.

"When you're this close," Smith said after his shopping day ended, "you've got to take the kick at the can. We owed that to the fans who've waited all these years. We have a team that can win the Stanley Cup. I believe it. Mike believes it. The players believe it."

Publicly, that's what they had to say. Privately, though, they were saying the exact same things as well. After announcing the trades and informing the traveling writers that all four new Rangers would be in the lineup the next night against the Flames, Watkins called Gutkowski.

"The coach is really happy," a giddy Watkins reported. "He's got the team he wants. He thinks he's gonna win the Stanley Cup."

The ease with which Smith and Keenan temporarily repressed their petty personal gripes and worked together to pull off this stunning lineup transformation defied belief. For two good offensive players in whom Keenan had no confidence and who were not going to be on the top two lines, the Rangers acquired a first-line right wing, a second-line left wing, a third-line right wing, and a highly dependable checking center who could win faceoffs and play on either the third or fourth lines.

The deals balanced the Rangers' depth chart for the first time all season (players acquired since Keenan's arrival are in italics):

First line: Graves-Messier-*Anderson.*
Second line: *Matteau*-Kovalev-*Larmer.*
Third line: Tikkanen-*MacTavish*-*Noonan.*
Fourth line: *Gilbert*-Nemchinov-Kocur.
Extras: *Kypreos*, Olczyk, *Hudson*, Hartman.

First defense pair: Leetch-Beukeboom.
Second defense pair: Lowe-Zubov.
Third defense pair: Wells-*Karpovtsev.*
Extra: *Lidster.*
Goalies: Richter, *Healy.*

It was a stunning transformation from the team Keenan bitched about in October. Gone from the twenty-man nucleus were Gartner, Turcotte, Patrick, and Amonte. In their place stood Anderson, Larmer, MacTavish, Matteau, Noonan, and Kypreos.

Keenan now had seven ex-Oilers who had won Stanley Cups in Edmonton (Graves, Messier, Anderson, Tikkanen, MacTavish, Beukeboom, and Lowe), Gilbert, who had won three Cups with the Islanders, and five former Blackhawks (Gilbert, Larmer, Matteau, Noonan, and Hudson).

Placing Anderson with Graves and Messier added defensive tenacity to the number one line. Fitting Matteau and Larmer around the gifted Kovalev improved the number two line's strength along the boards and its back-checking diligence. Putting Tikkanen with MacTavish and Noonan gave Keenan a bona fide checking line that could shadow and pester a foe's top guns. Having Gilbert and Nemchinov as fourth-liners, and Kocur as a heavyweight enforcer, testified to the Rangers' overall improvement.

For the moment, that is. No objective hockey expert believed that the Rangers had improved their future. Amonte was twenty-three and already a 35-goal scorer. Marchant was twenty. Anderson was an old thirty-three with a ton of Stanley Cup playoff miles under his hood. He was also an unrestricted free agent after the season who upon his arrival told Smith he planned to play the following season in Europe. MacTavish was thirty-five, another soon-to-be free agent who was contemplating retirement.

Matteau and Noonan were different. Matteau was twenty-four and a second-round pick by Calgary in 1987. Noonan was twenty-eight, a ninth-round pick of the Blackhawks in 1983 who had bounced between the minors and NHL throughout the late 1980s. Nobody believed that either player would have a better NHL career than Amonte, but Keenan explained to Smith that both young forwards had been terrific in the Blackhawks' run to the 1992 finals. Both overachieved and showed a hunger for winning. Both were physically stronger than Amonte, a critical factor in the debilitating 25-games-in-60-days run for the Cup.

A reunion with the demanding Keenan was a lifeboat for Matteau, a strapping French-Canadian from Rouyn-Noranda, Quebec, who was not a self-motivator and rarely played to his potential. At 6-3 and 205 pounds, he had the ability to be a physically imposing left wing, but he rarely played tough enough. He often lost loose pucks in the corners to smaller but hungrier players. He had already been dumped by Calgary and was now being discarded by Chicago.

Keenan would be good for him. For Noonan, too.

Noonan was another grinding winger who needed a steady poke from Keenan's cattle prod. He was a 6-1, 197-pounder from Boston with more natural talent than Matteau, but not significantly more. He caught Keenan's eye in the 1992 playoffs, when he finished fourth (behind Jeremy Roenick, Chelios, and Larmer) in team scoring, picking up 15 points in 18 playoff games after getting only 31 in 65 regular-season games. That was what Keenan loved, and remembered.

Anderson for Gartner was a no-brainer. For a guy whose fourteen NHL teams had never reached the semifinals, the Rangers added a player whose thirteen teams had reached the semifinals eight times, the finals six times, and had won five Cups. He was an integral part of Edmonton's success in the 1980s. He had the speed to outskate defenders, the strength to battle in the corners, and the mean streak to use his stick as an intimidating weapon, which was something Keenan admired. The altar boy didn't want choirboys gunning for the grail.

Anderson was another product of the Oilers' fabulous 1979 draft, a fourth-rounder taken after Edmonton had already selected Lowe and Messier. Anderson and Messier grew up together in Sather's system, triumphed together, bled together, skated together. Anderson was an erratic performer throughout his career who never seemed to care until playoff time. His skills had diminished far more rapidly than Messier's. Keenan correctly guessed that reuniting them next to the red-hot and hyperkinetic Graves would recharge both vets.

Hockey fans across the continent recognized MacTavish as the NHL's dinosaur, the last player to skate without a helmet on his head. Helmets became mandatory after MacTavish broke into the league with Boston in 1979–80, and he retained the right to sign a waiver each year freeing himself from the head gear.

The MacTavish deal surprised even Keenan, and he was in the room. With the deadline minutes away and Smith on a hot streak, the GM got on the phone with Sather and tried to pry two-way left wing Shayne Corson from the perennially financially strapped Oilers for a few prime prospects. Sather wouldn't budge.

"Well, who else have you got available?" Smith asked.

"Do you want MacTavish?" Sather replied.

The two GMs had talked about a trade involving the veteran two weeks earlier, but those talks quickly died when Sather asked for far too much in return. This time, however, Sather asked only for Marchant, whom the Rangers had selected in the seventh round of the 1993 draft. As the clock neared 2 P.M. Mountain Standard Time, the trading deadline, the coaches huddled. They considered the benefits of a savvy checking center. It meant Tikkanen could play left wing, his best position. It meant Kovalev could return to right wing, if necessary.

Smith then asked Pleau, the team's player development chief, to project Marchant's current and future contributions to the organization. Pleau agreed that he was a price worth paying for MacTavish.

"Okay, MacTavish for Marchant," Smith blurted out to Sather. "I'll phone Central Registry. We're almost out of time."

The final four weeks of the regular season was time on the Rangers' side. Still, they did not coast. Beginning with a 4–4 tie at Calgary in which Anderson scored two goals and Matteau tied it with fourteen seconds left in regulation, the four new Rangers mixed perfectly with the core group. The playoffs had been a lock since March 20, and so Keenan began subtly to cut back the ice time of his top players. Messier, Leetch, Zubov, and Graves still logged many minutes and Richter started 13 of the last 15 games, but Anderson, Noonan, Matteau, and MacTavish all took regular shifts each game and were given opportunities to play the power play, kill penalties, take critical faceoffs, and handle the last minutes of periods and games. It was Keenan's attempt to make them all feel integral parts of the project.

Graves capped a career year in Edmonton the night after the Calgary game. He scored two goals, his 50th and 51st, to tie and break Vic Hadfield's twenty-one-year-old Ranger record for goals in a season. Graves finished with 52, fifth-highest in the NHL. The Devils pulled even with the Rangers while the Rangers were in the middle of a five-game road trip, but the Rangers on March 29 held on to the top spot in Philadelphia. Leading 3–2, they yielded a Mikael Renberg goal with 4:37 left; exactly four minutes later, Larmer and Matteau set up Kovalev for a thrilling 4–3 win that capped a 3-1-1 trip.

The bus ride home was lively. After the pizzas were gobbled, the Rangers' favorite movie, *Stripes*, was popped into the VCR beside the driver that piped it into two dozen screens mounted overhead every few rows. Fifteen minutes into the Bill Murray comedy, however, Keenan ordered Todd to shut the tape off.

The players collectively moaned. "What's going on?" they shouted.

Silence. Players looked around, fearing the inevitable volcanic eruption from their head coach. But before anything happened, a few players started whispering, *"Stripes, Stripes, Stripes."* The chant grew louder as the giggles increased. Within a matter of seconds the entire bus was yelling, *"STRIPES, STRIPES, STRIPES."*

"Ah," Keenan muttered. "Turn the fuckin' thing on."

And now the chorus erupted anew:

"For he's a jolly good fellow, for he's a jolly good fellow, for he's a jolly good fellow . . . which nobody can deny."

Keenan grinned. This, after all, was his team.

He didn't have to go to his whip, and still the Rangers roared to an 8-2-2 post-deadline finish. They clinched first in the Atlantic Division, the top Eastern Conference seed, and the Presidents' Trophy with a 5–3 Garden victory over Toronto, six days before the end of the regular season. Keenan had talked all year about the regular season being an 84-game marathon tune-up. So the press wondered why he went all out so late in the regular season. Was the Presidents' Trophy worth such sweat?

"The only reason we want first place overall, the only thing I can think of," Keenan said, "is that we could play the seventh game of the Stanley Cup finals in Madison Square Garden."

4

Now I Can
Die in Peace

The Rangers and their rabid fans couldn't have picked a more delectable first-round opponent than their despised suburban rivals, the New York Islanders. This rivalry was born in 1972, when Long Island was awarded an expansion team. It became a legitimate battle three years later, in the first round of the 1975 playoffs, when the upstarts eliminated the established favorites in Game 3 of their miniseries. April 11, 1975, became one of the darkest days in Ranger history when J.P. Parise scored at 0:11 of OT, a goal that silenced the Garden like no other in this team's agonizing history.

The Rangers replied in 1979 with a phenomenal six-game semifinals triumph that preceded their final-round loss to the Montreal Canadiens, but the Islanders' Cup championships in 1980–83 overshadowed that upset. The Rangers hadn't returned to the finals since.

In the early 1980s, the less hockey-sophisticated but more decorous and sociable Coliseum fans outdid their unconscionable Garden counterparts, the ones who thought nothing of unfurling banners from the blue seats during the National Anthem scribbled with profane epithets aimed at the Flyers' Dave Brown or the Islanders' Denis Potvin. With equal measures of cruelty and cleverness, they mocked the Garden's rhythmic "Let's Go Rangers" cadence by reminding the team of its cursed legacy. "Nineteen-forty," they sang whenever the Rangers visited the Island. "Nineteen-forty." Fans throughout the league adopted the vindictive carol, and the Rangers were serenaded across North America for years.

Keenan's club did not hide from 1940. From the early training camp moment when he showed them the video of past victory parades, Keenan challenged them to accept the responsibility of killing the curse. Messier told his teammates to consider it an honor to be entrusted with the job of ending the fifty-three-year-old drought. The team ignored Ranger-Islander playoff history, rejected the notion that this blood-boiling rivalry would make a terrific series, and pointed to the fact that it had finished first over-all with 112 points while the Isles finished eighth in the East with 84 points, edging out the freshmen Florida Panthers by one point for the final Eastern playoff berth.

That was the first good omen. The Rangers didn't want to play Florida, a disciplined band of checkers coached by Roger Neilson and led by John Vanbiesbrouck, who had a phenomenal year in goal. They wanted the Is-landers, whom they had beaten 5–4 at Nassau on March 5, their first win on the Island since 1989. They wanted feisty, stick-wielding Ron Hextall, a marked enemy of Ranger fans since his Flyer days and a goalie strug-gling to regain his 1987–88 rookie form, when he carried Keenan's Flyers to the finals and won the Conn Smythe Trophy in defeat.

The Rangers got Hextall, and they pelted him. They drubbed the Is-landers 6–0, 6–0, 5–1, and 5–2. It was the second-most lopsided series in Stanley Cup history. Not only didn't the Isles score a goal on Richter in Games 1 and 2 at the Garden, they yielded the first three goals of Game 3 and didn't hold a lead until Game 4, when they blew an early 2–0 edge.

Leetch, Messier, Kovalev, Zubov, and Graves dominated offensively. Leetch, Beukeboom, Lowe, and MacTavish dominated defensively. As-signed the job of checking Pierre Turgeon, the Islanders' star center, Mac-Tavish held him to one assist and seven shots in the four games while scoring a goal and an assist himself. Richter stopped 21 and 29 shots for the back-to-back shutouts in the first two games, and 87 of 90 in the series. Healy, whose goaltending the previous spring had carried the Islanders to the semifinals, did not play, but he contributed a wealth of preseries tips to his teammates. "I know their team better than ours," he joked.

The four-game sweep signaled the Rangers' legitimacy. Favored top seeds are supposed to crush playoff pretenders. Serious marathoners aren't supposed to feel pain in the first few miles. By dispatching the Islanders so quickly, the Rangers got six days to reload for round two. Zubov got to rest the tender elbow over which Islander ruffian Mick Vukota broke his aluminum stick. Kovalev got to rest the backs of his calves, which were chopped at all series by checking center Benoit Hogue. Matteau got to rest an aching back that had absorbed a series of cross-checks in front of Hextall's net. Jay Wells got to rest his aching head, the one that absorbed a few sucker punches from a frustrated Vukota in the final period of the final game.

It took five more days for the East to complete its first round, and for the second-round pairings to fall into place. The Devils got Boston. The Rangers got Washington.

Ranger lore is filled with sad stories of good teams with fair Cup chances getting derailed by critical injuries to key players. Three times in the last twenty years the Rangers' hearts were broken by a fractured ankle: Jean Ratelle's in 1972, Ulf Nilsson's in 1979, Leetch's in 1990. This year, though, fate had it backwards. It was the Capitals who came into the series without their number two defenseman, Calle Johansson, who had been seriously injured in the previous round. Then, in Game 1, injuries floored one of their top scorers, Michal Pivonka, and their number one goalie, Don Beaupre.

The Rangers held serve in Games 1 and 2 at home, 6–3 and 5–2. On the day of Game 2, Viacom confirmed rumors that it was entertaining bids for its sports package—the Knicks, the Rangers, MSG Network, and the arena itself—starting at $1 billion. It needed the cash to pay down the $8 billion it had financed to buy Paramount Communications, the entertainment company that had purchased the Knicks, Rangers, arena, and cable network in 1977 for $60 million. Blockbuster Entertainment, ITT-Cablevision, Nike, the New York Times Company, and TCI Communications expressed early interest.

The already high stakes were now raised. It wasn't just the nation's sports eyes on Keenan's Rangers and Pat Riley's Knicks, who were busy making an NBA championship run of their own. Wall Street was now watching. Smith, whose Ranger presidency would have pushed him closer to the fiscal corporate game being played above him if he wasn't so focused on the team on the ice below him, tried not to let the pressure cascade upon him.

But he erred. Midway through the second-round series he agreed to be interviewed for a flattering series of articles that ran in the *New York Post* during the break after the Washington series. The headline, "How Neil Smith Put Rangers on Road to Cup," enraged Messier because he felt it was premature to start accepting praise for a job half done.

"We haven't won anything yet," Messier grumbled to Keenan.

Keenan never needed a reason to rip Smith behind his back, but this incident provided sufficient fodder for a few days. Keenan bitched to Watkins, who filtered the complaint to his boss. Smith reread the articles, concluded that in typical *Post* style the headline was far more inflammatory than the story beneath it, and told Watkins to assure Keenan it wouldn't happen again.

With the Rangers sequestered in Annapolis, Maryland, before Games 3 and 4 at the depressingly dark and unexciting USAir Arena in Landover, Colin Campbell dissected the tapes of Games 1 and 2, organized the statistics the team considered most crucial (scoring chances and body checks), and issued a warning. The assistant was Keenan's Xs and Os strategist, and he detected that although they had won the first two games by three goals each and delivered as many body checks as they absorbed, the Rangers had yielded more scoring chances than they generated. They were actually outplayed and outworked. They won because Richter greatly outplayed Beaupre in Game 1 and Rick Tabaracci in Game 2.

The Caps must have sensed that they weren't pummeled in New York. At practice the day before Game 3, right wing Peter Bondra and coach Jim Schoenfeld guaranteed victory over a team that was 6–0 in the playoffs and hadn't even been scared.

"We're going to win both games at home," Bondra boasted. "The Rangers aren't that good. They're not unbeatable. They have all these names from the past. They are past their primes."

"We will go out on the ice and win Game 3," Schoenfeld echoed.

They didn't come close. The Rangers passed another early marathon test. They needed to step up, and they stepped up, choking off the Caps' scoring chances, tightening their style of play, and routing Washington, 3–0. Bondra was kayoed midway through the game when he missed a check on Kovalev, hit the boards, and bruised his left shoulder.

Leetch was supernatural. He scored the first goal, set up Messier for the second, and controlled the game in a way Chris Chelios never could. He hit, rushed, sat back, and quarterbacked the power play flawlessly. After the game he revealed that a season of sweat under Keenan's iron fist had his weight at 184, down from 194; he said he felt lighter and quicker on his skates, but just as strong along the boards because of Keenan's season-long weight program.

Left unsaid was how contagious Messier's superstardom had become. Most sports superstars in the egotistical 1990s act better off the stage than on it. Their games detract from their videos and shoe commercials, or so it seems. Messier never fell into that trap, even when he lived it up off the ice as an Edmonton Oiler; the bigger the game, the better he played. He recognized his role, accepted his responsibility, and relished his opportunity.

Now, so did Leetch.

The Rangers lost Game 4 on the road, 4–2, but rebounded from their first poor playoff game by eliminating the Caps in a terrific fifth game at the Garden, 4–3, on Leetch's goal with 3:28 left in regulation. The indomitable defenseman dished out assists on the other three goals, and obliterated a bad, bad memory of a bad, bad goal exactly two years earlier.

On May 9, 1992, the last time the Rangers were Presidents' Trophy–winning Cup favorites, they held a two-games-to-one lead over the Pittsburgh Penguins. They led Game 4 at Pittsburgh, 4–2, midway through the third period. But with just over five minutes remaining, after Pittsburgh killed a major penalty, Ron Francis slapped a seventy-five-footer that somehow eluded Richter. The stunned Rangers never recovered. The Pens tied it in regulation, won it in OT, and captured Games 5 and 6.

Richter had been living with the memory of that goal for two years when Game 5 began with Graves scoring at 1:46. Less than four minutes later, Kevin Hatcher lofted a long pop-up intended to clear the zone from behind his blue line and kill some time off a Caps penalty. The puck flew down ice, bounced ten feet in front of Richter, and spun wackily to his right. He tried to react, but the puck floated by him and into the corner of the net.

"The only thing that went through my mind," Smith said after the game, "was not, 'Uh-oh, this is like Pittsburgh,' but that people are going to say, 'Oh, no, this is just like Pittsburgh.'"

Bad ice, bad ankles, bad goals. It was not hard for the Garden fans to conjure images of disaster. But this mentally tough team shook off the horrendous fluke goal. Graves scored two and a half minutes later, and Tikkanen made it 3–1 before the first period was over. After Washington rallied to tie, Leetch finished the Caps and the first half of the journey.

The easy half.

The Rangers' Eastern Conference finals opponent was easy to underrate. Although they play only eight miles from Manhattan in the Brendan Byrne Arena of the Meadowlands Sports Complex, a fifteen-minute drive (except during rush hour) through the Lincoln Tunnel, the New Jersey Devils had been the Rangers' weak sibling since their arrival on June 30, 1982. They were created by John McMullen, a naval commander from 1936 to 1954 who was born in Jersey City, grew up in nearby Montclair, and became a multimillionaire in the shipping and shipbuilding busi-nesses.

McMullen bought the moribund Colorado Rockies, who had spent six years in Denver after moving from Kansas City, where the expansion Scouts lasted only two miserable seasons. This transient franchise ex-pected to fill the nineteen thousand seats at the spanking-new Meadow-lands Arena, but after ten years it had only served as an additional day's rest stop for NHL teams on road trips to New York.

McMullen and Lou Lamoriello, his president-GM since April 30, 1987, were low-key, conservative businessmen who believe players are serfs who perform better and stay hungrier before they are tendered the large paychecks so prevalent in professional sports. Although McMullen cried poverty and managed to renegotiate his Meadowlands lease in 1986 and 1991, he believed in the sanctity of contracts and demanded undying loy-alty from his employees. He and Lamoriello, who owned a small slice of the team, eschewed the star system; they wanted the Devils to be a name-less, faceless collection of enterprising overachievers.

In 1993–94, under new coach Jacques Lemaire, the former Montreal Canadien great, they were just that.

Because Keenan's Rangers so dominated the New York scene, the Dev-ils completed a 106-point season under their rookie coach with hardly a mention. Because the Rangers had steamrolled the Islanders and handily disposed of the Capitals, few hockey people around the metropolitan area bothered to notice that the Devils survived a fabulous seven-game first round with the Buffalo Sabres by winning the deciding game at home, 2–1, just forty-eight hours after they lost Game 6 at Buffalo, 1–0, at 5:43 of a fourth overtime. Then, after losing Games 1 and 2 at home to Boston, they remarkably rebounded to sweep the next four.

The Monster of Madison Square Garden was pulling an eighteen-wheel bandwagon of fanatics-come-lately who had no grasp of hockey reality. All they knew was, the Stanley Cup was eight wins away. Few of them knew that a twenty-one-year-old rookie goalie named Martin Brodeur was every bit as good as Mike Richter, or that ex-Ranger Bernie Nicholls had given the team some badly needed offensive pizzazz, or that Scott Stevens had a regular season as good as Leetch's.

Nobody bothered to do the arithmetic. The Rangers finished with 112 points, 12 on the strength of their 6–0 sweep of the Devils. Had New Jersey won only two of the six games, they would have finished first over-all, 110–108. It took Messier, a close friend of Devil defenseman Ken Daneyko since boyhood and an usher at Daneyko's wedding, to temper the party and remind his teammates that they weren't even close yet.

The first thing he did was to discard the significance of the Rangers' regular-season dominance over the Devils. Messier knew from his years of playoff experience that head-to-head competition over an 84-game schedule was no comparison to seven consecutive meetings over thirteen days, a game every other day. Teams don't have time during the regular season to prepare specifically for an opponent. During the playoffs they do, and that would make a difference, especially for Lemaire's team. Unlike the Rangers, who applied pressure in all three zones and forechecked relentlessly, the Devils played a system of neutral-zone checking designed to trap their opponents, cause turnovers, and create transitional odd-man rushes.

The Rangers were punchers, the Devils were counterpunchers. When the Devils played their system well, they were difficult to play. They sat four players back in center ice and dared their opponents to charge two hundred feet up ice. They slowed the tempo, dumped the puck out of their zone and into their opponent's; a 3–2 game with just a handful of good scoring chances each was exactly what they wanted.

Messier reminded his teammates not to get impatient. Privately, though, he was. That's because in talks with his friends who played in the Western Conference, especially best friend Wayne Gretzky, he heard that the West finalists, the Vancouver Canucks and Toronto Maple Leafs (Mike Gartner was in the semis for the first time), were not going to pose the challenge the Devils would.

"I knew if we won this series," Messier admitted months later, "we'd win the Cup."

Keenan and Smith stopped speaking as the Rangers and Devils prepared to square off. Keenan was still angry about the series in the *Post,* he didn't want Smith patting the players on the back, and he didn't think the GM had any business hanging around now that his job was basically done.

Smith was irritated by a brief encounter at the team meal on the afternoon of Game 4 at Washington. After he served himself a plate of food at the buffet table and found a seat at one of the large, round tables near Wells and Kocur, he told Wells he had spoken to the league about disciplining Mick Vukota for the nonsense at the end of the Islander series.

"Oh, good," Wells said.

"Yeah, I'm going to make sure something happens with that," Smith replied.

At that moment, Keenan sat down at the table.

"From what I hear, it won't cost him any money," Wells said, meaning that Vukota's suspension might occur during the 1994–95 exhibition season, when players aren't paid.

"Oh, no," Smith replied. "It'll be regular-season games."

Keenan then interrupted. "You guys shouldn't be talking contract. It's the playoffs."

"What?" Smith said as Wells and Kocur began to giggle.

"I'm serious," Keenan said.

"Mike, you weren't listening to what we were talking about. You didn't hear what we were talking about. We were talking about what happened between Jay and Vukota."

"What about Vukota?" Keenan asked.

"We were talking about him getting suspended," Wells said.

"Oh," Keenan concluded.

Kocur and Smith left the table together a few minutes later. "Boy, he loses it sometimes," the player told the GM. And then Kocur, who grew up in Detroit's organization along with Smith, began to laugh. "Why don't you fire the fuck?" he joked.

It didn't matter now that Smith and Keenan weren't speaking; the GM had finished his job, and the coach still had his to do. Keenan sensed Smith's frustration, but he still didn't want him eating and chatting with the players, or skating with the spare players after practice like he did three or four times during the regular season. Keenan had neither time for nor interest in keeping Smith abreast of the team on a daily basis.

Game 1 foreshadowed one of the most competitive and melodramatic series in Stanley Cup history, a heart-stopping seven-game clash in which three were settled in double overtime, two after the Devils tied the game in the final minute of the third period with Brodeur off for a sixth attacker. New York and New Jersey simply stopped breathing from May 15–27 while Lemaire's Devils and Keenan's Rangers took turns controlling the epic confrontation.

Tragedy struck the Rangers' extended family on the day the series began. The body of Cecile (Ceil) Saidel, sixty-seven, an officer in the Rangers' Fan Club, was found murdered in her Bronx apartment. Saidel had been missing for six days, since she failed to attend Game 5 against the Caps. Her friends and clubmates knew something was up, for Saidel rarely missed a game and never without letting her friends know she'd be away. As with so many New Yorkers who grew up and suffered with this success-starved franchise, the Rangers were Saidel's family and hockey was her religion. Her senseless death played another macabre joke on the entire Ranger family.

The Devils struck first by winning Game 1 at the Garden in double overtime, four hours and seventeen minutes after the epic began. Three times the Rangers took one-goal leads, and three times the resilient Devils replied. They drained the adrenaline from the Garden on Claude Lemieux's backhanded chip shot during a frantic scramble around Richter's net with 42.7 seconds left to tie it at three apiece.

The first twenty-minute sudden-death period was tremendous. Richter made 11 saves, Brodeur nine. In the first four minutes of the second OT, the Devils threw eight more shots at Richter, and the Rangers managed only three at Brodeur. The Devils were the fresher team. Characteristically, they were the more patient team. And they won it by capitalizing on a gamble.

With Leetch already in the offensive zone after an attack, Beukeboom tried to keep the puck in at the left point. Instead, Bob Carpenter chipped it out. Stephane Richer grabbed it and counterattacked down left wing against Graves, who covered for Beukeboom. Richer muscled toward the front of the net around Graves, and shoveled a short shot that hit Richter's stick, popped over his shoulder, and tucked under the crossbar at 4:23.

"We weren't as sharp or as hungry or as attentive as we're going to have to be in terms of respecting this team," Keenan said in the postgame press conference that began a few minutes after midnight, "and being able to come up with the effort that's necessary to beat them. It's not a real strong aspect of being disrespectful. But there is an element of not being as desperate or not having the intensity levels that I feel they should have at this point in the playoffs."

The players digested the message. And then Messier set the tone.

Game 2 was a rout. In their first must-win game of the playoffs, on the game's first shift, Messier annihilated Scott Stevens with a check behind the Devil's net, stole a Lemieux pass for Daneyko at the side of the net, stepped in front, and stuffed the game-opening goal through Brodeur's pads as he shrugged off Daneyko's futile check.

"Everything that happened in the game after that happened because of Mark," Leetch said. "It becomes fun to stand back and watch a guy take over like that."

The Rangers nursed that 1–0 lead the way they know best: they pressured the Devils, outshooting them 25–11 through two periods. Although Richter only had to stop 16 shots, he made a gigantic glove save on Bill Guerin's power rush and break-in down right wing with seven minutes left in the second period. The Rangers broke it open in the third on goals by Nemchinov, Anderson (his first in 10 playoff games), and Graves. The 4–0 shutout, his fourth, tied Richter for the all-time single-season Stanley Cup record and pushed the growing battle through the Lincoln Tunnel even at one game apiece.

Game 3 was another two-OT heart-stopper, a four-hour, six-minute saga. It was a mean, dirty match. Bernie Nicholls viciously cross-checked Kovalev across the neck and side of the face, then shot the puck at his head. Both acts went unpunished. Afterward, Keenan angrily called for Nicholls to be suspended, and the Devils' number one center was shelved by NHL director of operations Brian Burke for Game 4 two nights later.

The Rangers badly outshot the Devils, 50–31, but didn't win until Matteau lifted a backhander through a scramble from the bottom of the slot off a screened Brodeur's pad and into the net at 6:13 of the second extra period. The huge left wing launched himself off the ice, jigged giddily when he landed, and threw himself into a jubilant mob of sweaty blue jerseys. In the crowded visitor's locker room, he reminisced about a Quebec childhood in which he dreamed of scoring a goal in the Stanley Cup finals. This came close, he said.

Keenan thought he had gained an advantage by crying for Nicholls's head, but he squandered the psychological edge the 3–2 overtime win had given the Rangers. Losing Nicholls gave the Devils a cause around which to rally. Losing the series lead sparked an urgency in their collective psyche.

The stage was set for Game 4, and the most frenetic forty-eight hours in the Rangers' Stanley Cup season. May 21 and 22 were the two days that once and for all ended any slim prayer that Smith and Keenan could coexist, two days that cemented Messier's reputation as the Rangers' rudder, conscience, and lifeboat between the team and its Napoleonic coach.

In Game 4, Keenan snapped. His cold-blooded, combustible style overwhelmed his judgment. A flurry of horrific errors in perspective blinded him from the mandate and nearly destroyed his Stanley Cup blueprint.

He benched Leetch after the defenseman committed a first-period penalty that led to a power-play goal.

He yanked Richter at 16:54 of the first period after the Devils made it 2–0.

He benched Noonan and MacTavish.

He sat Messier for long stretches of the Devils' 3–1 victory, a win that restored their confidence because they had triumphed without Nicholls. It was a loss that enraged the puzzled Rangers because they felt their maniacal coach didn't give them a fair chance to win a monumentally important game.

As he watched helplessly from the end of the bench in the second period, Richter felt surreal. There he was, in a game that could have given the Rangers a stranglehold on the series, sitting because he had given up two first-period goals. When he looked over he saw Leetch planted, too, and

Noonan, and MacTavish. At one point he and Leetch exchanged glances. Both simply shrugged.

Keenan's deployment of personnel lacked logic. Leetch did not play for a span of 6:53 in the first period and 8:06 of the second. If he was hurt, why did he play the last few seconds of a third-period power play, with the Rangers down 2–1? If he wasn't hurt, why did Esa Tikkanen start in Leetch's spot at the left point on a late-second-period power play, with the Rangers down a goal? How could the coach justify sitting his best player at the most critical juncture of a crucial game? And why didn't Messier log the ice time he usually does?

The coach provided no answers when he addressed his groggy team after the game. Instead, he yelled at them. "What the fuck are we doing? Do we want to win? Do you care? Does anybody have anything to say?"

There was dead silence until Olczyk, in civvies, tried putting a positive spin on the disaster. "Fuck, it's 2–2 and we're going back home. It's a three-game series now and we've got two at the Garden. C'mon, we've got to stick together."

Keenan erupted again. "Are you saying I'm not loyal?"

"No," Olczyk replied nervously. "I'm saying we've all got to stick together."

The dumbfounded Rangers were still scratching their heads as they showered and dressed while Keenan met the media minutes after it ended. Olczyk was teased for not standing up to Keenan and telling him he was disloyal.

Keenan was a bad witness at this postgame interrogation. He alibied, double-talked, and hinted at injuries he insisted the Rangers had no obligation to reveal. On why Leetch played so little: "Without getting into a lot of details, which is our prerogative, he wasn't 100 percent tonight. I don't want to elaborate." On why he pulled Richter: "The technical aspects of his game had to improve."

Leetch had hurt the rotator cuff in his right shoulder in Game 3. He told trainer Dave Smith in the medical room after Matteau's double-OT goal that he couldn't raise his arms, but he and the trainer decided not to tell Keenan about it that night; they would wait and see how it felt the next day at practice. When Leetch reported for work in the morning he was summoned to Keenan's office.

"Why didn't you tell the training staff you were injured?" Keenan asked, after being informed by Smith that Leetch wasn't 100 percent.

"I didn't know how bad it was," Leetch replied. "I told them I couldn't raise my arms."

The trainer was called in. He confirmed Leetch's story. They decided to use a pain-killing injection for the shoulder before Game 4. Leetch told Keenan he lacked strength, but had no trouble playing. When that shoulder took a massive clean hit into the boards from Claude Lemieux in the early minutes of Game 4, Keenan sensed problems and decided not to use his star defenseman regularly. He did not consult with Leetch before benching him.

Leetch wanted to play. The shoulder was pain-free and strong enough. He grew angry on the bench because he felt Keenan was punishing him for the first-period hooking penalty that led to the Devils' first goal.

"It's just part of his way of coaching," Leetch reminded himself. "But it's backfiring."

The composed defenseman grew angrier after the game, when several writers grilled him about an injury that had been carefully hidden from the Devils until Keenan's hint. He tried lying, but the New York writers who knew him best weren't buying it. Leetch, a perceptive guy, knew that, too. Through clenched teeth he simply said it was the coach's right to play the players he wanted to play. He admitted he had to play better, insisted his shoulder was fine, and walked slowly to the bus still biting his tongue.

Messier claimed his only pains were the usual bumps and bruises that inevitably arrived after over 100 games in eight months. He tried defending Keenan, too, but while he muttered a few clichés for public consumption, even before he climbed on the bus and listened to his teammates' whispered gripes he knew that a major problem had arisen that had to be addressed.

The Rangers were over the initial shock of the loss as the team boarded their bus for the ride home, but Richter from a few rows behind Keenan looked around and couldn't help noticing how quiet it was.

"Am I the only one who sees this was a bizarre loss?" he asked himself. "Did I get what happened straight?"

Richter, Leetch, and Messier car-pooled to Rye the next morning in Richter's four-door BMW. As usual, the radio played softly in the background. It was a Sunday morning without rush-hour traffic, so they flew up the West Side Highway. As they did, Richter and Leetch got most of their complaints off their chests. The two stars told Messier they couldn't believe Keenan would resort to such counterproductive mind games at this point in the year. "That's something he did early in the year, something we may have needed during the regular season," Leetch said. "Why now?"

"He didn't give us the best chance to win," Richter added.

Messier mostly listened. Richter and Leetch were repeating what half a dozen other guys had whispered to Messier on the bus the night before.

They spoke of how loyalty sometimes needed to be repaid, and of how they had come too far and gotten too close for Keenan to pull such a stunt now.

"I'll talk to him," Messier said.

Messier and Keenan spoke privately in Keenan's office almost every day. Messier relished being the conduit because it gave him the perfect opportunity to exercise leadership. He'd stroll in after a workout on the stationary bike, or before he hit the weights. He'd sit down on one of the cushioned chairs, or drop himself on the couch, and wait for Keenan to ask for a state of the Rangers.

"What's the beef today?" Keenan would ask. "What's the pulse? What's going on?"

Leetch and Richter did not ask Messier what he planned to say because that was not how it was done. Messier's job was to absorb his teammates' thoughts and opinions, digest them, and present them to Keenan constructively. Keenan had to be told the Rangers were angry, but he did not have to know that several players thought he concocted the injury alibi because he lacked the guts to publicly stand behind his controversial benchings. Keenan had to be told the players thought he showed no confidence in them, but he did not have to hear how many of them thought he was self-destructing.

Practice was delayed fifteen, thirty, forty-five minutes as captain and coach met behind Keenan's closed door. Messier never raised his voice.

"The team didn't feel you gave us the best possible chance of winning that game, Mike," said Messier, dressed in his underwear. "All the teaching, all the things you did during the season, they're already in the bank. We don't need that now. We need your moral support, your confidence. We need your loyalty and your backing."

Messier asked Keenan why he had benched Leetch and pulled Richter in the first period. Keenan described the conversation with Leetch and Dave Smith the day before. He told Messier he wasn't certain if Leetch was hiding a more serious injury from him, and he wasn't sure what to do.

"I was confused, too," Keenan said.

Keenan said he pulled Richter so early because he thought the team would respond to a switch to Glenn Healy like it had several times during the regular season. With the score only 2–0 in the first period, he thought there was time for the Rangers to rally.

Messier did the majority of the talking. He described how the pressure and physical intensity of the playoffs leaves even the most dominant players exhausted and emotionally fragile.

"Everyone at this time of year is tired, Mike," he said. "We've got a great opportunity here, we're so close. We just have to win this series and we'll win the Cup. You need to give us every chance to win."

Keenan convinced Messier that he grasped the message. He did not need to remind his captain that the last thing he intended to do was sabotage the quest, especially when they were so close to the Cup.

"It's your team, Mark, not my team," Keenan assured him. "We want to do well for each other, but not in response to what I'm asking them to do. I'm asking them to respond to what your teammates want all of them to do."

Keenan convinced Messier he was sincere. The longer they talked, the more enthusiastic and reenergized they became. Nobody in the Rangers' organization was under more pressure than these two well-paid hired guns, the saviors, both of whom were acquired solely to secure the Stanley Cup.

When he was convinced he had successfully channeled his teammates' anger into a fruitful dialogue that delivered the message, an extraordinary thing happened: Messier wept. He simply fell into Keenan's arms and cried as his coach hugged him tightly.

He composed himself, left the room, and walked back to the dressing room. Every eye followed him across the room, waited for some signal that the message had been delivered.

"That won't happen again," was all Messier said.

The Rangers practiced. Messier didn't elaborate on the meeting, but the spring in his step assured his teammates Keenan had taken the talk to heart. Keenan intended to tell his players exactly that the next morning, when he addressed them collectively again. That afternoon he had another closed-door meeting on his agenda.

Keenan asked Watkins what he thought of confidentially huddling with four of the most experienced beat writers: Frank Brown of the *Daily News,* Rick Carpiniello of the Gannett Westchester-Rockland papers, Mark Everson of the *Post,* and Joe Lapointe of the *Times.* Keenan wanted to inform them privately of the Rangers' injury report so they would leave the players alone and stop speculating.

"Don't do that, Mike," Watkins suggested. "That would be a big mistake. First of all, it would be wrong to invite some writers and not others. That would pose a problem for you. Second, somebody's going to write what you say."

Keenan argued briefly with Watkins, then ordered him to summon the four writers. Watkins told the coach he'd regret it, then escorted Brown, Carpiniello, Everson, and Lapointe into the same office where hours earlier Messier had wept.

"Put your notepads down," Keenan instructed. "This is off the record, although I know nothing's ever really off the record."

For the next twenty minutes, Keenan described his dilemma and sought the writers' assistance. He couldn't admit for the record that Leetch, Messier, Noonan, MacTavish, and Graves were hurt, but they were. He wanted the writers to tell him what he should do, since he claimed he didn't want to mislead the media.

He described Leetch's bad shoulder. He said Messier's rib cage was damaged. He said Noonan had hurt his knee. He said MacTavish hurt his shoulder. He said Graves had suffered a serious gash in his thigh.

Brown, who has covered the Rangers since 1973 and was the most senior member of the Ranger beat in the room, began doubting Keenan's sincerity when the coach leaned back in his chair, gazed out his window, and let out a woefully phony sigh. Keenan was acting too melodramatic, Brown said to himself. This was a coach who treated the reporters with disdain all year, who never once went off the record.

Brown distrusted the information, too, since it made absolutely no sense for an educated coach who understood the media's role to naively think he could confidentially reveal a list of injuries at so critical a time and expect it not to be leaked, unless he wanted it to be leaked. And he did. In this one brief scene he attempted to take the heat off his players, take the heat off himself for the Game 4 benchings, and stretch the truth or lie outright with the injury report.

Leetch's shoulder was bad; that much was already known by the media and Keenan couldn't deny it. Messier's ribs weren't bothering him, his groin was. Noonan's knee wasn't injured, his shoulder was separated. MacTavish's shoulder wasn't hurt, his foot was badly bruised. And the flesh wound in Graves's thigh amounted to a pimple in the scheme of things.

As Brown listened, he realized that the players who had finished practice were beginning to leave Rye. Keenan usually held his daily press briefings after the writers spoke to the players, but Keenan's secret meeting had potentially prevented the writers from talking to the players. As Brown wondered how he was going to handle this off-the-record information, Lapointe issued a warning: "Just because you're telling us this [off the record] doesn't mean it won't be printed," he said.

"Do what you've gotta do," Keenan replied.

The *News, Times,* and Westchester-Rockland handled the story properly, reporting the injuries (as Keenan described them) without mentioning Keenan as the source of the story. The *Post*'s Everson burned Keenan by reporting that the coach, "who never seems to do anything without ulterior motive, privately confessed" about the injuries. Everson wrote what Brown suspected but couldn't write because he had agreed to keep the meeting confidential as Keenan requested.

Keenan had manipulated the situation. He knew that regardless of whether he told the truth or lied, the Devils wouldn't rely on the information since everybody hides or feigns injuries at playoff time. It's part of the hockey culture.

Messier wasn't upset when he picked up the papers the next morning because he knew Keenan was simply trying to divert attention from the real issue of the day. Not one member of the media had the slightest idea about the Keenan-Messier summit meeting, which went unreported and unmentioned—except by the players, who were still eager to hear what Keenan had to say about his chat with the captain.

Keenan waited until the pregame meeting at the Garden before Game 5 before apologizing to the team for Game 4. "I made a mistake," he said. "We all make mistakes. Let's turn the page."

The Rangers couldn't, not that night, not after all that had happened. Although Graves, MacTavish, and Noonan knew Keenan's account of their injuries was untrue and was designed to create a smoke screen, and although Leetch knew Keenan was trying to make him a scapegoat for Game 4, the players hadn't recovered emotionally. They were a limp, shell-shocked unit trying to fend off a very talented and confident opponent. Leetch played an ordinary game. Messier failed to generate any offense. Noonan, the one Ranger legitimately hurt, played despite a slightly separated shoulder.

Nicholls scored a short-handed goal early in the first period. Brodeur stopped 20 shots over the first two periods. The Devils sensed the Rangers' tentativeness. It roused their confidence. As they broke their 1–0 lead open in the third period, the Garden turned from upset to frustrated to miserably angry. Tikkanen spoiled Brodeur's shutout with 2:37 left, but the Rangers lost 4–1 to the rejuvenated Devils and were one loss from elimination with Game 6 slated for the Meadowlands two nights later.

As he looked down from his perch high atop the building at the Seventh Avenue end and watched his team trudge off home ice, perhaps for the final time, Smith wanted to be sick. He bottled up his anger while he stood outside the dressing room. When the players and writers departed, he burst into Suite 200 and screamed at Gutkowski.

"Five years of work, Bob . . . we can't let this happen. How can that guy do what he did these last two nights?"

"What do you want me to tell you to do, Neil, go down and fire him?"

"No, I don't know what I want you to tell me. I don't know what we're gonna do."

There comes a crisis point in every championship team's season, no matter how cocky and talented the group is, when self-doubt overwhelms self-confidence. "Have we reached our limit?" the players silently wonder. They are afraid to say it aloud for fear of being ostracized, but they're all thinking the same things: "Have we fooled ourselves? Are we good enough to go further, and are we going to go further?"

On May 24, the Rangers reached their crisis point.

They trailed, three games to two. They faced a Game 6 the next night on the road against a team that had repelled their forechecking, stood up to their strength, and skated with their speedsters. Neither Leetch nor Kovalev had a goal in the series. Messier had one. Brodeur had held the Rangers' all-out pressure attack to one goal in two consecutive games, something that hadn't happened to the Rangers in the regular season. Still, Messier tried to make winning the series sound easy in Richter's car on the drive from Manhattan with Glenn Anderson and Messier's brother, Paul.

"All we have to do is win this game," he said.

As he walked through the dressing room that morning, Messier spotted too many uncertain eyes. As he circled the ice during the brisk workout, he sensed resignation. So when the media crowded around his locker and asked him to assess the team's chances in Game 6, the captain found himself making a very strange statement, one far stronger than he made to Richter, Anderson, and Paul Messier that morning. It was one that shocked his best friend three thousand miles away.

"We're going to go in and win Game 6," Messier said. "That was the focus this morning and it's the way we feel right now. We've done that all year, we've won all the games we've had to win. I know we're going to go in and win Game 6 and bring it back here for Game 7. . . . We have enough talent and experience to turn the tide. That's exactly what we're going to do in Game 6."

Wayne Gretzky was stunned the next morning in Los Angeles when he heard what Messier had predicted would happen later that night. Not because he didn't believe his former teammate could back it up; Gretzky knew better than to doubt Messier's abilities. He just recalled what the Oilers used to tell each other every year at playoff time: "Mess would always say, 'Don't ever give your opponent any little thing to ride on, or to get high about,'" Gretzky said. "He was a really big believer in that. I guess he just felt he needed to do something to rally his own teammates, and he didn't care about the opposition or what it would do to them because he needed to rally his own guys."

Exactly.

Messier was desperate. He still believed the Rangers could win two straight if they attacked hard enough to break through the Devils' trapping defense. But he didn't think most of his teammates still believed it. He didn't care how the Devils reacted, he just wanted his guys to wake up the next morning and feel a little bit more confident about their chances, knowing their leader had taken the outrageous step of putting his muscular neck squarely in a sullen city's guillotine.

The Rangers had to play Game 6 without Noonan, who was replaced by Olczyk, and without Beukeboom, who was suspended for viciously crushing Stephane Richer face-first into the corner boards in Game 5, a check that went unpenalized during the game. When the suspension was announced the morning of Game 6, it seemed that Keenan's call for Nicholls's suspension had now backfired in his face twice.

For the first period and a half of Game 6, Messier looked terribly mistaken. Although the Rangers wisely elected not to fall into the Devils' trap by forechecking relentlessly, they were badly outshot. Richter stopped eight shots in the first seven minutes, but was left helpless when Nemchinov inadvertently deflected Scott Niedermayer's centering pass from the right circle past the goalie.

Meadowlands Arena erupted. A vast majority of the 19,040—those numbers again—smelled blood. Those wearing blue feared the revival of The Curse. When Claude Lemieux tipped Niedermayer's slap shot past Richter late in the first period and the Devils skated off with a 2–0 lead, a premature celebration began.

Early in the second period, Keenan used his one timeout. He stood behind the bench but did not say a word. Messier was doing all the talking, imploring his teammates to stay alert, exhorting them to press on.

The Rangers stayed smart. They continued to trap the trap. They dumped the puck through the Devils' four-man neutral-zone box and patiently forced the Devils to skate two hundred feet. The only problem was, time was passing. Messier was worried. With 5:53 left in the second period, he and Nicholls drew unsportsmanlike conduct minors for a clash behind the Rangers' net.

Daneyko looked at his friend as Messier skated to the penalty box, and sensed triumph. "He thought it was over," Daneyko said. "I killed him for two periods, hammered him all over the ice. You could see he was frustrated. I saw it in his face when he took the penalty with Bernie. He thought it was over."

Midway through the second period, Keenan made a brilliant move. He moved Kovalev from center on the second line to right wing with Graves and Messier, linking the Rangers' three most explosive scorers on a line designed only to concern itself with getting the team back in the game.

With 1:41 left in the second period, it did just that. Messier took control of a loose puck and carried it over the Devils' blue line with speed, which forced Daneyko and Bruce Driver to yield too much room. One of the Devils' back-checkers missed an assignment, because Kovalev was wide open on right wing when Messier dropped the puck to him.

Kovalev wound up to fire a slapper from the top of the right circle, but when he looked up at Brodeur he spotted yards of open ice. So he crept closer, and from near the faceoff dot he unleashed a blur that whipped low past Brodeur's right pad and into the far corner of the net.

It was 2–1.

Tikkanen tripped Richer thirty-two seconds later, but it was still 2–1 after two periods because Messier and Graves killed the first 1:09 of the penalty. The goal had given the Rangers life, given the Devils reason to worry, and tempered an arena's party.

Between the second and third periods, for the first time all year—preseason, regular season, postseason—Keenan spent the entire fifteen-minute intermission with his players in the dressing room.

"C'mon guys, we can do it," he said over and over. "We can do it. We're going to go back for Game 7."

What followed was a third period for the ages.

Just twenty-eight seconds in, with Tikkanen still in the penalty box, Messier and Graves generated a two-on-one break that failed to connect. They killed the final seconds of the penalty, then took a rest.

On the top line's next shift, Kovalev led a rush through center ice and fed Messier, who steamrolled down right wing and flipped a low backhander that slithered between Brodeur's left pad and the near post. It was 2–2 at 2:48.

Halfway though the period, with the teams skating four aside, Keenan threw Messier and Kovalev out with Leetch and Zubov, an unparalleled attacking foursome. Forty seconds later, Leetch attacked and dropped a pass for Kovalev, who shot from the left wing. Brodeur kicked the puck into the slot. Messier, with Nicholls on his back, dropped the center to the ice and stuffed the puck into the net. It was 3–2 at 12:12.

As Leetch, Kovalev, and Zubov hugged Messier, there was pandemonium at the Ranger bench. Kevin Lowe had played a decade with Messier, and had chills seeing what Messier had just done. Mature veterans like Steve Larmer and Jay Wells became giddy fans, roaring with delight. And the show wasn't over yet.

Anderson took a senseless penalty for slashing Nicholls with 2:49 left. Lemaire elected to pull Brodeur during the penalty with the puck in the Rangers' zone. John MacLean had it in the corner to Richter's left. He tried a hard centering pass toward the slot. Messier intercepted it with his back to the Devils' open net 160 feet away, quickly pivoted, and from the face-off dot flung a bull's-eye.

His clearing attempt/shot on goal floated through the neutral zone, sat flat on the ice as it landed, slid briskly between the circles and stopped only after it hit the back of the net. Messier didn't follow the puck as it went in. He didn't celebrate with his teammates on the ice. He skated the width of the rink, leaned over the boards, and threw his torso into an orgy of excitement, relief, and disbelief at the Ranger bench.

Guaranteed.

It was Messier's finest hour, the pinnacle of a career in which he earned his reputation as the NHL's most clutch player. Three goals in the third period with his team down 2–1, a natural hat trick in the biggest game of his life with his team a period from Stanley Cup elimination, with his unequivocal promise threatening to choke him.

It was Cassius Clay before he knocked out Sonny Liston, Joe Namath before the New York Jets shocked the Baltimore Colts in Super Bowl III. It was New York's most chilling sports moment since May 8, 1970, when Willis Reed dragged his bum leg onto the Garden floor and spiritually led the Knickerbockers over the Los Angeles Lakers in Game 7 of the 1970 NBA finals.

"I played against Mark for nine years and nothing scared me more than when he got that real serious look of determination in his eye," Wells said in the game's aftermath. "In the third period, he had that. He was determined to back up his words and take the game into his own hands."

"That," a grateful Keenan added, "has to be the most impressive performance by any hockey player in the history of this league."

Messier tried dishing the credit to Richter, who stopped New Jersey's final 18 shots and was spectacular keeping the score 2–0 until Kovalev and Messier got going. But the night was his. He giggled when he was asked if he intended to forecast the winner of Game 7 two nights later.

"Well, I feel good about this team right now," he said. "We're going home and we have to remain focused and composed. This was a big game. But Game 7 is even bigger."

Even better, too. Considering the stakes, the rivalry, and the anxiety that tortured two front offices, two coaching staffs, forty players, and the 18,200-headed Monster for three hours and forty-six minutes, it was one of the greatest hockey games of the NHL's modern era.

The Devils shook off the devastating defeat two nights earlier, deployed their trap without mistakes, and kept the Rangers away. The Rangers rode the momentum and emotion, carried the weight of The Curse, and pressured the Devils tirelessly. It was 0–0 after one period despite wonderful scoring chances by both teams. Richter and Brodeur were indomitable.

As the second period neared its midpoint, progress was measured in inches of ice. Every pass mattered. Every check counted. Players who scraped loose pucks ten feet forward along the boards had terrific shifts. Defensemen who simply banked pucks out of the zone were patted on the back by their coaches when they returned to their benches.

At 9:24, Bruce Driver iced the puck trying to make a neutral zone pass. Messier won the ensuing faceoff deep in the Devils' end from Jim Dowd and worked the puck to Graves. Leetch got it below the goal line. Scott Stevens dueled Kovalev to a standoff away from the puck. Dowd had Messier. Leetch had Bill Guerin on him, but with a magical 360-degree spinerama Leetch shook free. With one quick motion he swept a six-foot backhander along the ice between Brodeur's pads.

It barely slid in. It was 1–0 at 9:31.

It stayed 1–0 for the final half of the second period. It remained 1–0 midway through the third. Richter stopped Nicholls's try from in front of the net. Brodeur stopped Graves's dangerous slap shot. Seconds took hours as the Rangers desperately and uncharacteristically sat on the slim lead, while New Jersey desperately and uncharacteristically pressed the attack for the tying goal as the clock dropped under two minutes to go.

With 1:05 left, Brodeur raced off to allow New Jersey a sixth attacker. With 0:18.6 left, Richter gloved and held a shot by Nicholls. What began a minute earlier as a roar of anticipation was now a thunderclap of expectation. The puck was dropped between Nicholls and Messier. All that was left between a berth in the Stanley Cup finals against the Vancouver Canucks was one more clearing pass, one more flurry withstood.

With less than ten seconds left and the Rangers running around in their zone after the puck, Richer frantically worked the puck to Lemieux, who from the left side of the net flung a cross-crease pass to Valeri Zelepukin near the right post. Stunningly, he was open. Incredibly, he chipped the pass in with 0:07.7 left.

Was there no limit to The Curse?

For fifteen minutes, while the Garden tried to rationalize what it had witnessed, the Rangers told each other to forget what had happened and get the next goal. All they were, they reminded each other, was one goal from the finals.

"We deserve to win this game," Richter told Healy.

"We're going to," Healy replied.

"Hey, we'll play all night if we have to," Messier told his mates. "We'll win this game."

The first overtime was tremendous, and costly.

The Rangers went all out for the win, outshot the Devils 15–7, but yielded the best scoring chance 13:15 into the extra session. When Leetch tried to keep a puck in the Devils' zone, Randy McKay and Bobby Holik counterattacked with only Beukeboom back. Beukeboom challenged, but did not commit to McKay. The right wing held the puck until he had no choice but to try a goalmouth feed for Holik. Richter, who is not very good with his stick, poked properly and broke it up.

"End it now," somebody screamed from his seat. "End our misery."

The Rangers lost Lowe with five minutes left in the first OT to a separated shoulder and concussion when Guerin cross-checked him into the boards. The night's fourth intermission gave everybody in the building enough time to visualize the worst and fantasize the best. It gave Stephane Matteau time to fix a broken skate lace, which made Matteau late coming onto the ice for the second overtime. League officials, thinking all the players had hit the ice, pulled the Prince of Wales Trophy out of an empty room and positioned it in the runway under the stands. When Matteau emerged from the dressing room he spotted the trophy and touched it for luck.

The period began at 11:18 P.M. At 11:26 P.M., Beukeboom grabbed a rare patch of open ice. The defensive defenseman who rarely strayed over the enemy's blue line with the puck carried it over the Devils' zone and fired a slap shot that crashed off the glass behind Brodeur's net.

Slava Fetisov, the Russian Master of Sport (equivalent to our Halls of Fame) who became one of the former Soviet Union's NHL pioneers when he joined the Devils in 1989, grabbed it behind the net, looked up from the right-wing corner, and tried to pass it up the middle of the ice. The clearing pass hit Tikkanen in the back of the pants and ricocheted into the left-wing corner, where Niedermayer and Matteau chased it.

It should have been no contest. Niedermayer on his worst day outskates Matteau easily. But after 104 minutes of hockey in a hot, humid building, Matteau got a jump on the Devils' defenseman and muscled him off the puck as both players' momentum carried them from left to right behind the net. Matteau controlled it.

Fetisov scrambled to the front of the net as Matteau pivoted behind the goal line a stride outside the post. Brodeur dropped to his knees, tried to squeeze his left pad against the post, and laid the fat shaft of his stick along the ice. Matteau, a left-handed shooter, from a few feet behind the goal line slid the puck in front just as Fetisov slid to block his lane.

The puck left Matteau's stick, briefly disappeared in the confusion at the crease, and . . .

On May 8, 1979, the Monster of Madison Square Garden counted down the final seconds of the Rangers' 2–1 series-ending Game 6 upset of the Islanders, and the arena atop Penn Station actually shook. Marv Albert, the Rangers' ace play-by-play man who soon advanced to national TV sports prominence, said it was the first time he felt the Garden vibrate since Game 7 of the 1970 NBA finals, Willis Reed's night exactly nine years earlier.

Howie Rose, a Bayside, Queens, native who as a boy lugged his tape recorder up to Section 429, Row G, Seat 11 of the blue seats, felt those good vibrations from the press box where he was working as radio station WHN's morning sports reporter. Fifteen years later he was a Ranger play-by-play man, Albert's backup, when he experienced the tremors again. At 4:24 of the second overtime, he joined the legion of announcers whose calls have become legendary.

"Matteau! Matteau! Matteau!" Rose sang deliriously after the puck somehow slithered past Fetisov, disappeared under Brodeur, and reappeared in the net. As the building shook, the decibel level grew frightening. Two piles of Ranger bodies dotted the ice. Matteau was immediately buried in the bigger heap, pinned to the glass near the Devils' bench, not fifteen feet from where their stunned opponents sat transfixed. The other mob scene converged around Richter, the true hero of the game, who already had the grand night in perspective. "Now we have the chance to win four more games," the goalie said to Keenan when they embraced at the bench.

The Black Aces scampered onto the ice in dress shoes and suit jackets worn inside out for luck. Smith and Gutkowski embraced up in the perch and refused to let go.

Messier accepted the Prince of Wales Trophy from NHL director of operations Brian Burke after the ceremonial handshakes at center ice, but the captain's experience tempered his exhilaration. He politely lifted it for the photographers, but quickly put it down. This was not the hardware of note, his actions said. Beating the Devils was our entry into the finals, nothing more.

The Monster knew it, too. "We want the Cup," they chanted. "We want the Cup."

. . .

The Vancouver Canucks who flew into New York on Sunday, May 29, for Games 1 and 2 were not the same team as the one that had qualified as the seventh seed of the Western Conference playoffs with a 41–40–3 regular-season record. They were now the Western Conference champions, having won eleven of their last thirteen playoff games, breezing in four straight past Toronto after losing Game 1 of the Western finals.

Right wing Pavel Bure, the "Russian Rocket," led the NHL with 60 goals during the regular season. Goalie Kirk McLean finished with a 2.99 goals-against average. Mean and rugged two-way center Trevor Linden best symbolized a balanced, disciplined group led by GM-coach Pat Quinn, the cigar-chewing former NHL defenseman. Quinn strengthened his team's depth at the trade deadline by acquiring defensemen Jeff Brown and Bret Hedican and center Nathan LaFayette for Craig Janney, who a week earlier had been awarded as compensation to Vancouver when St. Louis signed free agent Petr Nedved, the former Canuck who refused to re-sign and sat out most of the 1993–94 season.

These were not hockey's Washington Generals playing foil to the Rangers' Harlem Globetrotters for the final step of their remarkable quest for the grail. Game 1 proved that for anyone who thought this would be easy.

Kovalev scored a third-period goal to break a 1–1 tie, but for the third time in the eight games since the Devils series began, the Rangers blew a one-goal lead in the final minute of regulation. All three times it happened at the Garden, where the roar of an expected triumph was abruptly silenced, and followed by the worried murmurings of the anguished populace pleading for the ghosts of 1940 to stop the punishment.

"Not again," one middle-aged woman in a business suit pleaded from the exclusive club seats after right wing Martin Gelinas deflected center Cliff Ronning's poor-angled shot to tie it at 19:00. "Why are you doing this to us?"

The Rangers were by now extremely familiar with the feeling of regrouping before overtime. They aggressively stormed McLean's net for nineteen minutes of overtime, but the goalie stopped all 17 shots. Shortly after he made his 52nd save of the game (Richter had made 28), Leetch blew down the Canucks' zone, took a pass from Tikkanen, and wristed a high thirty-foot blur that McLean couldn't grab.

The crowd rose expectantly, then sighed when . . . PING . . . the puck hit the crossbar. It ricocheted hard to the top of the right circle, where Beukeboom tried to pinch. The speedy Bure easily beat him to the puck, lunged, and chipped it off the boards and out of the zone. Suddenly, Vancouver generated a pretty counterattack. With only Tikkanen back, Ronning stormed through the neutral zone and collected the puck on the left flank. Greg Adams skated down the slot on Ronning's right. Ronning waited, then feathered his pass for the left-handed shooter, who had a perfect angle. Adams one-timed a high shot over Richter's glove that floated a few inches lower than Leetch's and into the net with 0:31.1 left in OT.

McLean had stolen Game 1.

Messier asked the coaches to leave the dressing room immediately after the game. He closed the doors and convened the players-only meeting by saying, "I am 100 percent sure we will beat this team over a seven-game series. But these are things we have to do. One, we have to forecheck. Two, we have to get on their defense. Three, we have to get in on McLean and create more traffic in front of their net."

Strategic preparation was hardly Keenan's strength. He used to brag about never practicing a power play that was the NHL's best through the regular season and was equally proficient in the first three rounds. But Messier felt the Rangers needed more direction before Game 2. He did not think Vancouver's defense had the skill and strength to repel a ferocious forechecking attack. McLean made 52 saves, sure, but the Rangers didn't take enough quality shots.

The lecture was brief, but blunt.

The postgame faces reflected Messier's confidence. Nobody cared that forty-four of the fifty-five Cup champions had captured Game 1 since the finals became a best-of-seven affair. "It's not like we hadn't been here before," Matteau said, referring to the similar double OT loss in Game 1 to New Jersey.

Vancouver played far better in Game 2 two nights later than it did in Game 1, but the Rangers led 2–1 after the second period because they followed Messier's instructions. Doug Lidster, the former Canuck who pushed Karpovtsev out of the lineup by filling in tremendously for Beukeboom in Game 6 of the Devils series, scored the first goal by barging to the net. Anderson broke a 1–1 tie midway through the game by hustling to the net and tapping in Messier's shorthanded feed.

With forty seconds remaining in Game 2 after Beukeboom iced the puck, the Rangers were ahead by a goal. McLean was off for a sixth attacker, and Quinn called timeout to prepare his team for a faceoff to Richter's right: Linden against Messier. Linden won it to Bure, whose shot through a swarm of bodies pinballed wide as Richter looked behind him. The puck was cleared out of the zone. The crowd roared. The Canucks attacked again. The same frantic scene that had ended with Valeri

Zelepukin's goal one week earlier reappeared in front of Richter. Incredibly, Gelinas shook free at the goalmouth. Adams won the puck in the corner and hastily flung it to the net with Leetch and Beukeboom too high in the slot.

Gelinas one-timed it, but Richter stopped it. The winger controlled the rebound and tried to stuff it under the goalie, but Richter stretched his 5-11 frame to cover the six feet along the ice and left Gelinas no gaps. The clock showed ten seconds to go when the puck bounced off Richter and into the right corner, from where Leetch fired it 165 feet into the empty net with 0:04.8 seconds left to ensure the 3–1 win.

The Rangers won without Lowe, who had played Game 1 with a separated shoulder but needed a few days of rest and rehab. They won without much help from Kovalev, who had a horrid game and was benched in the second period. They managed to split at home despite scoring only four goals (not counting Leetch's empty-netter) on 94 shots over seven periods at the Garden. And they won despite losing Zubov in the final six minutes to a crunching check that battered his upper chest and rib cage, and knocked him out of Game 3.

Friday, June 3, was a travel day. The Rangers' six-hour flight on a lavishly catered MGM Grand DC-10 departed Newark Airport at 11:30 A.M. As the players reclined on their plush first-class seats and selected from a menu of salmon, turkey, or pasta primavera, they remembered that they hadn't changed time zones since March 27. As the jetliner floated over the Canadian Rockies while they munched on freshly baked chocolate chip cookies, the Rangers knew they were not going to have the regional fan support they enjoy at MSG East (Nassau Coliseum), MSG South (USAir Arena), and MSG West (the Meadowlands).

A few hours before the Rangers took off for British Columbia, Detroit Red Wings owner Mike Ilitch fired GM Bryan Murray, who could not escape responsibility for the Wings' demoralizing first-round defeat to the underdog San Jose Sharks. The firing came eighteen months after Murray almost lost his job to Keenan. In January 1993, six months before Keenan signed with the Rangers, he and Ilitch came to terms on a deal for Keenan to suceed Murray as GM-coach. When Murray and former Wings VP Jim Lites learned of the plan and challenged Ilitch, the owner got Keenan's permission to undo the deal and backed off.

Murray's firing went unnoticed as the finals moved to one of North America's most majestic white-capped cities. Vancouver had not reached the Stanley Cup finals since 1982, their only visit, when the powerhouse Islanders finished a four-game sweep with two decisive victories out west.

A province starved for its first Cup since the Canucks' birth in 1970 was well represented by 16,150 frenzied citizens clad in white and waving white towels, a raucous flock that sounded every bit as intimidating as the Monster back home.

Bure ignited another eruption one minute into the match. He took a Linden pass at the Rangers' blue line, sped between Wells and Lidster, and rocketed a blur that grazed Richter's skate and sailed between his pads. Two minutes later, he exploited another mismatch by drawing a tripping penalty on the lumbering Wells. Vancouver didn't score, but it maintained the momentum and continued stoking the emotion of its crowd for the game's first thirteen minutes.

Then, McLean blundered. Leetch at the left point flipped a harmless shot wide of the left post. Instead of letting it sail off the back boards, McLean tried to bat it into the corner with his blocker. He knocked it into his net. Across a continent, Ranger fans watched with bewilderment; this was the type of goal that had cursed the Rangers for years. Could this be our year, they dared ask?

Five minutes later, good fortune struck again. It struck Wells squarely on the nose. He and Bure lined up side by side for a faceoff in the right neutral-zone dot outside the Rangers' blue line. The puck squirted between them along the boards. Wells looked down, Bure's stick inadvertently flung up, and Wells dropped with a bleeding, broken nose. It was an accident, but it was a careless use of the stick according to veteran referee Andy van Hellemond. As a horrified crowd groaned and Quinn loudly protested, van Hellemond slapped Bure with a five-minute major penalty and automatic game misconduct.

Anderson scored a minute later on the power play. Leetch lifted a backhander over McLean late in the second period. Larmer was credited with a fluke goal twenty-five seconds into the third when his centering pass caromed off defenseman Dave Babych's skate and past a flustered McLean. Kovalev iced the 5–1 win late in the third period, leaving the Canucks looking very much like Stanley Cup rookies, which they were, against a group of experienced former champions, which many of the Rangers were.

With their white-clad fans more frenzied than three nights earlier, the Canucks started Game 4 twice as fast as they started Game 3, and they maintained the territorial edge longer because the Rangers couldn't get their offense going. Linden scored a power-play goal at 13:25, Vancouver's first power-play goal in eighteen attempts in the series. Ronning made it 2–0 at 16:19 with the teams skating four a side after Messier got a five-minute major for ramming Sergio Momesso head-first into the boards and Linden held Lidster fifty seconds later.

Keenan, who had been on his best behavior since the Messier meeting, couldn't help himself. He stormed into the cramped visitor's dressing room and began yelling. "You don't care," he ranted. "You're not trying. The work ethic isn't there. Is that not correct, Mark?"

Messier didn't say a word. With menacing eyes he focused an angry glare on Keenan, who immediately calmed down and stopped himself from short-circuiting again. "Oh, I didn't mean you're not trying," he backtracked.

The Rangers were oblivious to Keenan now. They were coolly confident, despite the deficit. When Leetch wristed a high shot over McLean's blocker at 4:03, the game began to turn. Just under three minutes later, it swung for good. The moment came fifteen seconds after Leetch missed wide on a breakaway, Bure got behind him on the counterattack, and Leetch was forced to drag him down from behind.

Referee Terry Gregson called it properly: penalty shot, only the seventh in the NHL's sixty-eight-year Stanley Cup finals history. Bure against Richter, four and a half months after the Canucks' sniper went 0-for-4 on breakaways at Richter in the All-Star Game, three days after Bure went five-hole on Richter in Game 3.

Richter elected to rely on his reflexes and not outguess Bure. He skated out to prevent Bure from trying a quick shot, glided back as the left-handed shooter prepared to make his move, and used his explosive lateral movement to stay with the puck as Bure deked backhand, forehand, backhand, forehand before trying to stuff the puck around Richter's right skate.

He couldn't. Richter concentrated on the puck, not Bure's stick blade. He did an incredibly quick split, a technically perfect move once Bure reached the lip of the crease with the puck, now on edge, still cradled to his blade. With his stick out along the ice, his body square, and his legs as far apart as a human male can spread them without shrieking, Richter made it Goalies 7, Scorers 0, in finals history by kicking the puck aside with the bottom half of his pad.

Zubov, who considered his season over after he injured his chest in Game 2 and had to be cajoled by the coaches into playing through the enormous pain, took the challenge to his manhood personally. Repeatedly matched by Keenan against Bure, his childhood friend who started stick-handling around him fifteen years ago in their Moscow neighborhood, Zubov won the majority of their one-on-one showdowns.

With 1:05 left in the second period, he drew a penalty when Adams boarded him. He shook off the hard hit, lined up at the right point, and tied the game 2–2 with a bullet that zipped past Graves's screen of McLean only sixteen seconds before the period ended.

Leetch emerged as the favorite for the Conn Smythe Trophy by dominating the tense third period. With 5:29 left and overtime imminent because of the teams' tight checking, Gelinas rammed Lowe into the boards. The veteran defenseman crumpled and Gregson called a roughing penalty. It was the fifteenth power play of the game; the Canucks were 1-for-10, the Rangers 1-for-4.

They made it 2-for-5. Leetch grabbed the puck in his zone and gained speed as he rushed through the neutral zone and easily blew past defenseman Brian Glynn. He saw Kovalev charging down the slot toward the net. Leetch faked like he was going to shoot, absorbed a vicious slash to his right arm from left wing Murray Craven, and feathered the puck past defenseman Jyrki Lumme to Kovalev, who artistically lifted it over McLean's glove hand from twelve feet away.

It was a breathtaking goal, Kovalev's third in the four games. The assist gave Leetch a series-leading three goals and five assists in the four games. He and Zubov then set up Larmer's game-clincher with 2:04 left, which rendered the final minute irrelevant. The white sea of supporters began filing out as the clock wound down, sadly certain they had seen their last game of the year.

"One more," Gutkowski said to himself from the press box as the Rangers congratulated each other on the ice. "One more."

The City of New York considered Game 5 a coronation, not a contest. The Monster of MSG did not consider defeat even a remote possibility. The wildest party in fifty-four years was scheduled to begin a few fashionably late minutes after 8 P.M. on Thursday, June 9, 1994, at the corner of 33rd Street and Seventh Avenue in Manhattan. No RSVP was necessary.

The players who weren't too excited to fall asleep for their afternoon snoozes made their celebration plans in the morning. Tickets had to be distributed, family gatherings planned, friends alerted. The PR staff fielded calls from the David Letterman show, *Good Morning America,* and every other self-respecting media outlet that hadn't already hopped aboard the bandwagon. The mayor's office wanted to make parade plans. The New York City Police Department had to prepare for a jubilant riot.

The dizzying thought of the Rangers winning the Stanley Cup eclipsed everything else going on in New York City. It even managed to blunt the repercussions of a shocking report. But on June 8, on the eve of what fig-ured to be the biggest night in Ranger history, CJRW, a tiny radio station in Summerside, a small town on Prince Edward Island in Canada's Atlantic Provinces, reported that Mike Keenan had agreed to become GM-coach of the Detroit Red Wings after the season.

The report, which was carried on the international news wires and cov-ered more thoroughly by every New York newspaper, was only slightly wrong. The deal wasn't done.

The Red Wings had endured a tumultuous 1993–94 regular season. Al-though they finished atop the Western Conference and were fourth overall with 100 points, GM Bryan Murray and coach Scotty Bowman clashed for reasons extremely familiar to Keenan-Smith watchers: the coach wanted half the team traded from the start, while the GM didn't agree with the coach's assessments. The coach was far too dictatorial. The GM made the wrong moves.

All season long the Red Wings told themselves they needed a goalie to buoy the league's most potent offense. On March 8, Murray acquired Bob Essensa from Winnipeg, although Bowman wanted Buffalo's Grant Fuhr. Essensa failed terribly. Bowman started him in Game 1 of the playoffs, but he played poorly in a 5–4 loss, was replaced by rookie Chris Osgood, and didn't start again. A 100-point season and high hopes in Detroit for the Wings' first Cup since 1955 ended miserably on April 30 when the San Jose Sharks won Game 7 of their first-round series at Joe Louis Arena.

Sometime in late May, before owners Mike and Marian Ilitch com-pleted their annual year-end review, Murray heard that Mike Keenan's agent and attorney, Rob Campbell, had contacted Ilitch's chief legal coun-sel, Jay Bielfield, to express Keenan's interest in Murray's job.

"I haven't heard from Keenan as such," Ilitch said at one high-level or-ganizational meeting. "Keenan has made contact with us through a third party."

This wasn't a novel pitch by Keenan, since he had previously signed a contract with Ilitch to replace Murray beginning with the 1993–94 season. Eighteen months after he was first talked out of the idea, on June 3, Ilitch fired Murray. Several days later, Murray got a sympathetic call from Jimmy Devellano, the Wings' senior vice president, who joined the orga-nization in 1982 as GM and was politely pushed aside and "promoted" to senior vice president by the Ilitches when Murray was hired in 1990.

"Bryan, I'm so sorry. I didn't have anything to do with it," insisted Jimmy D, who had remained one of Ilitch's trusted confidants although he had lost his hockey decision-making powers. "Keenan has been talking to the Ilitches. Mike [Ilitch] is very active in his pursuit of this guy."

On June 7, Bowman called Murray. He expressed his apologies and, like Jimmy D, swore he had no input into the Ilitches' decision. He offered as proof a conversation he had with the Ilitches several days earlier in which they informed him there was a very strong chance he would not be coaching the Wings in 1994–95. "How would you feel about not coaching next year?" Ilitch had asked Bowman.

"I'm ready to coach," Bowman replied. "I'm healthy, I feel good, I'm ready to go again next year."

"Well, there's a very strong possibility you won't be coaching. We'll certainly honor your contract and we'll put you into scouting."

Bowman dreaded Keenan's arrival. It was Bowman who had blocked Keenan's ascension to the NHL in 1983, when Bowman was Buffalo's GM-coach and Keenan led the Sabres' AHL farm club in Rochester, New York, to the Calder Cup. Devellano dreaded Keenan's arrival, too, for it certainly meant an organizational housecleaning. Although Jimmy D knew the Ilitches planned to take care of him financially, what little say he had left in the business end of the club was sure to be snuffed.

The facts they faced were these:

Bielfield and Campbell had held more than one highly confidential discussion on behalf of Keenan and the Ilitches during the Stanley Cup playoffs, most likely during the finals, but perhaps as early as the semis, before Murray was notified of his firing. No contract terms were finalized, but the general parameters of a deal were in place. Campbell told the Wings that Keenan expected to be released from his Ranger contract after the finals, or certainly given permission to accept a promotion to GM-coach of another team.

Three scenarios were proposed to the Red Wings' front office. In the first, Keenan became GM-coach, Bowman became scouting director, and amateur scouting director Ken Holland became assistant GM. In the second, Keenan became GM, Holland became his assistant, and Bowman remained as coach. In the third, Bowman remained director of player personnel and coach, Holland became assistant GM, and Keenan remained where he was, or went somewhere else. However much discussion had taken place, there was as yet no done deal.

For five days, through two huge Ranger victories at Pacific Coliseum, Murray's removal and Keenan's clandestine contact remained unlinked. Now that the story had broken, Smith did not know how to react. If the report was true, the Wings and Keenan were guilty of tampering and of disrupting the Rangers when they were so close to glory. But if it was true, it meant Smith would have Keenan out of his hair after the Cup was won, a delightful daily double. If it was false, it meant somebody devious had planted a story certain to stir controversy. And if it was false, it meant Smith would still have Keenan kicking around in 1994–95.

So Smith went jogging, five miles through Central Park at 9:15 A.M., and blended anonymously into the running scene. He wasn't nervous. He was euphoric. He felt like he did when he was eight years old the day before Christmas. Twenty-five miles away, Keenan's agent, Campbell, was riding the exercise bike at Rye. Between sets of free weights, when asked about the veracity of the Keenan-to-Detroit story, Campbell failed to deny it.

Smith simply declined to address it. "I've got more important things to worry about first, like trying to win the Stanley Cup," he said soon after he arrived at the Garden at 12:30 P.M. He showed up wearing the same charcoal gray suit he wore for Games 2, 3, and 4. After taking dozens of good-luck calls, he checked into a Garden security meeting where he learned 350 cops would be assigned to the game: three hundred outside the building, fifty inside.

They wouldn't be needed.

Game 5 brought back images of every cursed moment in this franchise's history. The game started wonderfully, the crowd responded emphatically, the air was filled with electricity. Ten minutes into the game, Tikkanen crossed Vancouver's blue line and fired a fifty-footer that beat McLean just as linesman Randy Mitton blew his whistle. Mitton ruled that Matteau was a stride offside. Although replays showed that the call was wrong, the goal was properly waved off by van Hellemond since the whistle had blown.

Before the argument began, while the Rangers were prematurely celebrating the goal, Sergio Momesso smashed Leetch into the boards and jabbed him with his stick. Beukeboom went over to defend his teammate. A fight ensued and Beukeboom was ejected for instigating it. Momesso got a slashing minor and fighting major for his attack on Leetch. Matteau got an extra roughing minor.

So instead of leading 1–0, the Rangers lost a goal, lost their number two defenseman for the game, and got a penalty. The night worsened from there. They were behind 1–0 after two periods, 3–0 when Geoff Courtnall and Pavel Bure scored in the first three minutes of the third period.

Heartlessly, the Rangers teased the ghosts of 1940. Lidster at 3:27, Larmer at 6:20, and Messier at 9:02 had fans reaching for their party hats—for just twenty-nine seconds. On the shift after Messier tied it, Richter allowed a pitifully bad shot by low-scoring defenseman Dave Babych to beat him. The Canucks won, 6–3.

Instead of dancing up the aisles, the Rangers trudged down the Garden ramp to the bus. They spent what was supposed to be their night of nights in Newark, at an airport hotel before chartering to Vancouver early the next morning. The flight was smooth, but the Rangers still flew into a storm.

The day before Game 6, Keenan denied the Detroit story and said he believed the source of the rumor was Doug MacLean, the Wings' assistant GM under Murray, who was also fired on June 3. MacLean lived in Summerside, where everybody knew everybody else. Surely, he insinuated, MacLean told someone who told someone working at the station, and the little radio station in the Maritimes went a little overboard with a piece of juicy gossip.

The next day, British Columbia went absolutely crazy. The locals knew they'd see the Canucks back in town Friday, but now to face the Rangers on Saturday, June 11, trailing only three games to two. This was truly Hockey Night in Canada.

The Rangers trailed 2–1 after two periods and Keenan couldn't cope. John Rosasco, a public relations assistant, found it preposterous that he was summoned to see Keenan during the second intermission. Rosasco's job in Vancouver that night was to escort the Ranger being interviewed between periods by one of the TV broadcasts to the correct booth set up adjacent to the Rangers' locker room.

Before the game, Rosasco was told that he was to bring MacTavish to one of the Canadian TV booths after the second period. He cleared it with Keenan before the game, just as he had cleared every scheduled interview with the coach before every game. Except now Todd told him, "Keenan's looking for you."

Rosasco found Keenan outside the dressing room.

"Are any of our guys on TV?" the coach asked angrily.

"Yes, MacTavish."

"I said no fuckin' TV." And then Keenan, who hadn't said anything like that to Rosasco, walked away.

ESPN reporter Al Morganti witnessed the entire bizarre little episode. "Now if you guys don't win the Cup, you know whose fault it is," he cracked as Rosasco shrugged and went about his business.

Game 6 was no contest. The Canucks were buoyed by their 16,150 albinos, who represented a country that now believed it could append a stunning chapter to the Fable of the Cursed Rangers. Vancouver whomped the Rangers, 4–1, in the most one-sided game of the series. The fans chanted

"1940" throughout the third period, then pulled out their history books and sang, "1928, 1933, 1940," the dates of the Rangers' three championship seasons.

At the final buzzer, the city went nuts. Fireworks spit out of the center-ice scoreboard, encasing the Coliseum in fog. Fans spilled into the streets of downtown Vancouver, rocking cars, honking horns, waving flags. This premature celebration turned the major thoroughfares into parking lots. It took the Rangers' bus over an hour to negotiate a ten-minute ride to their hotel, the Westin Bayshore, which overlooks Vancouver's Stanley Park.

Yes, that Stanley.

The NHL wisely scheduled two off-days between Games 6 and 7 of the finals to afford both teams a day to travel and a day to fully prepare for the climactic showdown. At the team meal after the game, Keenan approached Messier and Lowe with an idea. Since they were flying back to New York in the morning and due to land early in the evening, they would be idle for forty-eight hours before the seventh game's opening faceoff. Did the team need to see, hear, and read all about ghosts and curses and jinxes? Wouldn't two days hypothesizing about the thrill of winning and fear of losing detract from the intense mental preparation necessary?

"What if we went up to Lake Placid for two days?" Keenan suggested.

The concept intrigued Messier and Lowe. Fourteen years earlier, the sleepy little town high in New York's Adirondack Mountains played host to hockey's greatest miracle, the 1980 U.S. Olympic hockey team's gold medal–winning performance. Karma aside, the Rangers needed a break from the hundreds of reporters sure to invade Rye the next two days and dwell upon the possibility of the greatest choke in Ranger history. A hasty retreat to Lake Placid would shake all but the dozen regular beat writers off their backs.

But it would also show weakness, Messier said. It would send the wrong message. The Rangers were about to play one game for the Stanley Cup, on their ice, in front of their fans. The biggest game on the sport's biggest stage. Why run from it?

"This is the chance of a lifetime, Mike," Messier said. "Let's come back and enjoy it, instead of running from the situation. Let's come back here and do the things we did all year."

The coach, the captain, and his most loyal confidant tossed the concept around a little more. They talked about how Vancouver had seized the momentum, just like the Devils had seized the momentum. They agreed that forty-eight hours in New York wouldn't change the task: they had to beat the Canucks. It didn't matter to them that they had lost Games 5 and 6. They still believed the Rangers were the better team. The players recalled how their 1987 Oilers had let a three-games-to-one lead over Keenan's Flyers slip away before they won Game 7 in Edmonton. They reminded Keenan that they had pushed all year for the Presidents' Trophy in case they had to play a Game 7 at home. They beat the Devils in Game 7 at home. Now they were going to beat Vancouver in one, too. For the first time in the series, Messier said, there would be just as much pressure on Vancouver as on the Rangers.

"If they beat us three straight," the captain reasoned, "they deserve the Cup."

Sunday morning was supposed to be Parade Day in New York, but the only motorcade carrying Rangers was the one driving the beleaguered team back to the airport. The Keenan-to-Detroit story had been emphatically reported as fact by most of the major newspapers across North America all weekend. Several players whispered that Keenan had all but alienated himself from the players, and that Messier was running the entire operation.

What were the Rangers going to do?

"We'll just try to adjust," the always frank MacTavish said before boarding the plane. "As much as you can when you have your heart in your throat."

Doug MacLean could have been a source of the Keenan story, but on Sunday, June 12, it became apparent he wasn't the only source. A respected veteran hockey writer from Halifax, Nova Scotia, Pat Connolly, published a column in the *Halifax Sunday Daily News* in which he acknowledged having the same information that CRJW reported the day the station broadcast the news.

"A mole in the Keenan camp had whispered the same information into my ear last Wednesday [June 8] with a request not to release it until the Rangers clinched—or collapsed," Connolly wrote.

Connolly would not reveal his source that week, nor would he a year later. "My source was impeccable," Connolly said. "Obviously, I can't tell you who it is. But I can tell you the source has told me when Mike was leaving Philly, when he was going to Chicago, and when he was going to New York. It's somebody pretty close to Mike."

The next day, thirty hours before the biggest game of his life, Keenan faced approximately fifty reporters from across the continent and flatly denied there was any truth to the stories that reporters and columnists from New York, Detroit, Toronto, and every other NHL city had reported with quotes from reliable unnamed sources.

As a defense, he offered the possibility of sabotage. He hypothesized a scenario in which Devellano purposely planted the false story to detract and derail the Rangers' Cup run to harm Neil Smith. Jimmy D was Smith's boss from 1982 to 1989; they had had almost a father-son relationship, because it was Devellano who drafted Smith for the Islanders in 1974 and gave Smith his first break as a part-time scout in 1980. But Smith and Devellano hadn't spoken since the fall of 1989, soon after Smith left Detroit to become the Rangers' GM. Devellano blamed the falling out on the way the Rangers mishandled Smith's hiring and delayed the Red Wings' attempt to replace him. He never coherently explained why he took it out on Smith. The most logical explanation came from somebody who knew the eccentric little bachelor well: "Jimmy D takes young guys under his wing, but can't handle it when they want to leave the nest. He wants them to stay forever, and stay forever grateful to him."

Although Keenan's preposterous alibi eased some of the heat for one day, it failed to convince anybody who checked the story out. Devellano laughed when reporters called him that day for comment, especially since he knew Bielfield and Campbell had been talking for at least a week. Without confirming the stories that had been written about his boss's interest in Keenan, Jimmy D said any diabolical attempt to interfere with the Rangers' quest would have been easily deciphered by anybody with half a brain.

One day before the biggest game of his career, Keenan gave two of the best performances of his life. First he made his impassioned plea to the media, all but begging the writers who had quoted sources throughout the NHL to take his word that he hadn't contacted Detroit. Then he told his players the same thing. In an emotional fifteen-minute speech on the ice, he swore the Detroit story was a vicious rumor, insisted he'd be the coach for four more years unless he was fired, and reminded the players of how tirelessly they had worked since September for one shot at the Cup.

"Look where we were eight, nine months ago," he said. "All the things we've done, all we've gone through. Look where we are. If I said that first day of camp that we'd be here today, twenty-four hours before Game 7 of the finals, in our own building versus Vancouver, would we take it?"

After practice he replayed the video he showed them the first day of training camp, the one filled with scenes of New York City victory parades from the past.

"This is no time for the faint of heart," Messier said.

The Garden doors opened a few minutes before 7 P.M. on Tuesday, June 14. One of the early arrivals slowly circled the aisle between the loge and first promenade, stopping only to place a small clove of garlic on the cement wall in front of every section. Fans dropped lucky pennies and rabbit's feet into the hands of strangers during warm-up. Others rubbed huge metal horseshoes.

In the dressing room before Game 7, in a pregame speech that Messier later called one of the most inspirational he had ever heard, Keenan admitted he was a demanding coach, maybe too demanding. He paraphrased a quote from Stanley Cups past by saying that if the Rangers won tonight, they'd walk together forever. He again insisted he had never talked to Detroit, had no interest in any job other than the one he had, and would definitely be back in 1994–95 unless he was fired.

That touched the players. This close-knit group that often rallied around their hatred for their Machiavellian mentor didn't need to be strengthened any further. But for one night they bonded with their coach as they entered the biggest game of their lives.

"Mike," Messier said to Keenan before they hit the ice, "you can't be afraid to slay the dragon."

The Monster was at its boisterous best: exuberant and supportive, but not cocky. Unlike Game 5, nobody dared taunt the Canucks or the ghosts. A fear of failure that cloaked the Garden before the opening draw was quickly extinguished when the Messier line started strong. The Matteau-Kovalev-Larmer line had an impressive shift. The Rangers carried the first ten minutes and Keenan juggled his players masterfully. Eleven minutes into the game he used Larmer with Messier and Graves, Zubov with Leetch.

Messier got it going. He lugged the puck through the neutral zone near the right-wing boards, gaining speed as he crossed the red line. There are few scarier sights for a diminutive back-checking forward than the Rangers' freight train of a power center with his eyes on the net. Bure offered little resistance as Messier skated past him, then cut left toward the middle of the ice as he crossed the blue line.

Gerald Diduck and Dave Babych respected Messier's speed and backed off the line. When both defensemen concentrated on clogging Messier's lane down the slot, Messier dropped a pass back to the right for Zubov. The slick defenseman glided down the right circle toward the faceoff dot, attracting the attention of all six Canucks on the ice. Zubov thought about shooting, but when he looked up and saw McLean taking away his angle, he also spotted Leetch charging to the net from the left point, unnoticed because Messier and Graves had the Canucks tied up around the goalmouth. Zubov threw a crisp, precise, gorgeous diagonal pass through Vancouver's defensive position.

Slow-motion replay was needed to capture the climax to this play. The Monster's roar began to swell in its belly. People rose from their pews in unison as Leetch from the bottom of the left circle took his time, waited until McLean committed himself with a desperate dive across the crease, and then lifted the game-opening goal into the open top half of the net at 11:02.

The thunder had not yet abated when Lumme cross-checked Mac-Tavish. The Garden was still rocking forty seconds into the power play when Zubov, whose injured chest and bruised face had been hammered all series by sticks and elbows, led the power-play rush over the Canucks' blue line and distributed the puck wide to Kovalev, on right wing with the top line for this shift. Kovalev drew a defenseman toward him, then slipped the puck into the slot for Graves, the 52-goal scorer who hadn't scored a goal since Game 3 of the Devils series. Graves buried this one. Alone in the slot just twenty feet away, he looked McLean in the eye and snapped a low shot past McLean's stick side at 14:45. It was 2–0 after one.

Little had to be said between periods. "Keep playing the same way," a dozen Rangers chatted out loud. "Don't let up, boys. Don't let up."

Trevor Linden, who was the best player in this game, scored a short-handed goal at 5:21 of an evenly played second period to make it 2–1. Eight minutes later, during a power play, Noonan passed to Graves, whose shot was stopped by McLean. The rebound bounced around the crease, where John McIntyre tried to swat it away. He couldn't. Noonan and Messier poked at the rebound, and the puck somehow grazed McLean's pad, slid past his thigh, and found its way into the net.

Andy Bathgate never scored a playoff goal like this. Rod Gilbert never scored a playoff goal like this. Anders Hedberg never scored a playoff goal like this. Only Messier did. At 13:29 of the second period, Mark Douglas Messier scored the final goal of the 1993–94 season for the New York Rangers.

For the next twenty-six minutes and twenty-one seconds, which lasted two hours and felt like two days, eighteen skaters and a goaltender had to protect a two-goal lead from the Canucks and fifty-four years of ghosts and spirits and misery. The world's most famous arena was now the Vatican, with 18,200 parishioners on their knees in sweaty prayer.

In the radio perch, between the second and third periods, Howie Rose lifted the headset off his ears and handed the game back to Marv Albert, who graciously allowed Rose to work the middle period of the franchise's most historic game. "Coming up," Rose said off the air, "will be the longest twenty minutes of my life."

It started ominously. Linden scored again, on a power play after only 4:50. The period had very little flow, though. From the moment Linden scored, the Rangers did not hide their intention to simply work the final 15:10 off the clock. Midway through the period, Lowe, with a shoulder so badly separated it was amazing he could play, fired a shot from the blue line that hit the crossbar. Several minutes after that, with fewer than five minutes left until euphoria, Vancouver's Nathan LaFayette took a pass alone at Richter's doorstep, but hit the right post.

Had the demons conceded? Not without a fight.

The final ninety-one seconds were torturous. Pulses raced, stomachs ached, hearts fluttered. Four faceoffs in the Rangers' end over the final 1:31 afforded four gasps of oxygen, four pleas to the heavens, four opportunities for disaster. MacTavish won a faceoff from Craven, and the Rangers worked the clock to 0:37.8 before a frozen puck prompted a whistle. Messier won a faceoff from Linden, but Larmer cleared the puck out of the zone a little too hard. The clock showed 0:28.2 when the icing call stopped play.

Messier and Craven lined up this time. The Canucks gained control of the puck on Messier's first faceoff loss, but in the disorganized din of the crowd shrieks and player scrambles, Vancouver failed to take a shot at Richter. The puck remained agonizingly close to the net until it was iced with 1.6 seconds to go.

The end was near. As MacTavish and Bure lined up to Richter's right, there wasn't a devil on earth capable of quieting the bellow that had built for more than five decades. MacTavish knocked the puck into the corner, Larmer pinned it against the boards with his skates, the scoreboard read 0:00.0, and fifty-four years of bitter frustration burst like a volcano roaring to life.

Messier leaped like a little kid, looked out over the glass and found his family sitting in their usual corner of the arena. Richter hugged Leetch. Beukeboom, who hurt his knee in the first period and sat on the bench although he couldn't play, limped onto the ice behind his teammates, who raced to join the love-in at Richter's crease.

"Now I Can Die In Peace." What more needed to be said than that cardboard placard raised from the loge seats while the players spun each other around in unabashed joy?

For seven minutes the players cheered each other, lifted their fists to the fans, shook hands with the stubborn Canucks, and waited for the grail to appear. First, though, Leetch was awarded the Conn Smythe, becoming the first American ever to win the trophy first awarded in 1965. At 11:06 P.M.,

NHL commissioner Gary Bettman looked to the rafters and said, "Well, New York. After fifty-four years, your long wait is over. Mark Messier, come get the Stanley Cup."

For fifteen minutes they paraded the silver around the ice. When the scene shifted to the Rangers' dressing room, Graves stopped celebrating for a moment to solemnly remember why the Rangers wanted so badly to fulfill Keenan's mandate.

"Something happened about six weeks ago, to an avid Ranger fan, a lady by the name of Ceil Saidel," Graves said. "I think she took the Garden ghost and kicked it right out of the rafters."

The Rangers all year felt the pressure Keenan had applied. In winning, they understood the pressure the fans had felt. That cemented a bond few teams feel with their fans. The Rangers won the Cup so their devotees could live in peace. Said Lowe, "I don't ever want to hear 1940 again."

5

The Long
Goodbye

As he wiped the sweat, beer, and champagne from his scalp minutes after the Cup was won, a beaming Keenan swore he wanted to return for the 1994–95 season, and said he planned to return, "if they'll have me back." Smith didn't believe it for a moment. The morning after the Cup was won, two reliable NHL people whom Smith trusted finally assured him that the newspaper stories reporting negotiations between Bielfield and Campbell were correct.

"I'm trying to enjoy the Cup rather than focusing on this negative stuff right now," he told one informant. "But I'm so pissed, I'm thinking about hitting Detroit with a whopping tampering charge. Here's the clincher: instead of doing that, I can tell Rob Campbell I'm threatening to do that, then tell him to go to Keenan and say, 'Neil doesn't want to ruin your reputation. Let's not ruin your career. Take a job someplace else.'"

To Smith, it was a no-lose situation: He'd get Keenan out, which he wanted. He'd avoid a nasty scene, which he wanted. And he'd force the Red Wings—now run by Keenan—to compensate the Rangers with a draft pick for signing away their head coach.

Keenan envisioned a bubbly, happy press conference, too. Smith would step to the podium first. After thanking his coach for doing a fantastic job, he'd announce that neither he nor the owners could in good conscience stand in Keenan's way of a promotion since Keenan had accomplished the feat he was hired to accomplish in New York.

Keenan would speak next. After gratefully thanking Smith for the opportunity to coach such a fine nucleus of talent, he'd regretfully announce that the Detroit Red Wings had in the last few days made an offer too financially and personally lucrative to pass up. He'd explain how he missed his daughter, Gayla, terribly. By living in Detroit, he'd have more chances to see her in Chicago.

It would have been the phoniest press conference since Joey and Mary Jo Buttafuoco pledged marital bliss, but it never came close to happening. Viacom had no intention of severing a winning management team, not when their $1 billion asset was in play. Smith and Keenan learned that soon enough.

For one week after the Stanley Cup was won, the Rangers' most intense power play of the year remained on hold. Both men had enough common sense to enjoy the spoils of the achievement. Neither was in any condition to begin fighting while still basking in the glow from the parties that dominated the next forty-eight hours.

Whoa!

That's what thousands of lucky New Yorkers exclaimed that summer, the ones fortunate enough to get a chance to grip the black bottom base with one hand, steady the thin shiny rim with the other, and jerk the Stanley Cup overhead during the Rangers' Stanley Tour '94. Whoa! was the operative password, because the first thing you notice when you grab the trophy is how heavy and unwieldy thirty-six pounds of heaven actually is.

The second was the shiny silver's irresistible lure. All of New York wanted to touch, kiss, and caress the smooth spot where the names of the 1993–94 New York Rangers would soon be engraved. A city that had waited so long enjoyed its summer fling with the Cup like no other romance the Hall of Fame's prized jewel had ever seen.

The courtship began at 11:06 P.M. on June 14, the moment commissioner Gary Bettman handed the Cup to captain Mark Messier. After being passed from Ranger to Ranger, and even up to where the fans could reach out and touch it, the Cup was carried lovingly into the Ranger dressing room. Around 1 A.M., the beer- and champagne-soaked Cup was escorted upstairs to the Play-by-Play Restaurant for a party that was still rocking at 3:30 A.M., when a bunch of Rangers toted the Cup to one of their favorite after-hour haunts, the Auction House, on the Upper East Side in Manhattan. While hundreds of patrons, including actor Tim Robbins and Ranger great Rod Gilbert, drank from the oversized tumbler inside, thousands jammed the streets outside, halting traffic. Blue police barricades prevented even the limousines from pulling up in front of the tavern, so when a Ranger arrived, he and his entourage had to walk the last few blocks while the fans cheered and sang. It was one long nocturnal block party.

Spontaneous celebrations erupted throughout the city that night. A 1988 Honda pulled up at a red light on Fifth Avenue at 4 A.M. and blew his horn to the tune of, "Let's go Ran-gers": *Honk . . . honk . . . honk-honk;* from a 1994 BMW it heard the automatic Ranger reply: *Honk . . . honk . . . honk-honk-honk.* Fans carrying replica Cups fashioned out of cardboard and aluminum foil started their own outdoor processions when they couldn't get near the real grail.

A visibly wired Esa Tikkanen finally yanked the Cup off the bar, wobbled out East 89th Street, and shared the festivities with the revelers who couldn't squeeze into the tavern. The Cup was up all night. It found itself with Messier at Scores, the popular East Side strip joint, where it was the one featured attraction that the patrons were free to grope. Finally, at around dawn, Messier took Stanley home to his Upper West Side brownstone. Five miles downtown, Neil and Katia Smith staggered into their Greenwich Village apartment sometime around 7 A.M., after Smith dropped his mother off at the Plaza Hotel.

Gayla Keenan helped her father and Rob Campbell stagger out of their limo and into his Greenwich, Connecticut, home around 6 A.M., but Keenan wasn't ready to pass out yet. He turned on the stereo and played Frank Sinatra's version of "New York, New York" over and over, singing at the top of his lungs. Finally, Gayla Keenan put her dad to bed.

Watkins collapsed at 7 A.M. onto the bed in his room at the Southgate Hotel, a block from the Garden. Three hours later he staggered across Seventh Avenue and climbed up to the Rangers' PR office. The eight phone lines were already ringing off the hook. Everybody wanted a piece of the Stanley Cup champions.

The first reminder on Watkins's to-do list was a call to the Hall of Fame. He needed to know the rules or prohibitions regarding the Cup. "We'll get you a list of the obligations," director of communications Phil Dennis said. "Other than that, it's for the team to enjoy."

The Rangers' PR people were the only ones who reported for work Wednesday, the day after. Watkins, McDonald, Rosasco and his girlfriend, Jacqueline Middleton, administrative assistant Ann Marie Gilmartin, and two interns, Rob Koch and Karen Strelec, spent the day answering dozens of questions, fielding scores of offers, denying hundreds of media requests. One week earlier, on the day before Game 5, NHL corporate communciations VP Bernadette Mansur called Watkins to coordinate the league's attempt to begin marketing the Rangers' fantastic feat.

"If you win tonight, we'll do *Good Morning America* tomorrow morning," Mansur began. Watkins stopped her at once.

"Wait a minute," he said. "How am I supposed to get this done? If we win tonight, go hug Mess and ask him, 'Could you do *Good Morning America?*' Feel him out before the game?"

That was one of the many times the Rangers and NHL butted heads. The first was two days before Game 1 of the Finals, when the NHL insisted the Rangers bus their players to the Garden for Media Day and Keenan said no. It was Memorial Day weekend, the team was practicing at Rye, and there was no way he was going to have a busload of players sitting in traffic just for the press's benefit. It didn't matter to Keenan that the Canucks had agreed to cooperate. It didn't matter that the NHL wanted to accommodate the continent's media corps. Keenan wouldn't do it.

"Barry, it's mandatory," Arthur Pincus, the NHL's vice president of public relations, told Watkins.

"Arthur, we're not coming," Watkins replied.

"Barry, you have to come."

"Arthur, you tell that to Keenan. You tell a guy trying to win the Stanley Cup for the first time in fifty-four years that he can't run the team the way he wants."

The Rangers remained at Rye. Reporters had to choose one team to interview, or make the inconvenient trek from Manhattan to Westchester County forty-five minutes away.

Rob Burnett, head writer of the David Letterman show, called Watkins the day before Game 5 and invited the entire team for a guest spot the following day if they won. Watkins checked with Messier, who thought piling twenty-five players on Letterman's small stage was too much of a gimmick. "Why can't hockey players go on like regular people?" asked the captain, who wanted Letterman's people to pick a player or two for the spot. "It doesn't have to be me. But it can't be a goof, it's got to be serious."

Bettman called Gutkowski that day, hours before Game 5, to complain about the Rangers' stubbornness. Pincus and Mansur were also upset that the team nixed requests for the national network news-talk shows the morning after the Cup. Watkins conferred with Messier on that one, too, and was told that the celebrating was going to last far too long for any player to be in condition to do the *Today* show, or *Good Morning America,* or *Live with Regis and Kathie Lee.*

At the league's insistence, Watkins did ask Messier again, about three hours before Game 5. Messier thought about it, but still said no. After the loss, a furious Keenan blamed the defeat on the media for distracting the team's focus. He and Messier knew, though, that the players were also to blame, because while the networks were planning their Ranger Cup coverage, the Rangers were planning their Cup parties. Before Games 6 and 7, there were no tentative plans made by anybody.

Watkins and Burnett negotiated the Rangers' Letterman spot virtually all day Wednesday. At 4:00, less than two hours before taping, Messier, Richter, and Leetch were told to wait by the phone. At 4:30, Letterman's people agreed that the Rangers' three stars could appear in one spot. They rushed to the Ed Sullivan Theater, where Leetch strolled the Cup up and down the aisles. The pumped-up crowd went wild.

From Letterman, Leetch and Richter were driven to another studio for the Charlie Rose show. Messier took the Cup to the Garden, where the Knicks and Houston Rockets played Game 4 of the NBA Finals. At halftime, Messier carried the Cup onto the court. The Garden roared. Messier met up with Leetch later that night so Leetch could have an overnight with the Cup.

Early the next morning, Rosasco met Leetch at NBC's *Today* show studio at Rockefeller Center. The bleary-eyed defenseman and the somnambulant captain made it, but Stanley didn't. "Brian, where's the Cup?" Rosasco asked. "You were supposed to bring the Cup."

"John, you're lucky I'm here," Leetch mumbled. "I don't know where the Cup is."

Rosasco led the groggy Leetch from the *Today* show to WXRK-FM's studio for a radio spot with Messier and Richter on shock-jock Howard Stern's morning show. Messier was already there. Richter wasn't. He finally strolled in wearing shorts and a T-shirt, but carrying a freshly pressed suit for another gig later in the day. Producer Gary Dell'Abate saw this young guy carrying a garment bag and looked around for his soiled clothes; he thought it was the laundry man.

By early afternoon the Cup was resting silently below the Garden's scoreboard, perched inches above the Y in the Rangers' logo stenciled on the ice. For two hours it posed with one GM, three coaches, twenty-five players, four trainers, and three other trophies: the Smythe, the Prince of Wales, and the Presidents'.

Photo Day took forever. The exhausted players were in no hurry to climb into their pads and pants, and pull their white championship jerseys over their heads again, not even for the pictures in which they had waited all their lives to pose. McDonald and Rosasco kept counting heads and kept coming up short until a hungover Noonan finally showed up.

The first picture was by far the most important. It was the official Stanley Cup team picture. As the players were positioned by photographer Bruce Bennett, there was one frozen moment when Smith and Keenan were to be seated in the center of the first row. Although both had been around for nearly an hour, they had kept to their own cliques and hadn't acknowledged each other. Would they possibly sit side by side? Messier, the captain and franchise centerpiece, diplomatically took his spot between the warring generals.

Everyone else fell into place. Everyone smiled.

After the official group shots were complete, the media took its turn snapping team pictures. Then the players took turns posing for family portraits with the Cup. When the shoot was finally finished, somebody went to lift Stanley off the ice. The silver bowl and its many rings came free, but the oversized black coaster that serves as the trophy's base did not. It was stuck to the ice.

Eventually, it was freed and reattached. It had a unique date that night, a party at Restaurant National in Brighton Beach, Brooklyn, an unlikely bash hosted by the four Russian Rangers, the first citizens of the crumbled Soviet Union to have their names etched on the Cup. Karpovtsev, Kovalev, Nemchinov, and Zubov rented a huge banquet hall in Brighton Beach, a small enclave of homes and stores near Coney Island, which in the 1960s grew to become the largest neighborhood of emigrated Russians in the United States.

It was a phenomenal party. Keenan called it the best he ever went to in his life. Players drank borscht, ate caviar, and danced to the beat of Russian music. Leetch was one of the few Rangers to miss the gig. He was booked on TV again, this time with another carrot-top, on *Late Night with Conan O'Brien*. Smith and Graves missed the party, too, for they attended the NHL awards banquet in Toronto, where Graves won the King Clancy Memorial Trophy for humanitarian service.

Colin Campbell took the Cup home from the party. When he walked through the door well after midnight, he tiptoed into his nine-year-old son Gregory's room and stood the Cup at the foot of his son's bed. Gregory awoke the next morning and had quite a story to tell that day in school.

Friday, June 17, was beautifully hot and sunny, perfect for the 11:45 A.M. victory parade, New York City's first since the celebration of Desert Storm's success in the Gulf War in January 1991. A sea of Ranger red, white, and blue, 1.1 million heads strong, hailed the Rangers, who climbed into cars and onto floats at Battery Park and motorcaded up Broadway's Canyon of Heroes to City Hall, where Mayor Rudolph Giuliani chaired a 1 P.M. ceremony in the team's honor and rewarded the Rangers with keys to the city.

From there, Healy and Kypreos hopped into a police car with the Cup. They were late for a scheduled taping of MTV's *This Week in Rock,* so with sirens blaring they were sped uptown. Stanley also spent time that day on the set of NY-1, a New York cable TV station, and finished the evening at Gracie Mansion, where Mayor Giuliani hosted a dinner party for the champions. Tikkanen got to put the Cup to bed that night.

Sometime that day—the day O.J. Simpson's Ford Bronco became famous and Ranger radio analyst Sal Messina got married—Watkins was handed a phone message slip. One of the NHL's coordinators, Lori Busch, wanted to know how Watkins intended to get the Cup back to the league later that day so it could make it to Hartford in time for the Hartford Open golf tournament taking place the following week. "The Cup has to go on Monday," Busch said. "We have to talk about how we're going to get it."

This was the first Watkins heard about the Cup going to the PGA tournament. He was flabbergasted.

"Get it? I just assigned it. Monday it's going to a party at *Sports Illustrated,* Tuesday we're going to Yankee Stadium, they've already done a press release. Wednesday Messier is taking it to his Tampa Bay roller hockey team, they've already publicized it and sold tickets based on it being there. You can't have it Monday." They agreed to have the Rangers fly the Cup from Tampa Bay to Hartford on the twenty-third.

Tikkanen brought the Cup on Saturday night to the Waldorf-Astoria, where the Rangers held their official Cup-winning party for the players and their wives, the entire team staff, and selected high-ranking officials from the Garden and MSG Network. Through the cocktail hour and dinner, this was a staid corporate event. The band's background music blended soothingly with the quiet banter at the circular ballroom tables.

After dinner, something clicked. Perhaps it was the wine. Keenan began dancing on tables with Tikkanen and Tikkanen's wife, Lada. Wendy and Larry Pleau did a fine tablecloth mambo, too. Stanley's chalice was filled with champagne guzzled by the case. At 2 A.M. a tipsy Matt Loughran convinced the band not to stop, that he had the authority to approve an hour of overtime added to the team's hefty bill. When three o'clock arrived, Keenan and Graves headed uptown to Elaine's.

Sunday the nineteenth was a complete day of rest for the organization. The Cup spent the day in tony Greenwich, where Keenan held court at home and around the neighborhood. Keenan kept the Cup overnight and brought it to the Time-Warner Building for *SI*'s party, where Smith, Messier, Olczyk, and Kypreos also represented the Rangers. Kypreos decided that Stanley had suffered through enough formal banquets, so off it boogied to the China Club, where the paparazzi were all too happy to snap—for $20 a glossy print—a shining Stanley bumping and grinding with the beautiful people.

If Tikkanen was the Rangers' team clown, Kypreos was the court jester, their stand-up comic. Outgoing, talkative, and a clever needler, his teammates called him Kipper, but that wasn't much of a nickname. Hockey players since ice first froze under the dinosaurs had regularly bastardized a player's last name to find something endearing to call him, something like Kipper or Kipster or the horribly popular Kippy.

It wasn't until the blockbuster hit *Forrest Gump* was released the following season, and virtually every Ranger saw it, that they found the perfect handle for Kypreos. The Toronto-born left wing of Greek descent was Forrest Gump, for like Forrest Gump, he stuck his mug everywhere.

Take a look at the Stanley Cup celebration pictures. There's Kypreos. Who got to go to MTV? Kypreos. Who was one of the few Rangers at the *SI* party? Kypreos. The guy got more ice time with the Cup than he did in his three playoff appearances. He scored more quality moments with the Cup (four) than he did goals in 1993–94, three.

The spare forward was the first Ranger to jerk the Cup over his head during the celebratory laps around the rink and glide over to the glass so fans could touch it. And of the twenty jerseys worn in Game 7, his white No. 19 spent the summer and fall representing the Rangers in the Hall of Fame—although, to be fair to the Gumpster, Kypreos played no part in that decision. When the Hall asked the Rangers for a game-worn jersey to display, the team sent Kypreos's because they didn't want to relinquish the jersey of a more prominent player.

"Forrest always seemed to be showing up," Kypreos said. "Just like me."

Although he stuck his nose into everything, Kypreos was a well-liked Ranger with a big heart. While he and Stanley frolicked that night, a thirteen-year-old boy named Brian Bluver fought to stay alive. Twenty-four hours later, Kypreos became one of the most important people in his life.

Sometime Monday, Watkins accepted a call from Bill Bluver, whose son Brian was dying and desperately needed a heart transplant. TV analyst and well-read hockey author Stan Fischler, whose son Simon underwent a successful heart transplant a year earlier, had told Watkins to be ready for Bluver's call.

The Rangers' PR department gets dozens of desperate requests all the time. It is the most painful part of a PR person's job. How do you say no when somebody calls and requests some spiritual help for a dying youngster? But it is impossible to say yes all the time. Watkins tried to accommodate Bill Bluver. He promised him that they would try to get Messier to do something for his son next week, when the hoopla diminished, because Messier was going to be around New York all month.

That's when the father began to cry.

"No, no, no," he sobbed. "Next week could be too late. He's not going to make it. Anything you can do, please. We've got to try to save him, my boy is dying. He was fine. Fine. He's a regular boy, thirteen years old, a good boy. He's a big Ranger fan. He hasn't hurt anybody, he hasn't done anything. We don't know why this has happened to him. He was a healthy boy, and all of a sudden they say his heart's no good and he could die. We don't know if he'll get another heart. We're waiting. We need a heart. Please. Please. Whatever you can do."

Watkins called Messier, who was due at Yankee Stadium with Leetch, Kypreos (naturally), and the Cup for the game that night. Since Brian Bluver was uptown at Babies Hospital, a part of Columbia-Presbyterian Medical Center, Messier and Kypreos decided to leave an hour earlier and pay a surprise bedside visit. Leetch had a prior engagement and couldn't make it.

Bill Bluver thinks his son's life was saved that day. Because when Messier visited the gravely ill boy and gently laid the Cup beside him, he promised Brian he'd see the day the Rangers raised the Stanley Cup banner to the rafters.

Four days later, Brian Bluver received a new heart. Seven months later, on Opening Night, Brian was the Rangers' honorary captain, seated on the bench with the players when the banner was raised to the ceiling.

"Every day I reminded Brian to hold on and hang tough because we had a date with the Rangers when they raised the banner," Bill Bluver wrote Watkins in a heartwarming letter of thanks for Kypreos and Messier. "This, I am positive, contributed to his inner strength and brought him through. In closing, our sincerest gratitude to yourself and the entire Ranger organization for giving our son 'Your gift of life' by winning the Stanley Cup."

Their heroism accomplished, Messier and Kypreos headed to the Bronx, where the Yankees were playing the Minnesota Twins that evening. The normally subdued Leetch, who threw a ninety-mph fastball when he pitched for Avon Old Farms High School, acted like a little kid. "This is great," he kept giggling hours before the game. Each Ranger got to throw a ceremonial first pitch while Stanley stood majestically on the diamond and accepted thunderous applause from the crowd. The Cup then joined its teammates in owner George Steinbrenner's box (the Boss was absent) for the game. Messier placed the Cup, still wearing the press credential jokingly assigned to it by the Yankees, between Kypreos and Leetch.

"It likes an aisle," Leetch said.

Messier baby-sat Stanley that night and flew with it the next day to Tampa, where the Roller Hockey International team he owns, the Tritons, played. The NHL mercifully gave the overworked Cup a rest the next day, for Stanley spent a week in Hartford, first posing at the PGA Hartford Open and then sitting in a display case at the draft. It looked tired, a little beat-up, like it had been in a scuffle.

But the real scuffle had not yet begun.

The effort to engineer an uncontested Smith-Keenan divorce began in earnest on Monday, June 20, when Rob Campbell called Smith. The two men had known each other for years, and trusted each other. At first, however, Campbell did not openly admit he was talking to the Red Wings. Smith did not openly admit he wanted Keenan out. They carefully inched closer to their positions, then began exploring ways to sever the relationship without rancor, and with Viacom's blessing.

Smith's desire to rid himself of one of hockey's finest coaches didn't surprise Campbell. It had happened in Philadelphia and Chicago, too. Smith's complaints to Campbell throughout the year about his incorrigible client's behavior were all too familiar. Campbell maintained a neutral position whenever the GM called, no easy task since he got paid by his client, but he needed to retain Smith's trust. He always sympathized with Smith whenever Smith bitched about Keenan's disrespectful nature and grating personality. "I know he's not the easiest guy in the world to deal with, Neil," Campbell said in one conversation midway through the season. "Try not to let Mike bother you. That's just the way he is."

"But he's such an asshole."

"I know. Mike's a high-maintenance guy. Just let him run his team."

Smith and Campbell agreed on June 20 to let Smith propose a cordial parting with Keenan to Gutkowski. Smith felt he could tote enough information on Keenan's advances to Detroit to convince Gutkowski that the coach had to go. That was fine with Campbell, because he and Keenan were already talking to the Garden president behind Smith's back, jeopardizing Smith's status in Gutkowski's eyes by reporting everything Smith had said in confidence to Campbell about Gutkowski.

And on June 20, Smith had said plenty. Smith sensed from his partici-
pation in several interviews with the Garden bidders (Gutkowski wasn't
invited to any) and from the MSG grapevine that Gutkowski was going to
be released when the corporation was sold. In his fervent desire to impress
upon Keenan and Campbell that their major ally was a lame duck, Smith
exaggerated. He told Campbell he knew somebody high in Viacom who
assured him Gutkowski was out.

That was a bluff. Smith had nothing but a strong hunch and a keen sense
of the political winds.

The first major salvo in the Keenan affair was launched by Smith on
Wednesday, June 22, when he and Gutkowski met in Gutkowski's office.

"Bob, I know beyond a shadow of a doubt that Mike was talking to Detroit during the playoffs," Smith said. "But more importantly, Mike's
gonna be destructive long-term for the organization. Look at what happened against the Devils; there was a mutiny. There's no way this guy will
succeed with this team again. He'll destroy it, just like he destroyed Philly
and Chicago. We should let him go to Detroit."

Gutkowski had heard all year from Keenan about his serious problems
working with Smith, and from Smith about his serious problems working
with Keenan. Yet the New York Rangers had won the Stanley Cup for the
first time since 1940. The franchise for which he possessed ultimate responsibility when sitting around Viacom's boardroom had under contract
one of the best GMs and best coaches in the business. Gutkowski thought
it was insane not to keep the tandem intact, even though he knew how
much the men fought, how deeply they despised and disrespected each
other.

"Well, I'm going to have to hear what Keenan has to say about this,"
Gutkowski said, "and then I may have to make a decision."

Smith was incensed. "Bob, I've got an employee problem here. I'm the
president of the Rangers and I have a problem with an employee. Why do
you have to talk to my employee?"

Smith persisted. He described his vision of the farewell press conference in which the Rangers would appear grateful and magnanimous. He
emphasized the value of compensation from the Wings. He also told
Gutkowski he didn't know if he could stand another year like this one, Cup
or no Cup. "Bob, I don't want to go through another year of hell with this
guy."

"Are you telling me he goes or you go?"

"No, I'm not telling you that. If I have to, I'll work with this guy because I don't ever really want to leave the Rangers. But I sincerely believe

it's in the best interest of this franchise to let him go. He will destroy this organization. Anyway, the guy's already been talking with Detroit."

Gutkowski did not budge. He told Smith he had a meeting scheduled for the thirtieth with Viacom CEO Frank Biondi, and would do nothing before that meeting. He said Viacom would probably tell him to keep the team's assets intact. He also told Smith he'd probably be meeting with Keenan.

"I'd appreciate it if you'd let me know what he says," Smith said, fighting back the frustration and outrage over his boss's decision to meet with Smith's coach.

Gutkowski assured Smith he would, but he never did. He did take a call from Campbell not long after Smith left his office. "It's imperative that we meet," Campbell said. "Mike and I want to talk to you. We have proposals. We want to do it as soon as possible. Neil told me he knows people high in the organization, that you're going to be gone, that he's going to have the power base. We need to talk to you as soon as possible."

They scheduled a confidential meeting for two days later, the twenty-fourth, and elected to hold it at Gutkowski's apartment in the Essex House, on Central Park South. For two days Gutkowski considered his predicament. He knew he was probably going to lose his job, but he was still employed by Viacom. He still ran the Garden, which meant he was accountable for Smith's and Keenan's actions. He wasn't sure Smith had a source high in Viacom, but he believed enough of what Campbell said to be angered and disappointed in Smith's end-around.

Everyone was on his own now, he told himself. There were no allies. There was no protocol.

If MSG were not for sale, perhaps he could have forced the issue. Maybe he would have agreed that one of the two men had to go. But it was, and he didn't. He had grown up a Ranger fan, and he understood better than Smith or Keenan how New York's diehard hockey community felt the last eight days. The overwhelming feeling of joy and the relaxing sense of relief provided an intoxicating mix of emotions that deserved to linger all summer. Gutkowski didn't want to halt the celebration any more than he wanted to split a strange but effective GM-coaching duo.

On Friday, June 24, he learned just how difficult that would be. Keenan and Campbell arrived with a list of seven proposals, seven resolutions to the problem. Before he listened to their pitch, he issued the same preamble he had given Smith.

"My interest is to keep everybody in the same position," Gutkowski said. "And sometime soon I'm going to have a conversation with Viacom and put this out on the table. And there's a very strong possibility they're going to say, 'Nobody's going anywhere.' I want to say this up front. Now I'll listen to your proposals."

First, Campbell and Keenan each took several minutes making several key points. Campbell insisted he had not talked to Detroit during the playoffs. He blamed the speculation on the negotiations with Mike Ilitch in January 1993. Keenan reminded Gutkowski that the two men he considered his closest allies, Stanley Jaffe and Gutkowski, were either gone (Jaffe) or close to gone.

Keenan ripped into Smith. He reminded Gutkowski of the GM's overly optimistic preseason assessment of the team's Stanley Cup chances, his reluctance to make the Larmer trade, his stubbornness before the trade deadline. Gutkowski reminded Keenan that Smith had pulled off a complicated Larmer deal, and worked with him to pull off the trades that shaped the team for its Cup run.

He also told Keenan he had spoken to John Davidson, the intelligent, popular, and very well-informed MSG-TV analyst on Ranger telecasts, about the GM's job. Davidson, whose superb goaltending carried the Rangers to the 1979 finals, where they fell to Montreal, had been in the Ranger family for twenty years and had been rumored for the GM's job before Smith was hired. "Could you work with JD, Mike?" Gutkowski asked.

Gutkowski had begun considering Davidson as a candidate to succeed Smith a few weeks earlier, while on the golf course during the semifinals, after Smith freaked out over Keenan's Game 4 antics. If Keenan left, Smith needed to have a successor in mind when Gutkowski asked. If Smith left, Gutkowski needed to have a successor in mind when Viacom asked. It's how the chain of command works.

Was Davidson a consideration of Gutkowski's? Absolutely. He was a possibility the season before, after the Rangers missed the playoffs. Was he ever offered the job? Were there serious conversations between him and Gutkowski? Absolutely not. The only conversation between the two occurred on the putting green, when Gutkowski said, "Hey, JD, if Neil goes, would you have any interest in becoming general manager?"

"I hope nobody goes anywhere," Davidson replied. "But if the position was ever open, would I have some interest in talking about it? Sure."

Keenan assured Gutkowski that he liked, respected, and could work well with Davidson. (He didn't tell Gutkowski that in October, without Smith's knowledge, he had asked Davidson to become his part-time goalie consultant—not to tutor Richter and Healy, but so Keenan could have an ally close to Gutkowski's ear. Davidson, wise to Keenan's motive, said no.) Gutkowski warned Keenan that replacing Smith with Davidson was not his intent, again reminded the coach and the agent that his status was extremely uncertain, and said he believed Viacom preferred to keep the front office intact.

Gutkowski then asked to hear their proposals. Campbell outlined the following scenarios:

1. Keenan stays, Smith goes.
2. Keenan goes, Smith stays.
3. Both Keenan and Smith stay.
4. Both Keenan and Smith go.
5. Keenan becomes GM-coach.
6. Keenan stays as coach with new GM.
7. Keenan leaves the Rangers via a breach of contract.

As a way of saving Gutkowski's job, strengthening his foothold in the organization, and providing himself an airtight ally, Keenan also floated this interesting proposal: he'd be willing to tell Viacom he would stay if Gutkowski was kept on as Garden president.

"I'm flattered by that, Mike," Gutkowski replied. "But that's not the way I want it. But thank you for offering."

The suggestion offered circumstantial proof that Keenan had agreed to join Detroit and was completely seduced by his own importance: Why would a coach who repeatedly insisted he wanted to remain a Ranger attempt to bully a multibillion-dollar corporation that considered the Rangers a fleck on their portfolio, especially after Gutkowski had told him they planned to leave the team intact? And how out of touch was he to think he could put any conditions on his staying when he had four years remaining on a contract that had already paid him nearly $1.5 million?

The meeting lasted approximately ninety minutes. Keenan and Campbell ultimately said they wanted the right to explore options if Gutkowski couldn't prevent Smith from wresting power from him, or Gutkowski's guarantee he'd survive to protect them from Smith.

Gutkowski offered neither. He assured Keenan he was safe until his meeting with Biondi on the thirtieth. He promised Campbell and Keenan he'd outline their propsals. "I'm going to tell him the complete magnitude of what's going on," he said. "A couple of things could happen: they could let me go outright, or Frank could say, 'Bob, you make the decision.' And understand that my decision could very well be, 'I'm sorry you guys don't get along. But find a way.' I'll make a recommendation if he wants me to. But my sense is that Frank will say, 'Nobody's going anywhere.' What I

Mike Keenan: the demanding coach never lost sight of his mission—to win the Stanley Cup—and cared little whose egos got bruised or toes got stepped on along the way.

(Photo: Bruce Bennett; copyright New York Rangers)

One of the NHL's greatest all-time scorers, Mike Gartner often had to look to the heavens for help in tolerating Keenan's treatment of him.
(Photo: Brian Winkler; copyright New York Rangers)

Goalie Mike Richter blossomed into a star under Keenan's whip, but he had no answer to questions about why Keenan would yank him and bench his best players in a vital semifinal game against New Jersey.
(Photo: Bruce Bennett/B. Bennett Studios)

Matteau! Matteau! Matteau! Only Stephane Matteau, raising his stick at left, seems to know that the puck has gotten past Martin Brodeur for the goal that put the Rangers in the 1994 Stanley Cup finals. (Esa Tikkanen is the Ranger causing havoc in the crease.)
(Photo: Bruce Bennett; copyright B. Bennett Studios)

Sergei Zubov, the Rangers' leading scorer in the 1993–94 season, was prodded to play through his injuries in the playoffs and assisted on the Rangers' first two goals in Game 7 against Vancouver.
(Photo: Bruce Bennett; copyright New York Rangers)

The Ranger bench explodes at the moment The Curse is lifted and the Monster of MSG celebrates the 1994 Stanley Cup championship.
(Photo: J. Leary/B. Bennett Studios)

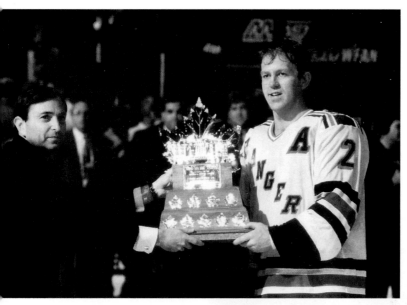

Brian Leetch accepts
the Conn Smythe Trophy
as most valuable player
in the playoffs from
commissioner Gary Bettman.
The important trophy is the
one that came next.
(Photo: Bruce Bennett/B. Bennett Studios)

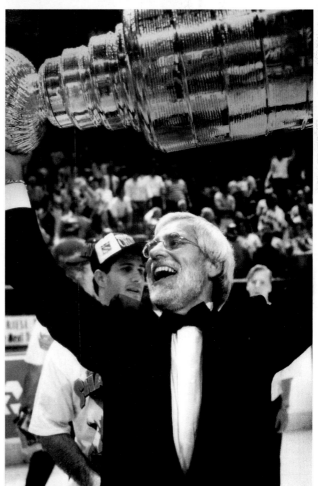

Madison Square Garden
president Bob Gutkowski
holds the Stanley Cup aloft
on June 14, 1994. The Cup
proved far easier to bear
than the burdens in the
month that followed.
(Photo: B. Winkler/B. Bennett Studios)

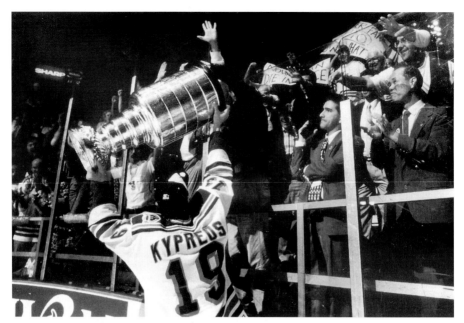

Nick Kypreos—a.k.a. Forrest Gump—brings the Cup over to where the
Garden faithful can enjoy their long-awaited prize.
(Photo: Bruce Bennett/B. Bennett Studios)

Mark Messier enjoys the attention in the locker room after delivering the
Cup. His father and agent, Doug, is visible over his left shoulder.
(Photo: Scott Levy/B. Bennett Studios)

Neil Smith with the trophy he dreamed of bringing to New York, never suspecting that the circumstances would seem so nightmarish as he went through them.

(Photo: B. Winkler/B. Bennett Studios)

Black Aces Mike Hartman and Ed Olczyk—who is not wearing alligator shoes—hold the hardware that, thanks to Mike Gartner's kind intercession, would soon bear their names.
(Photo: Bruce Bennett/B. Bennett Studios)

Alexei Kovalev, with friends and troll, harnessed his great talent and became a dependable scorer during the playoff run.
(Photo: Scott Levy/B. Bennett Studios)

Mark Messier, the coach's advocate, confidant, and pipeline, shares a moment with Mike Keenan not long after Messier had cried in Keenan's arms.
(Photo: John Giamundo; copyright New York Rangers)

Esa Tikkanen brings the Cup to the fans lining East 89th Street outside the Auction House Bar. Tikkanen told the fans, "We're just holding it for you, it really belongs to you."
(Photo: Lorraine Semenkewitz)

A rare photograph: Keenan and Smith together holding the Stanley Cup, at the post-draft party in Hartford, after their conversation about how to work together in the coming season. The Rangers' security chief, Dennis Ryan, stands between them.
(Photo: Nicole Wetzold)

Steve Larmer (in shades), Brian Leetch (holding the Cup), and Mark Messier along the parade route through lower Manhattan.
(Photo: Jim McIsaac; copyright New York Rangers)

Captain, hero, leader, messiah—Messier proved to be all these things as he taught the Rangers how to win the ultimate prize.

After fifty-four years and a three-month lockout, a new championship banner was finally raised at Madison Square Garden.
(Photo: Bruce Bennett; copyright New York Rangers)

Defenseman Kevin Lowe, one of the many former Edmonton Oilers acquired by Neil Smith, provided veteran stability on the ice and in the locker room.
(Photo: Bruce Bennett; copyright New York Rangers)

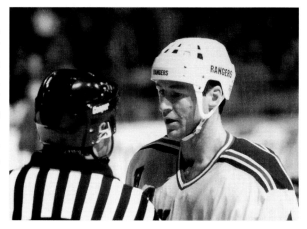

Colin Campbell faced an impossible challenge in his first NHL head coaching job: replace Mike Keenan, hold tight through a three-month delay, weather injuries and personnel moves, and defend the Stanley Cup.
(Photo: Bruce Bennett; copyright New York Rangers)

Center Petr Nedved, exchanging words with Rob DiMaio in the '95 playoffs, tempted Neil Smith with his talent, but puzzled Colin Campbell with his efforts.
(Photo: Bruce Bennett; copyright New York Rangers)

The captain settles an old score and tries to inspire his team-mates in this fight against Kevin Haller of the Philadelphia Flyers.
(Photo: Bruce Bennett; copyright New York Rangers)

Glenn Healy's strong regular-season play gave Campbell a dilemma for the playoffs, one that was resolved when Healy could not duplicate those efforts in the postseason.
(Photo: Bruce Bennett; copyright New York Rangers)

Pat Verbeek was Neil Smith's one significant acquisition as the season approached its trade deadline, a sharp contrast with the multiple deals he made in '94 that solidified a contender into a champion.
(Photo: Bruce Bennett; copyright New York Rangers)

Jeff Beukeboom provided the Rangers' most consistent physical presence behind the blue line.
(Photo: Bruce Bennett; copyright New York Rangers)

Adam Graves, hindered all season by a bad back, tussles with Eric Lindros in the playoff semifinals. The size difference between the two demonstrates the problem posed by Philadelphia's Legion of Doom.
(Photo: Bruce Bennett; copyright New York Rangers)

Mike Richter's downcast look says it all as the season winds down two rounds too soon.
(Photo: Brian Winkler; copyright New York Rangers)

need from you, Mike, and you, Rob, is a promise that nothing happens on your part until I get back."

Campbell and Keenan each gave Gutkowski his word.

Two days later, on Sunday, June 26, Campbell made something happen. He called Smith and asked to meet with him immediately in Toronto. He had an idea. Smith was out of ideas, and was so desperate to hear a new one that he agreed to fly up that afternoon. But when he and Campbell sat down in an airport hotel room, Smith didn't hear anything he hadn't already thought of and rejected.

"Can't you, as president and GM of the Rangers, give Mike permission to leave?"

"No, I can't," Smith said. "You know that."

Campbell convinced Smith that something had to be done fast. The draft was two days away in Hartford, and the agent told the GM he wanted to get Keenan signed there. Campbell never mentioned Detroit by name, but he constantly referred to Marian and Mike and Jimmy D. No reading between the lines was necessary.

"I'll check with the people I know high up," Smith said. "But I think I have to go through Bob."

The following afternoon, Gutkowski told Davidson at a charity golf outing in New Jersey that even if Biondi left him the authority to make the decision when they met on Thursday, he would not allow either Smith or Keenan to leave, and not only because Viacom wanted to present an intact management team while it tried to finish its sale. "There's no way I can represent to our fans who waited all these years for us to come up with a winning combination that, 'Ya know what? We're splittin' it up,'" Gutkowski said. "It worked last year. So we'll try another year of this."

Gutkowski returned home late in the afternoon. He wasn't home twenty minutes when the phone rang. It was Smith.

"Bob, I just got the phone call I dreaded I'd get, but I knew I was going to get," Smith said. "Rob Campbell called and said they want out, they can make a deal with another team—he didn't specify which one—and Rob was flying to Hartford that night to work out a separation."

Gutkowski became enraged. Not at Smith, whom he believed did get that threatening call from Campbell, but at Keenan and Campbell for failing to wait until after his meeting with Biondi, as they had promised.

"We've got to let him out, Bob," Smith said.

"We're not letting him out," Gutkowski yelled, sensing Smith's indignation. "I told you that. You call Rob Campbell back and tell him, 'Don't you fly to Hartford, because no one's going anywhere.'"

Gutkowski slammed down the phone. Five minutes later, it rang again. It was Keenan. Gutkowski didn't wait to hear what the coach had to say.

"Mike, what the fuck is going on? You guys gave me your word that you wouldn't do anything. I just got a call from Neil saying you're forcing the issue and Rob Campbell wants to fly in and let you out of your contract. You and I agreed on this."

"That's right, we did," Keenan answered. "I do want you to know what's going on. And what I tell you, you have to protect me on. But Neil Smith flew up yesterday to Toronto and had a face-to-face with Rob. And again he reconfirmed that you were going to be out, and he was going to have total control of the Rangers, and he was going to get me out. And we're not taking this anymore. I'm not going to go through this with this guy. We've got to get out."

Keenan's version of Smith's position was untrue, a desperate attempt to portray Smith as a back-stabber. Keenan wanted Gutkowski to think Smith knew something Gutkowski didn't. Smith knew he wouldn't be able to fire Keenan even if Gutkowski was fired, not unless Biondi approved it, and Campbell knew it, too. But Keenan apparently hoped to paint Smith so badly that Gutkowski would try to get approval from Biondi to fire the GM.

Gutkowski could not fathom Smith's flying to Toronto for a rendezvous with Campbell without telling him. Suddenly, the Garden president realized this sordid saga had turned three professionals into hopelessly immature kids fighting over who'd get to stay in the treehouse. Gutkowski now believed he wouldn't get the truth from Smith, Keenan, or Campbell.

Still, he listened. Later that evening he took a call from Campbell, who had flown from Toronto to New York and was with Keenan in his Greenwich home. Campbell wanted Gutkowski to believe yesterday's Toronto meeting was solely Smith's idea. "Bob, he suggested backdating a letter and putting it into the contract saying that if a GM job opens, he'd be free to leave. He said he talked to someone higher up who said he could get that done."

Gutkowski's head spun. At one point he asked Campbell, "What did Neil say when Neil called you back after I told him to tell you I wasn't going to let Mike out?"

Replied the agent, "Neil said, 'I told you he'd fuck it up.'"

Gutkowski didn't believe Smith would say that. He had concluded by now, however, that Smith was so angry at being denied permission to broker Keenan's exit that he had grown obsessed with ridding himself of his nemesis any way possible.

More significantly, Gutkowski now saw how Campbell was playing one executive against the other to further his client's goal. Campbell had Smith believing he was a willing and sympathetic co-conspirator doing whatever he could to circumvent Gutkowski. At the same time, Campbell repeated Smith's ugly comments about Gutkowski to the president, portraying the GM as a disrespectful and disloyal enemy who claimed to have an ally over Gutkowski's head at Viacom.

"I don't care if you guys hate each other," Gutkowski told Keenan and Campbell that night. "If I'm here, I'm going to do everything I can to make it work again. I'll stay in the middle again."

Gutkowski called Biondi the next morning and told him their meeting couldn't wait two days, that the Smith-Keenan problem had become a crisis needing immediate attention. Biondi agreed. Before departing for Viacom's headquarters, Gutkowski approached Ken Munoz, the Garden's legal counsel.

"Ken, did Neil Smith talk to you about backdating a letter? Would it be possible for Neil to do something like that?"

"Neil did ask about the possibility," Munoz said. "I told him we couldn't do something like that and Neil said, 'Yeah, I know we can't.'"

From Munoz's description of the conversation, Gutkowski concluded that Smith and Campbell had discussed the possibility of secretly adding an escape clause to Keenan's original contract. But it didn't sound like an idea Smith had pushed terribly hard for.

Gutkowski admitted to himself he didn't know what to think anymore. Everyone had his own agenda. Nobody trusted anybody. But Biondi had to be told what was going on.

The twenty-minute meeting at Viacom's midtown Manhattan headquarters was anticlimactic. "Frank, I've done everything I could, but this is an extremely ugly situation," Gutkowski said. "In my judgment, I don't want to let either one of them go. But it's so ugly, I would be prepared to make a decision. I've told both these guys that."

"Let me make it easy for you," Biondi said. "Nobody's going anywhere. And if you want me to talk to Neil Smith, I'll be happy to."

Gutkowski said that wouldn't be necessary, that both men planned to call him before the draft commenced early that evening. Before Gutkowski finished, Biondi told him that his contract, which had three months remaining, was being extended for one year.

Keenan and Campbell phoned almost as soon as Gutkowski returned to Penn Plaza.

"Nobody's going anywhere," Gutkowski stated. "I talked to Biondi. So you guys work it out. I've got an extension, so I'm going to be around at least for another year. The company's being sold. Mike, you can't go anywhere, and Neil can't get rid of you."

Gutkowski didn't reach Smith that day, but Smith got the news before the draft from Campbell. He grabbed his draft notebook and presided at the Rangers' draft table. When the first half of the draft ended after 11 P.M., Smith helped host a cocktail party thrown by the Rangers for their draftees, the scouts, and the media. He faked a few smiles, deliberately avoided Keenan, who was holding court near the vegetable dip at the opposite end of the small banquet room, and fumed the rest of the night.

The second half of the draft concluded the next day. When it ended, Smith and Keenan decided it was time for a heart-to-heart. Both realized they had been buried in a huge corporate game with stakes far too large to risk jeopardy. Viacom didn't care that Smith despised Keenan's personality. Viacom didn't care that Keenan felt vulnerable because Stanley Jaffe was gone and Gutkowski was on shaky ground. The Garden was in play, and individuals didn't matter.

They shook hands at the bar, briefly discussed the draft, and spoke pleasantly about their summer plans. Once both men relaxed, they delicately discussed ways to decrease the tension.

"Mike, we can't keep using Watkins as the middleman," Smith said. "The message always gets mixed when it goes through him. Why can't you pick up the phone if you don't like something and tell me?"

"I agree," Keenan replied. "You, too, have to be able to come to me if you're pissed off about something. If I'm going to work here, we can't exist like this."

"I agree," Smith said. "I've gotta tell you one thing, though. I don't give a shit, you can go to any team you want. You're never going to be as good a coach without me as GM, and I'm never going to be as good a GM without you as coach."

"You're right," Keenan said.

They outlined the way they wanted to defend the Cup, the moves they had to make to improve the team. They briefly discussed moving training camp from Glens Falls to Lake Placid. They agreed to stay in touch.

Smith felt great. For the first time since the Devils series he actually felt excited about working with Keenan. So did Gutkowski, who heard of the chat from Smith and said he was thrilled to hear the two executives acting like adults again. As far as Gutkowski was concerned, the issue was dead. But a few days later while Smith and his wife, Katia, were enjoying a two-week vacation at their Key West, Florida, condominium, Campbell called.

"Don't put any stock in what Mike said that night," Campbell told Smith. "You know when next season starts it'll be the same old shit."

•   •   •

The Stanley Cup itself was looking bad by late June. It was slightly off-center. It needed a tune-up, so one was scheduled for mid-July. That still left time for Joe Murphy, the Rangers' longtime equipment manager, to bring Stanley home to the Bronx for a visit to the Provenance Rest Nursing Home. The nuns who respected another Holy Grail liked this one, too.

On July 1, Ed Olczyk brought the Cup to Belmont Park racetrack, where fans got to take a picture with Stanley for a $2 donation to Ice Hockey in Harlem and the Backstretch Employees Assistance Team. Kentucky Derby winner Go for Gin stuck his head in the empty goblet and got his photo taken free of charge. The following afternoon the Cup made it to a pool party in Armonk, New York, a Westchester suburb fifteen minutes from Rye, at the home of Dr. Ron Weissman, one of the Rangers' physicians.

Watkins couldn't give the Cup away over the Fourth of July weekend, so the Long Island community of Massapequa enjoyed one special block party and barbecue. "It spent three-fourths of the weekend sitting in my living room, all alone, ready to be shipped to Montreal to get fixed. But nobody picked it up."

Bruce "The Masseuse" Lifrieri, the team's full-time massage therapist, got it for a day and Stanley toured White Plains. One customer in a pizza parlor, a typical skeptical New Yorker, refused to believe Stanley's identity. "That's not the Stanley Cup," he huffed. "It doesn't even look like it."

Yes, the Cup needed a face-lift. A week later it was back in Montreal, at Boffey Silversmith. Louise St. Jacques, the Hall of Fame's Cup engraver since 1978, repaired the base, banged out a few dents, soothed a few nicks, and polished the shiny armor.

For approximately ten days beginning July 1, Keenan was in Italy with his daughter, Gayla. Smith was in Key West with his wife, Katia, trying to push the last two weeks out of his mind. But Campbell wasn't finished. He raised the possibility of a breach of contract when he asked Smith, "What if Mike doesn't get his bonus check on time?"

Keenan earned $608,000 in bonuses for winning the Cup. According to his contract, Keenan's bonus check and the bonus checks of all the players, coaches, and staff members were due no later than thirty days after the Rangers' final game. The due date was July 14. Could Smith make sure Keenan's check did not arrive on time?

"That's crazy, it's impossible," Smith said. "I signed off on the checks before I left. All I do is check to make sure the bonuses are correct. I check them against the contracts. Then the figures go to finance. I have nothing to do with the checks now."

Campbell dropped the subject, and Smith went back to the beach. From Key West he began his early courtship of several NHL free agents. One who caught his eye was Bob Probert, the 6-3, 215-pound Detroit Red Wing right wing whose drug and alcohol problems had checkered his career as a ruffian who could skate. Probert's arrest for drug smuggling, his one-year NHL suspension, his deportation by the U.S. Immigration Department, his reinstatement, and his drug and alcohol relapse made him a very high risk.

"Try to get him," Keenan told Smith.

He did. But so did the Chicago Blackhawks. So did Detroit, which had lost his rights by failing to tender a qualifying contract by July 1. On July 14, Mike Ilitch called Probert's agent, Pat Ducharme, asking Ducharme to do the right thing and not make the Wings pay for their administrative error after all Detroit had done to help Probert through his personal problems.

"Mike, the problem is, no matter what you pay Bob, he's got a problem with Scotty Bowman," Ducharme said. "He doesn't want to play for Scotty."

"I'll get rid of Scotty," Ilitch said. "I'm hiring Mike Keenan here, anyway."

When Ilitch made that claim, it didn't make sense. Twenty-four hours later, it did.

At 2:20 P.M. on a quiet Friday afternoon before another summertime weekend, the fax machine outside Munoz's Garden office began to hum. HENDRON, the logo of Campbell's financial company, was at the top, followed by a copy of a fax that had also been sent to Smith's empty office.

July 15, 1994

New York Rangers Hockey Club VIA FAX
4 Pennsylvania Plaza
New York, New York
10001

Attn: President and General Manager

Dear Sirs:

Re: Employment Agreement made April 15, 1993 by and between Michael Keenan (the "Employee") and the New York Rangers Hockey Club (the "Club"), a division of Madison Square Garden Centre Inc. (the "Corporation") hereinafter collectively referred to as the "Agreement"

As you are aware, I represent Michael Keenan. As you are also well aware the Agreement provides for the payment of the following incentive bonuses applicable to the 1993–94 NHL regular season and playoffs:

(a) First in overall record in NHL; and

(b) First in Eastern Conference; and

(c) First in Division; and

(d) NHL playoff rounds won (including winning the Stanley Cup); and

(e) Bonus equivalent to one player's share pursuant to the Collective Bargaining Agreement currently in effect between the NHL and NHLPA [National Hockey League Players' Association]; and

(f) One player's share of any uniform team bonuses (i.e. team segment bonus).

As a result of the Club's performance in the 1993–94 NHL regular season and playoffs all of these bonuses have been earned but have not been paid in accordance with the express provisions of the Agreement. The failure of the club to pay these bonuses totalling approximately $620,000.00 constitutes a fundamental and material breach of the Agreement by the Club.

I have been instructed by Mr. Keenan to advise you that in view of the Club's above-mentioned fundamental breach and repudiation of the Agreement, Mr. Keenan accepts the repudiation with effect as of this notice. Accordingly, the Agreement is ended and Mr. Keenan has no further obligation as employee or otherwise, to the Club under the Agreement.

> Yours very truly,
>
> Robert C. Campbell (signed)

cc: Madison Square Garden Corporation
Two Pennsylvania Plaza
New York, New York 10121
Attn: Executive Vice President and General Counsel

Munoz was stunned. He quickly found Gutkowski, who tried but failed to reach Smith because the GM was on a day-long bicycle ride with Katia. For the next sixty-five minutes Munoz and Gutkowski studied the fax, Keenan's contract, and their legal position before replying with this fax:

Dear Rob:

I have just received your telefax, dated today, regarding Mike Keenan's incentive bonus in respect to the 1993–94 season.

Please be advised that we have prepared Mike's aggregate bonus check. As is normal practice, Neil Smith was intending to personally delivery [sic] this bonus check to Mike. However, as you are well aware, Neil is on vacation in Florida and will be returning next week.

The Club is ready, willing and able to deliver Mike's relevant bonus check. Please contact me immediately, withdrawing your telefax and instructing me as to where Mike would like the bonus check delivered.

Frankly, we are very surprised by the tone and substance of your letter. A de minimis delay of less than one day to effectuate the delivery of a check hardly constitutes a material breach of any agreement, let alone an agreement covering the exclusive services of a key employee. I note, for the record, that there is no "time-is-of-the-essence" clause in Mike's employment agreement, nor was any such clause discussed in the course of our negotiations last year. The club therefore totally rejects your argument that Mike's employment agreement is in some fashion "ended." We fully expect Mike to comply with all terms and conditions of his employment agreement. Please be further advised that the New York Rangers hereby reserve all of its rights and remedies, at law and equity, that it may have against Mike in connection with any breach by him of his obligations under said employment agreement.

Sincerely,

Kenneth W. Munoz (signed)

cc: Michael Keenan
Neil Smith

Gutkowski's assistant found Keenan on his car phone at approximately 3:50 P.M., ten minutes before the scheduled start of Keenan's press conference at the Toronto TV studio of The Sports Network.

"What the fuck's going on, Mike? Are you kidding me, or what?" Gutkowski hissed.

"You guys are in breach," Keenan responded. "I'm a free agent. I told you this was going to happen." At that point Keenan's car drove into a parking lot. The call was disconnected. Eventually they connected again.

"You owed me a phone call," Gutkowski said. "After everything I tried to do for you, and as honest as I've been, I don't like what you're doing. In fact, I hate what you're doing. You owed me a phone call, even if it was a half-hour before you were going to do this. You owed me at least that much."

Keenan was in no mood to argue. He was late for his date with the media, a date he scheduled that morning by calling TSN and asking for a vacant studio to make a major announcement. He stood before the group of reporters and cameras. With TSN, ESPN, and a few Canadian networks broadcasting live, he declared himself a free agent.

"I want to make it explicitly clear that I have not resigned from the position," he stated. "The New York Rangers did not fulfill their contractual obligations. And as a result of that breach, I notified them that I am accepting the breach in the contract. At this point I am open to anything that might possibly be open in the National Hockey League."

The next four days were obscene.

On Saturday, Keenan and Campbell flew from Toronto to Detroit and met with Bielfield and the Ilitches. They then drove twenty minutes across the Canadian border, through the Windsor Tunnel, for Keenan to see his former players at Graves's wedding in Windsor, Ontario. The coach was invited to the affair, but chose not to attend because he didn't want to overshadow Graves's day. Instead, he took a room in the hotel and said goodbye to some players. He didn't explain why he did what he did, and because the situation was still so delicate, nobody asked.

The meeting with the Ilitches went poorly. Mike and Marian Ilitch did not feel good about Keenan's desire to join the Red Wings, not after the call they received earlier that week. A few days before Keenan declared his breach, Bowman phoned. "I hear Keenan's already got a deal with St. Louis," he warned.

Money wasn't the problem in securing Keenan; control was. The Ilitches told Keenan they wanted Devellano to remain with the club, even if it meant Jimmy D taking a nonhockey role. They told Keenan they wanted Ken Holland to become assistant GM.

It was no way to court favor with Keenan, not with St. Louis lurking. But at this point the Ilitches weren't certain they wanted to hire a man who was talking to the Blues while he was talking to them, just as he had talked to them while he was coaching the Rangers in the finals. They knew they didn't want a man who wanted to clean house and rebuild the organization from scratch. They agreed to talk again, but they never did.

The St. Louis Blues had a coach, Bob Berry, with whom they weren't thrilled. They had a GM, sixty-five-year-old Ron Caron, who had already announced that the 1994–95 season would be his last. They were coming off a dismal four-game first-round playoff defeat, which delighted a league of governors who despised the Blues for their irresponsible free-spending ways throughout the 1990s.

The Blues had failed in their bid to sign Keenan before the rival Blackhawks did in 1988. Caron and president Jack Quinn loved the idea of stealing Keenan from Detroit, since eight years earlier the Red Wings had swiped coach Jacques Demers from St. Louis on a technicality: Demers had never received a signed contract from St. Louis.

On Sunday, Keenan and the Blues agreed to a six-year, $12 million contract. On Monday, the Blues introduced Keenan at St. Louis's new Adam's

Mark Hotel and swore they hadn't contacted him or his agent before his press conference on Friday. It was a ridiculous claim, since it meant that in forty-eight hours they managed to convince Berry and Caron to step aside, convince Keenan and Campbell that their club gave Keenan a better chance for success, negotiate the highest deal ever given an NHL head coach, and consummate the deal.

The weekend looked like a smoke screen, with Keenan purposely finding a snag in his negotiations with Detroit so he could conveniently look elsewhere right away.

The Rangers didn't buy Keenan's whirlwind tour, either. While Keenan traveled the Midwest over the weekend, they plotted their legal options. They officially asked comissioner Gary Bettman "to conduct a full investigation into the circumstances surrounding Mr. Keenan's reported agreement with the St. Louis Blues and reported contact with the Detroit Red Wings."

Bettman ordered written position papers from the Rangers, Keenan, Detroit, and St. Louis by 10 A.M. Thursday.

"I have no need to talk to Gary Bettman," Keenan huffed.

On Tuesday, July 19, only thirty-five days after the Stanley Cup was won, the Rangers held a bizarre press conference in which Smith, Gutkowski, and Munoz sat three abreast on a dais and aired their dirty laundry. An hour before they met the press, Smith and Gutkowski spoke for the first time in nearly a month. Gutkowski had been waiting four weeks to ask Smith if he had traveled to Toronto to meet with Campbell.

"Yeah, Bob, I did," Smith said.

"Well, it's done," replied Gutkowski, who did not ask about the substance of the conversation because he wasn't sure he'd hear the truth. "Keenan's gone now. We'll try to shake this thing off and go back to our relationship for the good of the Rangers. Now we've got to go out and hammer Keenan as best we can."

First, though, Smith had a question for his boss that had been bugging *him* for weeks. "Did you talk with JD about my job, Bob?"

"Yes, I did," Gutkowski replied swiftly. "As a possibility. Did I ever offer him the job? Absolutely not. Neil, if you had taken a walk, or I ultimately made the decision you had to go, I needed to be prepared."

Smith reluctantly accepted the explanation. He was an emotional wreck at the press conference, but he hid it well. He toed the company line, said very little, and carefully avoided saying anything about how he had tried scheming with Campbell to get Keenan out. Gutkowski avoided that black mark on the saga, too. Their agenda was simple: bash Keenan, who had embarrassed the Garden, the Rangers, and Viacom, and was the one participant who did not obey the corporation's instructions.

"My personal feeling is, I'm extremely embarrassed for Mike Keenan and the way he has handled himself," Gutkowski told the New York media. "I think, in all truth, Mike Keenan would always want to be coach and general manager of any team—coach and general manager and president and vice president and treasurer."

While the Rangers fired back in their press conference, they also fired back in court. They filed an eight-count civil suit in U.S. District Court in which they sought an injunction preventing Keenan from working for the Blues. In the legal brief, which became public record, they humiliated Keenan further by appending the full text of his contract, making him seem even greedier than he already appeared to be. Gutkowski puncutated that concept when he complained about how Campbell had failed to phone asking for Keenan's bonus check. "He didn't hesitate to call me regarding problems Mike Keenan might have had. And he called me regarding Barbra Streisand tickets . . . but when it came to a check for a significant amount, I found it interesting that their fingers could not do the walking."

Asked whether Campbell requested complimentary seats, Gutkowski replied, "Everybody pays for Streisand tickets. As a matter of fact, I think he was one day late paying for the Streisand tickets."

The position papers had to be filed with Bettman by 10 A.M. Thursday, so Wednesday was quiet. On Thursday, Bettman accepted the parties' statements and scheduled a hearing for 10 A.M. Monday. The Blues and Rangers had ample reason not to want to endure Bettman's scrutiny. Smith didn't need for the league to know how he tried to team with the agent of the coach he despised to get the coach out of his contract. The Blues certainly didn't need the league to tell them they had acted prematurely by signing Keenan.

And Keenan didn't need to have his position paper scrutinized. It was a vicious declaration. Gutkowski and Smith, both of whom read the copies they were given, said he made outrageous claims, most of which he could not substantiate and some of which, they insist, were outright lies. They also said Keenan included several mean-spirited statements Smith had made in confidence to Campbell about Gutkowski.

Keenan claimed Smith called Campbell to schedule the secret Toronto rendezvous. He stated that neither he nor Campbell had any contact with Detroit before he claimed his breach on July 15. He claimed Smith bragged about a contact high in Viacom's front office. However Keenan thought Bettman would react to his charges, he certainly couldn't think his claim of breach and declaration of free agency was going to sit well with the commissioner, a lawyer with common sense.

The various sides decided to try to circumvent an official hearing by reaching a settlement. They spoke on Thursday and agreed to meet the next day. Jack Quinn, the Blues' president, and Mike Shanahan, the chairman, represented St. Louis and repeatedly excused themselves to call Keenan and/or Caron. Gutkowski and Smith represented the Rangers. The meeting at the Essex House lasted all night.

The Rangers wanted left wing Brendan Shanahan, a Graves clone, but the Blues said that was out of the question. St. Louis wanted to get rid of Brett Hull, their highly paid superstar right wing, a player who clearly did not fit Keenan's hardened mold. His was the first name thrown on the table by Quinn. Smith and Gutkowski countered by asking for Petr Nedved, the twenty-two-year-old Czech center.

"That's certainly not out of the question," Quinn said. "But we can't just give away Nedved. We have to ice a team in St. Louis. So why don't we try to expand the deal? For example, how about if we offered you Hull and Nedved for Larmer and Beukeboom?"

Smith said no immediately. He wouldn't have made that trade even if the Rangers weren't due compensation for Keenan. He couldn't lose Beukeboom. He didn't want Hull's $3.5 million salary clogging his 1994–95 payroll, and he didn't feel the individualistic Hull would mix well with the players already on the team.

At one point, Smith and Quinn went off alone, leaving Gutkowski with Shanahan. Smith and the two Blues wanted badly to cut a deal that would avoid Bettman's hearing. Gutkowski was still fuming over the Keenan betrayal and wanted to exact his pound of flesh from the Blues.

Quinn offered Nedved for Beukeboom. Smith rejected that and countered with Doug Lidster. Quinn asked Smith for both Tikkanen and either Lidster or Karpovtsev. Smith excused himself to chat with Gutkowski. "We can get Nedved for Tikkanen and Lidster, Bob. I think it's a good deal. Lidster is thirty-three, he doesn't have much left. Tikkanen is twenty-nine, but with all his physical problems he has a year, maybe two left. Nedved is a potential superstar."

Smith called Pleau for a second opinion. "Neil, any hockey guy would make that deal," Pleau said.

The Rangers and Blues shook hands at 11:30 P.M. and put the settlement in writing, thinking they had just saved Bettman the trouble of an inquiry and each other the embarrassment of a hearing. Smith called Brian Burke and asked the VP for a conference call with Bettman, NHL legal counsel Jeff Pash, the Blues, and the Rangers.

Burke called Bettman. He found the commissioner watching TV in bed with his wife, Shelli, at the Sagamore Resort on Green Island, in Lake

George. The Bettmans were away for the weekend attending the visiting days of their son's and daughter's camps at Lake George.

"St. Louis and the Rangers want to make a deal," Burke said. "They want us to take a conference call. They've made a trade to resolve it."

"No," Bettman said.

"They're insisting on doing it now," Burke replied. "They want to resolve it and they're done."

"But I'm not done," Bettman said. "They can't get me involved, invoke the commissioner's jurisdiction, and then make it go away. If they want to make a deal, I want to see it, make sure I'm comfortable with it, and make sure the league's interests are vindicated."

The Blues and Rangers wanted to meet with Bettman the next day, but Bettman's daughter was in her camp play. "I'm not ruining this whole weekend," he said. "I'll drive back first thing Sunday morning, no earlier. Tell them I'll meet them at the NHL office at noon on Sunday. If it doesn't settle Sunday, we'll hold the hearing Monday."

Bettman said goodbye to his children Saturday night, awoke with his wife at dawn, drove her to their Rockland County home and continued into Manhattan to hear what Keenan, Smith, Gutkowski, Quinn, and Shanahan had to say.

The meetings lasted twelve hours. Arthur Pincus, of NHL public relations, made sure each faction had its own conference room: the Rangers, the Blues, Keenan. Bettman interviewed each participant separately. The sides huddled alone, and with each other.

Bettman did not elicit testimony that strayed from each side's position paper. By far the most interesting aspect of the long, long day was each side's insistence that Bettman place a gag order on the decision. Enough mud had been thrown all month. There was enough left at their feet to last a lifetime. They all wanted to be sure nobody grabbed one last handful.

At a few minutes after midnight on Monday, July 25, Bettman issued his decision:

- Keenan was fined $100,000 for conduct detrimental to the league, suspended for sixty days, then allowed to join the Blues as GM-coach on September 24.
- The Rangers were fined $25,000 for going outside NHL jurisdiction and filing a civil lawsuit. They agreed to drop their lawsuit against Keenan and pay Keenan the money they owed him, which was approximately $208,000 ($608,000 in 1993–94 bonus money, not $620,000 as Campbell claimed in his letter, minus $400,000, which

was the share of his $500,000 signing bonus Keenan had to return for not fulfilling four-fifths of his contractual term).

- As compensation for the loss of their coach, the Rangers accepted a trade of Petr Nedved for Esa Tikkanen and Doug Lidster.
- The Blues were fined $250,000 for negotiating and signing Keenan on July 17, while he was under contract to the Rangers.
- The Red Wings, who were not required to attend Sunday's meeting, were fined $25,000 for negotiating with Keenan on July 16, while he was under contract to the Rangers.

Since it was in nobody's interest to admit the Campbell-Bielfield connection, nobody did. The Rangers didn't press the matter, since that might have prompted somebody to question the Campbell-Smith connection, which certainly left the GM in less than a favorable light.

Short of requesting phone records, which Bettman had no interest in doing, or cross-examining the participants under oath, which he had no authority to do, the commissioner could not prove the Red Wings or Blues had tampered with Keenan. He could not prove Keenan had breached his contract with the Rangers by seeking employment elsewhere during the playoffs. And he could not prove Smith had violated any NHL bylaw with the way he attempted to rid the Rangers of Keenan.

The case was closed.

The Stanley Cup—if not the league's image—was freshly polished when Montreal native Kevin Lowe claimed it from the silversmith on July 20. Stanley next endured a six-week odyssey in which each Ranger got the Cup at his home, played with it for a day or two, and shipped it to the next guy on the list. Brian Noonan had it in Boston, Mike Hartman in Detroit, Greg Gilbert in Chicago. Nick Kypreos hosted a party in Toronto, Jay Wells threw a bash in Buffalo, Stephane Matteau showed it off in Quebec. Neil Smith got it in early September and asked his lawyer, John Hughes, if the Cup needed a yarmulke to attend the bar mitzvah of Hughes's son, David.

Each time the Cup was transported it was carefully packed in its baby-blue trunk, the one stuffed with form-fitting, cushioned foam to keep Stanley from bouncing around. The case is too big for the trunk of an average car or back seat, so whenever a player carted the Cup by car he had to leave his trunk half-open and tie it down with rope. The Cup's case would stick out of the opened trunk, but the Hall of Fame required that Stanley itself be removed from it whenever it was on the road; the Cup had to sit with the driver. Buckled with a seatbelt, of course.

Stanley's long, hot, summer ended on September 12, when Smith secured the Cup in its case and slipped in a hand-written note to Boffey Silversmith, instructing Louise St. Jacques of the forty-four names to be etched onto the trophy:

NEW YORK RANGERS 1993–94
Neil Smith Pres. G.M. Gov. Robert Gutkowski Gov.
Stanley Jaffe Gov. Kenneth Munoz Gov.
Larry Pleau Asst. G.M. Mike Keenan H. Coach
Colin Campbell A. Coach Dick Todd A. Coach
M. Loughran Tm. Op. B. Watkins Dir. Comm.
C. Rockstrom Scout T. Feltrin Scout
M. Madden Scout H. Hammond Scout D. Bennett Scout
M. Messier Capt. B. Leetch K. Lowe A. Graves
S. Larmer G. Anderson J. Beukeboom G. Gilbert
G. Healy M. Hudson A. Karpovtsev J. Kocur
A. Kovalev N. Kypreos D. Lidster S. Matteau
C. MacTavish S. Nemchinov B. Noonan E. Tikkanen
M. Richter J. Wells S. Zubov D. Smith Trainer
J. Murphy Trainer M. Folga Trainer B. Lifrieri Trainer
E. Olczyk M. Hartman

Despite all that had happened since that glorious night, they would still walk together forever.

Paid in Full

6

Under normal conditions, their dramatic Stanley Cup championship would have been a tough act for the Rangers to follow. From the start, however, it was clear that in the 1994–95 season conditions would be anything but normal.

An unsettled labor situation was threatening the scheduled start of the season. The NHL Players' Association had played the previous season under an expired contract, and the increasingly contentious discussions over a new collective bargaining agreement were headed toward an impasse.

For the Rangers, those storm clouds were overshadowed by a contractual matter of their own. As part of the five-year, $13 million deal Mark Messier had signed soon after he joined the club, the Rangers made a written promise to renegotiate if they won the Stanley Cup.

Neil Smith fully intended to honor his commitment. But before he could even volunteer his intent, he received a fax from Doug Messier, Mark's father and agent. Doug was in charge of Team Messier, which also consisted of Mark's older brother, Paul, and their accountant, Barry Klarberg. The fax reminded Smith of the Cup clause and Messier's desire to cash it in.

Smith was ready to deliver. The only question was, at what price? The clause that had been hastily written into Messier's contract three years earlier was vague; all it granted was "the right to request renegotiation if the Rangers won the Cup." Smith and Doug had rushed to finish the pact and never specified the value of this prerogative.

Messier was home in Hilton Head, South Carolina, when Keenan departed. He followed the summertime fireworks from afar and recognized that his renegotiation had to wait until Smith hired a new head coach and Viacom sold the Garden to its new owners. Messier was not consulted, but he had no problem with Smith's obvious choice for Keenan's successor: assistant coach Colin Campbell, who signed a four-year deal (which included a one-year option) worth $1.85 million.

Nineteen days later, at a press conference in ITT's Sheraton New York hotel, Viacom chairman Sumner Redstone announced he had sold Madison Square Garden to a partnership of ITT Corporation and Cablevision Systems Corporation. The price was reported to be a staggering $1.075 billion, $300 million more than most Wall Street analysts felt the entertainment package was worth. It was $75 million more than the next highest bid, which was from Liberty Media Corp., a subsidiary of Tele-Communications, Inc., the United States's largest cable operator.

When the deal officially closed on March 10 of the following year, it was at a slightly lower price, $1.009 billion. The network was valued at $400 million, the building at $350 million, the Knicks $150 million, the Rangers $100 million. Still, this was hot property: not the teams, but the building and network.

Although ITT put up $600 million to Cablevision's $100 million, ITT chairman Rand Araskog and Cablevision chairman Charles Dolan agreed that within a year after the deal closed, the corporations would each own a 50 percent stake in the asset. Cablevision agreed it would pay its remaining share in cash, or relinquish a TV subsidiary called Rainbow Programming to ITT. Cablevision didn't want the building or the teams, it wanted the network. Owning MSG-TV gave Cablevision a monopoly on the programming of pro baseball, basketball, and hockey in the New York metropolitan area. Dolan's company already owned SportsChannel, which for years had been outclassed by its closest competitor, the MSG Network. With the Garden purchase, Dolan now owned cable rights to the Mets, Yankees, Knicks, Nets, Rangers, Islanders, and Devils.

Gutkowski knew that the sale meant his term as Garden president was in its final days. Although Viacom's Biondi was technically still in control, ITT chief financial officer Bob Bowman was the new point man for the ownership group. Bowman wanted Gutkowski out; so did Dolan.

Gutkowski ignored the guillotine over his head and huddled with Smith to plan the Messier contract negotiations. Team Messier stated its asking price in early August, after the Keenan smoke had settled but before Viacom finished listening to the final round of bids: $18 million guaranteed over three years, $6 million per year. "Mark's worth as much as Gretzky," Doug Messier told Smith and Gutkowski. "And he's got at least three good years left."

Having saved approximately $500,000 per year on the head coaching slot with Keenan out and Campbell in, the Rangers had some money to work with. Messier was due to make $2.65 million in 1994–95 and $3.25 million in 1995–96. The Rangers didn't for one second believe this would get a deal done, but they were prepared to double the $5.9 million if Messier was prepared to offer them one more year. With Viacom's approval and the tacit consent of ITT-Cablevision, the Rangers made their first serious offer in late August: $12 million for three years. Team Messier scoffed.

The elder Messier and Klarberg maintained a regular dialogue with Gutkowski and Smith throughout the first week of September, but little progress was made. The Rangers listened to Team Messier's claim that Mark deserved to join Gretzky and Mario Lemieux as the league's highest paid players. They listened respectfully while Doug repeatedly insisted the Rangers would not have won the Cup without his son's leadership.

They agreed that Messier certainly deserved plenty more for delivering what he had promised. But $12.1 million more? In exchange only for Messier's willingness to sign for 1996–97, a season in which he would turn thirty-six? Smith didn't think Messier had three world-class years left in him: two, yes, but not three. Neither did Gutkowski, who tried to avoid looking overhead at the inevitable ax while trying to hammer out a deal before training camp opened on September 9.

In their talks, Gutkowski toed the hard line. But in his heart, he believed Team Messier's numbers were reasonable. "If he and his father had come in [when he was traded to New York] and said, 'We guarantee you'll win the Stanley Cup in 1994, but you have to pay us $6 million a year after that,' we would have said, 'Where do we sign?' Now that we did win, we had to be respectful of that. He felt very strongly he did what he said he was going to do, and it was a statement by this organization to take care of them."

Neither side felt a sense of urgency when training camp opened without Messier on September 9 at Rye. Nobody said so, but an extended vacation was part of the captain's reward for delivering the Cup. The two sides maintained a steady dialogue, but failed to make much progress. The Rangers found that whenever they inched up, Doug Messier did, too.

"Doug, you're going the wrong way," Smith told him when Doug repriced his son at $7 million per year if the deal was only going to last two years.

Tensions began to build between the two men, so Smith backed off. It made no sense to dicker with Messier when Gutkowski had to get approval of every step of the negotiation from ITT and Viacom. "Gut, why don't you try dealing with Doug directly?" Smith asked. "This way we'll cut out a step."

Whenever Gutkowski sought advice or approval from the corporate bosses to take the next step with Messier, he felt himself sucked into the same vacuum Keenan and Smith found themselves in three months earlier. Biondi didn't feel it was his place to approve a massive contract that ITT-Cablevision was going to inherit, so he advised Gutkowski to talk to Bowman or Dolan. Neither had benefited from the Stanley Cup, so neither felt any allegiance to Messier for having won it.

On September 19, Gutkowski called Bowman. The Rangers had not significantly increased their $4 million per year offer, and now needed to tender a good-faith bump-up. "Bob, we have to go to $5 million per for two years," Gutkowski told the financial chief. "I know they're not going to accept it, but I think we have to get to this level now."

Gutkowski remembered Bowman's answer: "If that's what you've gotta do."

Gutkowski also called Dolan. He vividly remembered the response of the man with whom he had directly competed during the years they ran the metropolitan area's competing cable sports networks. "Being the brain surgeon that he is, he said, 'Why don't you offer five million for one year?'" Gutkowski recalled. "And I said to him, 'Chuck, this is the big-time now. That's not going to work.'"

Charles F. Dolan, a sixty-eight-year-old Cleveland native, might not have known how to avoid tangling with Messier, but the man knew how to wire a city for cable television. In 1961 he established the nation's first cable TV system, now known as Manhattan Cable. In 1971, he founded Home Box Office, the cable industry's first premium channel. In 1973, he organized Cablevision Systems Corporation to provide cable service to a small area of Nassau County; twenty years later, it was the nation's largest system.

Dolan's vision of TV's future made him a fortune over three decades. But as profits of his sports premium service, SportsChannel, soared in the 1980s and 1990s, the quality of its broadcasts paled in comparison to MSG Network's. Dolan spearheaded the woefully unsuccessful 1992 Summer Olympics pay-per-view joint venture with NBC called the Triple-cast; Cablevision promised 2.5 million subscribers and delivered fewer than 250,000.

"I'll get back to you," was how Gutkowski remembered Dolan's reply to his condescending take on Dolan's suggestion. In the meantime, the Garden president upped the Rangers' offer to $10 million for two years. Because they had just gotten their first significant increase, and because they regularly leaked misinformation to a media eager to print anything sounding legitimate, Team Messier implied that a deal was imminent when they spoke to the media two days later.

Dolan got back to Gutkowski all right; he got back at him for winning the 1988 battle over the Yankees' TV rights with a twelve-year, $486 million bid, and for their ugly 1988–89 fight over how Cablevision marketed MSG Network on its cable systems, a battle that saw Dolan remove MSG from his company's systems for several months. The next day, Biondi summoned Gutkowski into his office and said, "The new owners want a change in management. They never authorized you to go to $5 million [per year] for two years."

At that moment, Gutkowski realized he had been blindsided by Bowman. The Messier negotiations provided a convenient excuse, because Gutkowski knew that ITT did not believe he maximized revenues in his three years running the building, and they wanted to hire their own man to serve, as Gutkowski had, as the link between ownership and the presidents of the Knicks, Rangers, and MSG Network.

And so he was out. Biondi allowed him to resign and said management would honor the one-year $500,000 extension he had received in June as his severance package.

"They had such a lack of knowledge," said Gutkowski, who ran the Garden for three years after running the network for six. "They were going to have to get somebody in there who'd be able to tell them what they wanted to hear. I would never be able to tell them what they wanted to hear."

Dave Checketts, the Knicks' president, was named interim president of the Garden. Checketts, thirty-eight, from Bountiful, Utah, joined the Knicks on March 1, 1991. His résumé included the GM's job in Utah and a brief stop in the NBA front office. He was widely respected as a man who could run a business, lead people, and rebuild organizations. As head of the Knicks, he regularly clashed with Gutkowski. Checketts never liked Gutkowski's insistence upon MSG Network's autonomy, especially when its analysts criticized his team.

Team Messier's gut reaction to the Gutkowski dismissal was displeasure.

"We were very close to completing something yesterday," Doug Messier told the press from the Hilton Head compound, although that statement was untrue. "What I was told, and I don't know why, is that this was like starting all over again."

Checketts and Smith got along very well as parallel presidents under Paramount and Viacom. They relied on each other's business advice and commiserated whenever one or the other felt choked by the corporate red tape that prevented him from running his team without interference. Smith had no reason to worry that his peer was now the man to whom he had to report; since Checketts knew very little about hockey, his promotion necessitated Smith's return to the Messier negotiations.

On Checketts's first day on the new job, he labeled Messier's contract his number one priority. On Checketts's second day, NHL commissioner Gary Bettman announced that the league would not start the season in nine days without a new collective bargaining agreement. The commissioner called the delay an indefinite postponement. Since Bettman and Players' Association executive director Bob Goodenow were nowhere near a contract, and since Bettman on September 1 had followed through on an August 1 letter threatening to roll back preseason benefits, the NHL owners' intent was obvious: they planned to lock out the players.

The Checketts-Smith duo and Team Messier did not meet until September 26, when the sides huddled all day and night at the Regency Hotel. Checketts and Smith needed the six days after Gutkowski's removal to convince ITT-Cablevision not to hardball the hardheaded Messier. An entire sports city felt in his debt. An entire team swore by him. Virtually every member of the media said or wrote, "Pay the man."

Five million dollars a year for two years was certainly not going to get the guy signed. It was, Checketts and Smith warned their new corporate bosses, certain to sully the new owners' image.

From Hilton Head, Mark Messier spoke daily with his family and almost daily with the media. He expressed no animosity toward the Rangers, and sincerely felt none. The weather was gorgeous down south, training camp and the exhibition season were unnecessary bores, he was staying in shape, and he was confident the deal would be done in time for him to play and practice with his teammates a week before the regular season opener on October 1.

Team Messier believed they were in a perfect bargaining position throughout the process. They would have still held the upper hand in late September, except for one miscalculation: they hadn't figured on a lockout and the possibility of a lost season. Unlike many young players who were willing to stand firmly behind the NHLPA because they had years to recoup the money they'd lose, Messier's career was near an end. There would be no way to recover a lost year, not at his age.

Team Messier had to strike a deal quickly or risk losing their superstar's bargaining power. They couldn't, and they did. On September 29, they negotiated with the Rangers for the last time before the lockout. They dropped their request to $13 million for two years or $17.5 million for three. The Rangers offered $12 million for two or $17 million for three. Team Messier rejected it.

That same day, Smith signed Richter to a four-year, $13 million deal. Richter's agent, Herb Pinder, wisely predicted the lockout's effect and structured a deal in which Richter received very little of his total compensation in first-year salary. Richter took $1 million to sign immediately, a bonus that was payable prior to the lockout. His salary would be a well-below-market $1.5 million for 1994–95, $3.0 million in 1995–96, $3.6 million in 1996–97, $3.9 million in 1997–98, plus incentive bonuses. The lockout jeopardized only $1.5 million.

On September 27, four days before the scheduled start of the season, the NHL presented the union with a revised proposal that included a form of revenue sharing in which a luxury tax would help the free-spending teams buttress the small-market franchises; a rookie salary cap; changes in free agency; and an end to salary arbitration.

The union rejected it almost immediately the next day. That night, the provocative Chris Chelios exemplified the players' rancor toward management when he said on national TV and radio: "If I was Gary Bettman, I'd be worried about my family, about my well-being right now. Some crazed fan or even a player might take it into his own hands and figure that if they get him out of the way, this might get settled." The Blackhawks' defenseman apologized the next day, but the undeniable tone of the message cast an ominous shadow over the talks.

The lockout officially began when the 12 season openers scheduled for Saturday, October 1, were wiped off the slate. The first 75 games through October 14, were postponed, as Bettman sat in New York and Goodenow was in Toronto briefing more than a hundred of the seven hundred NHLPA members.

Strategically, the lockout greatly benefited the Rangers. Although Colin Campbell knew he was the obvious candidate for the job the day Keenan left on July 15, the new head coach hadn't been hired until August 9. He had only one month to prepare for the season. The whirlwind celebratory summer was too short for most of the players, who didn't wind down until July 1 and found themselves having to wind back up to get in shape for September 1.

Campbell could have called his first month in charge Camp Crippled. Three days into the veterans' on-ice workouts, Sergei Zubov suffered a sprained and partially torn medial collateral ligament in his left knee.

Surgery wasn't necessary, but he was lost for four to six weeks. Ten days later, Joey Kocur underwent arthroscopic surgery to remove bone spurs above the rotator cuff in his right shoulder. His shoulder had bothered him for nearly a year, but the doctors tried rest and rehabilitation before operating. He was lost for six weeks.

Four days after that, Kevin Lowe underwent surgery to repair the left shoulder he separated in Game 7 against the Devils the previous spring. Rest and rehab didn't work for him, either, so now he, too, was lost for four to six weeks. And two weeks after Lowe was hospitalized, the heart of the Cup-winning nucleus took a catastrophic hit, as Adam Graves underwent surgery to repair a herniated disk in his lower back, which put him out for eight weeks.

If not for the lockout, the Rangers would have opened their defense of the Stanley Cup without their top left wing, their third and fourth defensemen, and their enforcer. And that's assuming Messier would have played.

Emotionally, the Rangers wanted to play. From the June 14 moment when Messier carried the Cup off the ice and into the dressing room, the monster of MSG looked eagerly forward to their next date on the ice, Banner Night. For fifty-three years, only three solitary banners hung from the Rangers' ceiling: the tired, old Stanley Cup championship flags from 1927–28, 1932–33, and 1939–40. They would finally have company.

The date was supposed to be Monday, October 3, against Pittsburgh. The Rangers' PR event night staffs starting planning for the extravaganza in July. But the lockout put everything on hold.

Fiscally, the Rangers had to play. ITT-Cablevision had spent too much money to watch one of its two new teams and one of its two new arenas sit unexpectedly idle. Unlike most team owners, who lost only revenues against expenses, the Rangers took a triple hit from the lockout. Every home game missed also meant a Garden booking date squandered and a live network event canceled.

The Rangers were doves throughout the three-month war, but they were understanding partners. They preferred a salary cap to a luxury tax, but they were going to be among the league's biggest spenders no matter how the new collective bargaining agreement shook out. To them, the system was irrelevant. To their brethren, the system was vital. So they stood back and watched the teams with more at stake dominate the agenda.

By mid-November, 24 games per team had gone from postponed to canceled. Players were scattered across the continent. Graves, the Rangers' player rep, was recuperating following his back surgery. Some Europeans, incuding the Rangers' Kovalev and Karpovtsev, returned to their former teams in their native lands. Gretzky took Messier, some of his other NHL friends, and a team of stars on a goodwill tour to Europe in December. Leetch, Richter, and a handful of teammates rented the ice at Rye most weekdays and scrimmaged by themselves.

The negotiations dragged on. The All-Star Game, scheduled for January 21 in San Jose, was canceled. After a stormy four-day period in which the owners came incredibly close to canceling the season altogether, an agreement was finally reached on January 11. It called for unrestricted free agency for players thirty-two or older who had played at least 40 games in four or more seasons (the age would drop to thirty-one in year four of the six-year deal); restricted free agency for younger players after three years, with the player's team retaining the right to match an offer, or receive compensation if it chooses not to; salary arbitration after five years, or once a player reaches age twenty-five; a rookie salary cap; and the right of either side to reopen the agreement after the 1997–98 season.

It was a great deal for both sides. The NHL's average salary had skyrocketed since 1990, from $220,000 to $570,000. The players who correctly complained throughout the 1980s that the owners were taking too large a piece of the pie could no longer make that claim. In exchange for a collective bargaining agreement with enough cost-conscious measures to placate the owners, the NHLPA kept a salary cap out of its sport. And the owners, who show paper losses each year while they watch their investments double and triple in value, got a great deal, too; with the restraints sewn into this agreement, a team would have to be run by incompetents not to succeed. That's because Bettman's shrewdness won the Lords of the Rinks something as close to a salary cap as possible: a cap on premium free agent activity. Once a team signed a prominent free agent—and forfeited two to five first-round draft picks as compensation, depending on the salary—it could not sign another one because it would no longer have draft picks to relinquish.

On Sunday, January 12, players began rushing back to their reopened training camps. The league released a revised schedule of 48 games, to begin on January 20 and end on May 3. It left time for the full four rounds of playoffs to begin May 6 and end June 30. The schedule contained no interconference games. This meant that the Rangers would not meet Mike Keenan's St. Louis Blues unless both teams reached the 1995 finals.

Like most of the seven hundred players who had overwhelmingly ratified the agreement, Nick Kypreos felt ambivalent about the three-and-a-half-month ordeal. He was thrilled to be playing again, for sure. But he had made it to the NHL because he refused to be pushed around. Now he was

returning to the NHL because he and his fellow players allowed themselves to be pushed around; for the love of the game, they allowed the
owners to extract every last nickel from their pores. That's all Kypreos
could think of as he passed through United States Customs in Toronto before boarding his plane for La Guardia Airport.

"Anything to declare?" the U.S. customs agent asked.

"No," Kypreos said. "The owners took it all."

Messier had a more historical perspective on the players-owners battle,
one grounded in his years working for Oilers owner Peter Pocklington. It
was Pocklington's short-sighted business vision, Messier believed, that inadvertently blew the lid off NHL salaries. Compared to the NFL, NBA,
and major-league baseball, NHL players were still indentured servants
until Pocklington decided he could no longer afford Wayne Gretzky.

After the Oilers' fourth Cup in 1988, The Great One was making
$900,000 Canadian dollars per year. No NHL player dared ask for more.
When Pocklington traded Gretzky to Los Angeles and pocketed $15 mil-
lion, magnanimous Kings owner Bruce McNall jacked Gretzky's salary to
$3 million.

It soon became apparent that Pocklington cost himself and the NHL a
large fortune, because Wayne's exodus raised the salary ceiling. If Gretzky
was worth $3 million, which he was, then the superstars just below him
were worth $2 million. And the B-plus players were worth $500,000, not
$200,000. And the NHL salary scale was changed forever.

The notion wasn't lost on Messier as he prepared to resume his negotiation with the Rangers. When asked if the owners needed a salary cap,
Messier replied, "The NHL had its salary cap. They had Wayne in Edmonton."

Anticipating the end of the lockout, Messier flew to New York from
Hilton Head on Monday, January 9. He skated with eight teammates that
morning. That same day, Barry Klarberg got a call from a high-ranking
Ranger official who warned Team Messier that if the season resumed, their
client had better report to camp. He had a contract. The Rangers were doing
their best to honor the Cup clause. Holding out was no longer an option.

"It was okay last time," Klarberg was told. "But not this time."

ITT-Cablevision wanted the "don't push us" message sent for effect.
They had already approved $12 million for two years or $17 million for
three, more than Smith ever thought he'd have to pay. Since the sides had
closed to within $1 million for a two-year deal and $500,000 for a three-
year deal (Messier was now holding firm at $13 million for two years or

$17.5 million for three), there appeared to be no reason why Messier would not be signed before the opener.

But there was. When Smith and Doug Messier met five days before the opener, on Sunday, January 15, Smith heard Doug talking as if the lockout had never occurred. Team Messier still wanted $6 million for 1994–95, even though the new agreement called for all players to receive 58.5 percent of their salaries, the prorated portion of the shortened season. And 58.5 percent of $6 million was $3.5 million.

The $2.5 million gulf posed a major problem, one that did not go away easily.

The following evening, after the Knicks-Nets matinee on Martin Luther King Day, the sides faced off for three hours at the Regency. They tried to avoid antagonizing each other, but it was difficult. Doug's combative style irritated Smith and Checketts. Paul Messier's repeated statement, "You need the Big Guy. You're not going to win without the Big Guy," didn't help. And the supremely confident and headstrong Messiers bristled whenever Checketts or Smith wondered how far Mark's skill level would fall in three years.

The Rangers proposed leaving the third year subject to their option. If the sides agreed, the Rangers would pay Messier $6 million for each of the three years, with years one and two guaranteed. Year one would be prorated, of course, with no signing bonus.

"We're not giving you a signing bonus because we're not trying to entice you to sign it," Smith said. "You already have a contract."

When Team Messier refused to consider a prorated share of the first year, the proposal fell flat. Checketts and Doug Messier excused themselves and tried different variations of the same theme, but the sticking point still remained.

Publicly, Mark displayed a happy face. He skated hard in workouts, described the negotiations optimistically, and carefully avoided answering the "What ifs?" Like, what if there was no deal by Friday, the night of the opener? "I feel confident we'll have a deal by Friday," he said on Tuesday.

Privately, Messier wasn't happy. He wanted that third year, badly. The sides were supposed to talk again Wednesday afternoon, Mark's thirty-fourth birthday, but the NHL waiver draft ran two hours late. It ran two hours late because the Rangers tried sneaking two players into their last protected spot. They wanted to protect reliable defensive left wing Greg Gilbert, and thought they could because Smith didn't plan on protecting Mark Osborne. The free agent left wing had agreed to terms with the Rangers and was in their camp, but since he had not yet signed his contract he was not technically theirs.

Smith hoped to sneak him through the draft before any GM noticed, protect Gilbert, and then sign Osborne. It didn't work; the other GMs screamed foul, an argument ensued, and the Rangers were forced to protect only one. Smith and Campbell hastily chose Osborne because people had been asking about him, he had a smaller contract, and they thought that Gilbert, thirty-three, a year older than Osborne, was less likely to be selected.

But he was—by his old boss, Keenan. Pittsburgh took center Mike Hudson, one of the Black Aces who provided depth, comic relief, and a competitive push to the borderline Rangers trying to stay in the lineup.

"Back to hell," Gilbert joked before heading off to St. Louis.

Checketts and Smith rescheduled negotiations with Team Messier for Thursday, because Wednesday night was the Rangers' preseason dinner at the St. Regis Hotel. It was also Ring Night.

Smith designed the 10-karat gold, diamond-studded rings over the summer. It was a beautiful piece of sports jewelry, with the diagonal Ranger name in blue across the face, the team logo on one side, the Cup, the Garden, the New York skyline, and each player's name engraved on the sides.

On the underside there was a special touch: a circled 1940 with a slash through it.

Unbeknownst to many of the players and most people in the organization, Smith had the rings in his office drawer for months. He was not going to distribute them until the lockout ended, until the Rangers were a team again. He finally did it that night over dinner. After the players were seated, twenty-six waiters entered the room, each carrying a plate under a silver-domed lid. When the players lifted the lids, they uncovered a carved wooden box containing the item each had waited his whole life to own.

Eyes watered. Mouths opened. For a moment, silence. Then unrestrained excitement.

"I couldn't get it out of the box. I just kind of stared at it for a second," Jay Wells recalled. "I looked around the table to see what the other guys were doing. A lot of them had it already on, flashing it around."

"I put it right on my finger," Leetch said.

"Now I can believe I won the Stanley Cup," Kovalev said.

"When you get a ring on your finger, it's like having a library of films right on your finger," Messier explained. "Every time you look at it, a whole new movie comes up. Experiences of the past that will be with them the rest of their lives."

The ring wasn't the only dream to come true that night. The Cup was back in the Rangers' possession, back from the engraver and ready to participate in Banner Night. For the first time, each Ranger got to touch the

Cup with his name on it. Players softly ran their fingers over their names, each hand-engraved by Louise St. Jacques using the same iron hammer and engraving tools that have been passed from silversmith to silversmith since 1893, when the Cup was born. St. Jacques worked nine hours over three late-summer days to complete the job that overwhelmed every player.

This was a bittersweet moment for Olczyk and Hartman, two Black Aces Smith had included on his forty-four-man list. The NHL stuck to a literal interpretation of its regulations and disqualified both players from appearing on the Cup because neither had played 40 regular-season games, or at least one game of the finals.

Smith protested. Olczyk played in 37 regular-season games; he suffered a broken thumb in January or else he would have played in at least 40. Hartman was simply too low on the depth chart to play 40, but he played in 35, reported to work every day, practiced every day, and was a Ranger every day of the season. The rule designed to catch unworthy names would have caught these worthy players in its net if not for the unselfish Mike Gartner.

As an ex-Ranger, he knew that Hartman and Olczyk were legitimate members of the team. As president of the NHL Players' Association, he had the clout to raise the issue. As a reasonable and respected man, he got Bettman, another fair man, to listen, so after the NHL and the NHLPA agreed on the major points of its new contract, Gartner asked Bettman if he could settle "a few minor issues." Adding Hartman and Olczyk to the Cup was one of those minor issues.

The two Rangers, who had spent all summer trying to accept the painful reality of their omission, were told by Smith on that night that the Cup was going back to the engraver, back because Smith and Gartner had convinced Bettman to do the right thing. Their names would be added to the roster of players who have won hockey's ultimate prize.

Campbell took the Cup back to Rye after the team dinner. The next morning, before the Rangers' last full practice prior to the start of their first defending Stanley Cup season since 1940–41, Campbell stood the Cup in the center of the dressing room. He reminded the returnees of what it took to win it, and what it would take to win it again. He instructed the newcomers—Nedved, Glen Featherstone, and Osborne—to relish and respect the opportunity to win it a first time.

He did not challenge the team as Keenan would have. He did not icily stare his players down and tell them 1994 was history, as Keenan would have. Keenan would have locked the Cup in a closet and told his players they hadn't won anything yet, that the 1994 title didn't include any freebies for 1995.

While the Rangers dined at the St. Regis, Team Messier huddled in Paul's apartment plotting a new approach to the stalled talks. They found one. Mark wanted the third year guaranteed so badly that when the sides met Thursday, with Mark on hand after practice, Team Messier's new two-year number was $14 million. "If you don't want to give me what I want for three years, just give me what I want for two years," Mark said angrily. "Then me and Gretzky will be free agents the same year."

"That's not our intention, Mark," Smith replied.

Twenty-four hours before the Rangers and Buffalo Sabres were to open the 1995 NHL season, twenty-four hours before Banner Night and the culmination of a summer of celebration, the captain was angry. The lockout had cost him leverage and some of his overwhelming public support. There was no way he was going to boycott the Rangers' season-opening celebration; he knew he owed it to his teammates and the fans to be there. No matter where the negotiations stood, he wanted to be there. He had to be there.

But still, he was angry.

The morning skate at Rye in preparation for the opener against the Sabres kept Messier from the bargaining table. Before the Rangers and Team Messier met, Checketts spoke to Bob Bowman and got ITT to approve this bargaining chip: the Rangers offered to guarantee Messier $6 million this season and $6 million the next, hold the option to a third year at $6 million, but turn the option year into a guaranteed third year if the Rangers won the Cup in 1995 or 1996.

Team Messier loved the challenge, just as the Rangers thought they would. But they tried to extract a concession on this proposal. "You've got to tell us if you're taking the option year by the All-Star Game next season," Doug demanded. "If you don't, we want $1 million as a buyout."

That additional money wasn't the biggest roadblock, even though Checketts and Smith both doubted that ITT could be persuaded to cough up a penny more than $12 million. The major obstacle remained Doug Messier's refusal to accept for his son what the 699 other NHLPA members were forced to swallow: prorated salaries.

Mark joined his father, his brother, and Klarberg in Smith's office at 4:40 P.M. The respectfully combative tenor of the talks remained the same once Mark entered, until the captain threatened to hold out. He was not talking about the opener; although dozens of reporters waited outside the Ranger dressing room two hours before the opening faceoff to hear if Messier was going to be signed and in the lineup, there was no air of uncertainty in Smith's office. Both sides knew Messier was going to play that night no matter what. But the next night at home against Montreal was another story.

"I'm gonna play tonight. I won't let my teammates and my fans down," Mark said. "But I don't know about tomorrow night."

After Checketts and Smith reminded Messier that he had a valid contract, Team Messier continued fawning over their meal ticket. Paul raved about Mark as if he actually believed his younger brother was the Messiah. He spoke of the Rangers as if they were a peewee outfit. "You're not going to win the Cup this year without the Big Guy," he said at one point. "Don't the owners realize what he means to the team? Or will he have to sit out and let them lose their first 20 games to find out?"

For ninety minutes they parried without a breakthrough. Smith was asked at one point if he would go above 6-6-6 to compensate for the loss of Messier's first-year salary due to prorating. "No," he said. "ITT signed off on 6-6-6, but nothing more. They think we're crazy to be where we are."

Mark had to get dressed for the pregame warmup. He left Smith's office at 6:10 P.M., walked one flight up, and was led by Watkins into the dressing room. He made no comment. Reporters immediately asked Watkins if he had signed.

"He's playing," the director of communications announced. "They're still talking downstairs. There's no announcement yet. Mark will be available after the game."

Watkins was on edge all night. This was the culmination of six months of effort by him and events presentation manager Jeanie Baumgartner. Watkins began outlining his vision of Banner Night in late July; for the thirty-year-old lifelong Ranger fan, this was the final scene of a dream come true. Fifteen years after he watched the Rangers fall to the Montreal Canadiens in the 1979 Finals from Section 416, Row C, he helped choreograph the Rangers' celebration of the team's links to its zealous constituency.

"Neil," Watkins told Smith one day in early August, "Opening Night has got to be for the fans. Whatever we do, we have to thank them somehow. They waited fifty-four years."

"Absolutely," Smith agreed.

Watkins understood the Rangers' legacy. Banner Night had to acknowledge the past, honor the present, and celebrate the fans. He and Baumgartner wanted to script a forty-minute program that included several prominent alumni, a handful of the most loyal season-ticket holders, and the current team.

Season subscriptions manager Susan Marenoff found five longtime season-ticket holders in her files: Christopher Armstrong, Evan Dobkins, Burt Gwirtzman, Hal Macklin, and Frank Negri. Smith called each one, thanking him for his unwavering support and asking if he would be able to participate in the banner-raising ceremony.

"Who is this?" asked Armstrong, certain that he was the butt of a prank.

"It's Neil Smith, Mr. Armstrong. Of the Rangers. Honest. This is no joke."

Armstrong asked for the GM's number and called back. When Smith's assistant, Barbara Dand, answered "Neil Smith's office," Armstrong was stunned.

Gwirtzman, sixty-nine, was the fan whom the Rangers believed had held season tickets longer than anybody in team history. He became a subscriber in 1939–40, when his father bought two seats to the 24 home games at the old Garden on 49th Street and Eighth Avenue for $48. "That doesn't sound like much," he said, "but our rent was $33 a month."

Choosing the alumni was easy. With John Davidson as master of ceremonies, the Rangers had a link to the 1979 team that reached the finals. Watkins and Smith immediately agreed that no alumni were more revered by the fans than Hall of Famers Ed Giacomin and Rod Gilbert, who represented the 1960s and 1970s in Ranger lore, were two of the most popular Rangers ever, and were the only two Rangers whose numbers were retired and hanging from the Garden ceiling. Ron Greschner represented the 1970s and 1980s, and was an obvious choice. So was Harry Howell, who from 1952–69 played in 1,160 games for the Rangers, more than any player in franchise history, and was also a Hall of Famer.

All four happily said yes. Giacomin, though, was not content only having his expenses paid. He wanted a $1,000 appearance fee. Watkins was stunned. None of the other players made such a request, but after receiving approval from Smith he agreed to compensate the popular goaltender.

That wasn't the end of Watkins's negotiations with Giacomin. When the lockout postponed the regularly scheduled October 3 event, Watkins stayed in touch with each of the four alumni, checking their schedules, and reminding them that once the season got underway, the new date of the event would be determined quickly. Arrangements would have to be made hastily.

Giacomin lost interest in the idea. Early in January, a few days before the lockout officially ended, he said he no longer cared to participate—at least not for $1,000. When the lockout ended, Watkins realized the alumni theme would look preposterous without Giacomin on hand.

"Neil, he's got to be here," Watkins said. "You can't have ex-Rangers representing the franchise and not have Giacomin."

"Then do whatever you have to do," Smith replied. "I want him here. I agree he has to be here. Do whatever it takes."

It took $2,500 plus expenses. Twenty-four hours before the ceremony Giacomin finally agreed to fly up from his Florida home, listen to 18,200 of his favorite people chant ED-DIE, ED-DIE again, and help raise a banner.

Before finalizing the script in September, Watkins briefed Messier. The last thing the Rangers wanted, the PR man said, was to slight the 1993–94 group that had won the Cup while feting the franchise's past.

"Mess, we don't want it to be, 'Thanks for winning it, guys, now go get lost while we celebrate,'" Watkins explained. "What do you want for the team? How do you want the team involved?"

Although Messier was holding out, he, Leetch, and Watkins met to discuss how the Rangers wanted to celebrate. Lowe and Messier remembered how they had started a tradition in Edmonton by skating the Cup around the rink prior to the season opener, a reprise to the season-ender that marked closure for the Cup celebration. Leetch didn't like the idea, but he was overruled. They all loved the idea of the Cup descending from the center-ice scoreboard, on a table, while the players circled under it at center ice.

Baumgartner choreographed the array of video features that greeted the exhilarated crowd when the doors opened at 6:30 P.M. The electricity in the building matched the night of June 14, with one exception: everybody knew the outcome. The Cup was in the building, the banners were in place, and they were all going up as planned.

The nation got a peek at the 1993–94 championship banner one week before the opener, the day the second training camp opened, when Messier appeared on *Late Show with David Letterman.* As Messier sat with the host, the banner dropped from the rafters of the Ed Sullivan Theater, to the delight of the audience.

Letterman contributed to the Banner Night festivities with his "Top 10 Perks of Winning the Stanley Cup":

10. For one full year, people have to call you Stanley.
 9. Goodbye dull family station wagon, hello Zamboni.
 8. Harder for other teams to score goals with that giant Cup in the crease.
 7. Fifty free stitches from doctor of your choice.
 6. Chance to move to St. Louis for bigger money.

5. Olczyk now entitled to buy a vowel.
4. Three words: free Streisand tickets.
3. When jammed into your steering wheel, Stanley Cup works better than "The Club."
2. Although it has nothing to do with this list, I'd just like to take a moment to say, "Potvin sucks!"
1. My friend, you can't drink beer out of a Nobel Prize.

That and dozens of other clips from the nation's reaction to the Rangers' dream season entertained the impatient patrons for nearly an hour. At exactly 7:34 P.M., the lights dimmed. A ten-minute video of the Rangers' playoff highlights led into Davidson's introduction, the appearance of honorary captain Brian Bluver behind the bench, and the personal introduction of every Ranger, in numerical order except for the captain. Leetch and Richter drew the loudest ovations until only "the Big Guy" remained cloaked behind the white pillows of machine-generated smoke.

Messier emerged, raised his hands in celebration as he skated onto the ice, and thrust a finger in the air. For now, the Rangers were still number one.

Davidson introduced Howell and Greschner, who lifted banners commemorating the 1993–94 Atlantic Division Champions and the 1993–94 Regular Season Champions. Gilbert and Giacomin arrived next, to raise the 1993–94 Eastern Conference Champions banner to the ceiling.

When the thunder subsided, the scoreboard took everyone back to Parade Day, and the subsequent commemoration at City Hall, where the GM put the title into perspective. "It was always a dream to bring the Stanley Cup into New York City," Smith said that day. "And we did it because we wanted to be New Yorkers. We love New York City. And we know we have the best fans in the whole world. We did this for you. The fans. Thank you."

As the crowd cheered, the video cut to Adam Graves, sitting casually in the Garden recording for the fans the team's last word before The Moment: "The bottom line is that Ranger fans, the people of New York, will never, ever, ever have to hear '1940' ever again. Thank you."

And with that, the building turned black. Synthesized music serenaded a dazzling and brief laser light show that highlighted the soft blue smoke accentuating the familiar silhouette descending from the scoreboard. The Rangers lining the center faceoff circle gazed skyward as the Stanley Cup—their Stanley Cup—floated slowly to the ice.

"It was strapped in there pretty good," Messier noted. "Believe me, I was looking at that contraption."

At 8:03 P.M., the Cup reached ice level. At 8:04, the 1993–94 Stanley Cup Champions banner was hoisted. The Garden rocked, louder than ever. Richter and Leetch stood transfixed, truly in awe of the overwhelming response to their achievements. Lowe kept turning his head, looking everywhere, savoring the proudest moment of his career. When the banner neared the roof, Messier nodded and clapped.

The fireworks exploded. Tina Turner singing "You're Simply the Best" boomed out of the speakers. Messier grabbed the Cup as he had on June 14, started a lap, and handed it off to Leetch. It went to Graves, to Wells as Messier directed traffic, to Larmer, Olczyk, Kypreos, Richter, and Messier again.

At exactly 8:08 P.M., 220 days after the celebration that was fifty-four years in the making, Hockey Hall of Fame representatives Phil Pritchard and Scott North in their navy Hall of Fame blazers and prim white gloves lifted the Cup off the tablet, grabbed it by its wide, black base, and escorted it back to Toronto.

"We were the ones to bring it out, and tonight we took it back," Pritchard said. "That completed the cycle. Closure."

The game itself was anticlimactic. The usually bad Garden ice was horrible. The plodding tempo was reminiscent of an exhibition contest, which this was, considering that the teams had been in camp only seven days. The crowd seemed uninterested, almost distracted after Larmer scored the season-opening goal early in the first period. The defensive-minded, well-schooled Sabres played without injured star Pat LaFontaine, but got an early third-period goal from Donald Audette—a slapper Richter should have stopped—to break a 1–1 tie and nursed it for a 2–1 win.

Afterward, a sweaty Richter stood in the players' lounge and accepted belated Stanley Cup kudos from the state's new governor, George Pataki. Richter signed a couple of pucks for the governor's sons, nodded when Pataki fawned over him for a few more seconds, and then remembered to say, "By the way, congratulations yourself."

Before trying to downplay his contractual predicament, Messier admitted how tough it was getting mentally prepared to play Game 1 of the season after such a wonderful ceremony. "I wouldn't lie to you to say that it wasn't tough to come out of those clouds and bring it down to the task on hand," he admitted. "If I said it wasn't a factor, I would be lying."

He did lie, though, when asked what had happened in Smith's office earlier that day.

"I was pretty pleased with the way the talks went," he insisted with a straight face. "In fairness to the Garden and Mr. Checketts and Neil, a deal like this takes time to get everything organized. I felt good leaving the meeting, encouraged that a deal's imminent."

Before Friday night's talks had ended, the Rangers had sweetened their offer slightly, so Messier didn't deliver on his threat the next night. He scored the late third-period goal that broke a 2–2 tie in the Rangers' 5–2 triumph over the Canadiens, Campbell's first win as an NHL head coach. "Truthfully? It's a relief," he said.

In the back of his mind, though, Campbell was worried about his unfocused group of players, who were watching the Messier negotiations closely. New owners often mean new direction and new decisions. Was ITT-Cablevision going to play hardball? Were they hoping to force the unrelenting Team Messier into submission, or an ugly showdown?

Smith was growing restless. Neither he nor Checketts could convince the owners the Messiers weren't bluffing. The stubborn determination and indomitable mental toughness that Mark showed on the ice were paralleled in the supreme confidence and unwavering beliefs that Doug showed at the negotiating table. The man was a terrific representative, for he was not a typical player agent with a factory of clients quickly churning out deal after deal with GMs he did not want to upset. Doug Messier's only client was his flesh and blood.

By Sunday the twenty-second, the Rangers had agreed to prorate only the $2.65 million that Messier had coming to him under his current contract. They offered to pay the other $3.35 million in the form of a signing bonus payable in one lump sum, upon execution of the contract. They guaranteed $6 million for 1995–96. They were still haggling with Team Messier over the $6 million option year for 1996–97, the buyout by the 1996 All-Star Game, and whether another Cup triggered a guaranteed third year at $6 million.

The sides met at the St. Regis on Tuesday, where Checketts outlined the offer he described as final. On ITT's ledger, it was an $11.9 million expenditure over two years: $1.55 million in salary (the prorated portion of $2.65 million) and a $3.35 million signing bonus in 1994–95, $6 million in salary for 1995–96, and a $1 million payoff if the Rangers elected to release Messier. They agreed to the 1996 All-Star Game as the deadline for notification and they agreed to guarantee the third year if Messier delivered the 1995 or 1996 Stanley Cup (even if they had initially chosen to buy out the third year).

Team Messier liked the added value of the huge signing bonus. They considered the $1 million buyout an acceptable alternative to the third guaranteed year, since the 1996 All-Star Game was only a year away and they were certain Mark would still be playing at a superior level. Another Cup worth another $5 million guaranteed? Why not? Winning is what he lived for.

On Wednesday the twenty-fifth, hours before the Rangers dropped a 3–2 verdict to the Pittsburgh Penguins to finish their season-opening four-game homestand at 1-3-0, Team Messier accepted the deal.

Since ITT had taken a lot of grief for butting heads with Team Messier before capitulating to the Gretzkyesque contract, Checketts and Smith decided to prominently herald the new deal. On the morning after the agreement was reached in principle, the Rangers called a 5 P.M. press conference. It started at 6 P.M. It nearly didn't start at all.

The two sides gathered in Smith's office to review the provisions before the ceremony in the Garden's interview room. They spotted a problem: Doug Messier's recapitulation of the complex contract did not match the Rangers' bottom line. Team Messier had miscalculated the prorated salary, and had reached a 1994–95 salary figure that was $110,000 too high. Since Mark had approved the higher figure, Doug wanted the higher figure.

"I made an honest mistake, but I already told Mark what he was getting," Doug said. "So with the deal as you have it, he's not getting what he wants."

Checketts and Smith were outraged. It took nearly an hour to settle the spat, convince Mark that the Rangers' numbers were accurate, and watch the attorneys fine-tune the preliminary documents that would be prepared for signature in the weeks to come.

For Messier, the press conference was an emotional moment. When Mark had joined the Rangers in 1991, his mother and father severed their ties to Edmonton and moved into one of the houses on the Messier family's Hilton Head compound. His sister Mary Kay and brother, Paul, moved with Mark to New York to handle Messier Management International, their rich and famous brother's marketing arm.

It's not that the Messiers didn't trust outside help, although anyone bred in the Edmonton Oiler chain would be forgiven for being suspicious of financial mistreatment by management. They simply felt safest around each other. The captain of the Stanley Cup champions tried to call his dad every day. He called his brother almost every day, and had breakfast with him near Mark's Upper West Side brownstone whenever the Rangers were home.

Messier rented the two-story, two-bedroom, two-thousand-square-foot apartment for two years, then bought it. He liked the fact that it was on the first floor, and had a courtyard with a large garden. He liked being a recognizable personality in the world's most exciting city, a town that gave him by day what he returned on the ice by night.

Mark purchased two acres of prime beachfront property in Hilton Head a short time before he was traded to the Rangers. There were two homes on this lavish compound, one for his parents to live in full-time, and one plush hostel for him, his brother, sisters, nieces, nephews, and his son, Lyon. The pool, tennis court, and thirty-two-foot fishing boat off the pier were for everybody.

Lyon Messier is eight. He lives in Manassas, Virginia, not far from Washington, with his mother, a woman Messier encountered in 1986. Quietly, while his Edmonton Oilers were dominating the NHL, this devout believer in the sanctity of family accepted responsibility for his son, and tried to provide more than just financial support.

"That's just the way things happen," Messier said. "I love the kid. He's a great kid. He's a hockey player, too. A great hockey player. He's a center and a wing."

Lyon's parents remain cordial. Lyon sees his father at games in Washington, Philadelphia, and New York. He spends six weeks every summer at the compound, swimming with his cousins. Messier tries not to think of what his son misses without a full-time dad. "As he gets older he can make those decisions. He's definitely set with his mom. It's best for him right now."

The father has been single all his life, and he surely knows about playing the field. He delved into New York's trendy scene the year he arrived. He dated Madonna twice. He won't talk about those evenings, except to admit they were "interesting."

Everything about New York interested Messier. That's why he came. He was intrigued by Gretzky's success as pro hockey's lightning rod on the West Coast. His competitive juices longed to test the East Coast, the nation's toughest media market, the NHL's least-successful original franchise. He wanted to experience New York's twenty-four-hour pace, its culture, its intensity. He had already done everything he could do in Edmonton with Gretzky. Then, after Gretzky left, he took over the Oilers' captaincy and won another Cup. What was left to experience in Alberta, where he was born and raised? What reason was there to stay after Pocklington refused to pay him what he was worth?

Messier needed a new challenge to fall in love with hockey again. He needed the pressure magnified by the seven metropolitan newspapers that covered every game, the six TV stations, the dozens of radio stations.

He insisted his teammates stare 1940 in the eye from the day he arrived.

On October 5, 1991, when he stepped onto the Garden ice as a Ranger for the first time and received a standing ovation, this is what Messier said to himself as he lifted his stick to the sky with his right hand: "Something will have to go drastically wrong for us not to win a Cup."

Three seasons, two humongous contracts, and one Cup later, in front of a pack of reporters with whom he dealt virtually every day, he could not describe how great it felt.

"A lot of things in the last three years have happened, most of which have been fantastic and great, not just for myself but for the organization," he said softly, with a voice that trembled. "The experience that I've had the last three years has been tremendous. But, uh . . . but, uh, I'm really happy I'm going to be here for the next two or three years. The commitment that the Rangers have made to me is pretty overwhelming. I guess I'd like to thank . . . there are a lot of people to thank . . . Oh, man . . . Is it hot in here, or am I just crazy?"

Messier began to cry. He briefly tried holding back, but he knew there was no point. He didn't have to say anything. The tears rolling down his cheeks revealed his love for New York and an overwhelming appreciation for the riches and devotion he had earned. The pack of reporters remained respectfully silent. The cameras clicked for two . . . five . . . ten seconds before Neil Smith mercifully jumped in with a few remarks. Then Dave Checketts, who had stepped into the Rangers' lives only five months earlier, asked for the mike. "This is what makes the Rangers great," he said. "This was a very difficult contract to work out. But Neil Smith as usual conducted himself professionally. Mark was terrific. And let me say this about Doug Messier: He has got nothing on [NBA superagent] David Falk. He's a gentleman. A very tough gentleman. I enjoyed getting to know him. I think what Mark said to me as we left Neil's office today was the most telling. Neil said, 'Are you happy, Mark?' And Mark said, 'I'd be a lot happier if we were 3-1.'"

Hungover

The stupendous amount of money that marked Messier's Stanley Cup bill paid in full wouldn't enlarge the captain's role in the organization, because Messier's job couldn't get any bigger. In his Rangers tenure he had already gotten one coach fired and had saved another from committing professional suicide. Since he had held out of the September training camp, the start of the 48-game regular season marked the time to forge his working relationship with Campbell.

The Messier-Gretzky Oilers of the 1980s toppled the traditional barrier between players and staff, as GM-coach Glen Sather solicited input from his team leaders and had no qualms about his two superstars volunteering their opinions and even challenging his authority when necessary. That's all Messier knew about player-management relations when he came to the Rangers. It took several years for the key personnel in the Rangers' organization—most notably Smith—to accept that Messier had no personal agenda whenever he offered his opinion on strategy, suggested a trade, or criticized a player. His sole reason for offering advice was to improve the team's chances of winning the Stanley Cup. Roger Neilson never fully understood that. Colin Campbell did.

They were both Oilers in 1979–80, when Messier was a pup and Campbell was a grizzled veteran simply hanging on from year to year. They shared a friend in Gretzky. Later as an assistant coach responsible for Xs and Os, Campbell had discussed strategy with Messier hundreds of times. They adapted to each other easily because Campbell's common sense, desire to succeed, and professional survival instincts all led him to welcome Messier's input.

They never had to discuss if Campbell's door would be open like Keenan's was; both men knew it would be. Messier was going to be Campbell's best forward, a reliable twenty- to twenty-five-minute offensive force, his power-play and penalty-killing anchor. He knew how to subtly assist head coaches with problem players, he knew how to police the dressing room, and he knew how to handle Stanley Cup defenses. Campbell was a rookie coach trying to defend a Stanley Cup for the first time in a monstrous market his captain kept in the palm of his hand. He needed Messier more than Messier needed him.

"If I didn't know him and he didn't know me after two and half years of hockey . . . He either was going to accept me or not," Campbell said.

Colin John Campbell was born on January 28, 1953, in London, Ontario. He grew up with a brother and two sisters in Tillsonburg, a farming town of fifteen thousand located a hundred miles west of Buffalo and twenty miles north of Lake Erie. His mother, Gwen, raised four children and was a nurse for forty-five years, until her retirement in 1992. His father, Jack, was a lineman for the town's public utility company when Colie was a boy, then became the manager of Tillsonburg Memorial Arena until his death in 1990.

He watched his two working-class parents survive without a financial safety net and learned the value of hard work and honest effort. Jack Campbell, who was a pretty fair amateur hockey player in the days of the six-team NHL, died of lung cancer. He smoked cigarettes for years in a town where teenagers like his son Colin earned money in the summers harvesting tobacco, one of the region's bountiful crops. Colin and Heather, his wife of nineteen years, and Heather's three brothers still make money that way. They own and operate four farms that grow tobacco and ginseng.

"I don't smoke, I don't like smoking, but it's your choice," said Campbell.

Colin met Heather at Annandale High School, where he starred as a football tailback before he left to play Junior A hockey for the Peterborough Petes. He was a slow, steady, colorless, defensive defenseman drafted for the Ontario Hockey Association team by Roger Neilson. The coach admired

Campbell's spunk and courage. Campbell stood only 5-9, but he carried a squat 190 pounds. He excelled due to gritty determination on a team that in his two junior seasons won one OHA regular season title and one play-off title.

Campbell entered the NHL while Boston's Big Bad Bruins and Philly's Broad Street Bullies were bloodying the landscape. The willingness to take a sucker punch was a valued skill in the early 1970s, so the Pittsburgh Penguins drafted this fireplug in the third round of the 1973 draft.

As a twenty-one-year-old rookie, Campbell played for the WHA's Vancouver Blazers. He started the following season with the Penguins' American Hockey League farm club in Hershey, Pennsylvania. One day he and a teammate eyed an airfield with a landing strip that stretched almost to the back door of the local bar. Campbell took ten hours of flying lessons over the next six weeks, got called up by Pittsburgh, and finished the 1974–75 season in the NHL. He returned to flight school that summer and earned his pilot's license two year later. He and his brothers-in-law own a two-seat Chipmunk they use for recreational flights over the Ontario countryside, although Campbell hasn't been in the cockpit since the summer of 1994.

"I'm a danger to everybody," Campbell joked. "Even myself."

Campbell sandwiched two stints with Pittsburgh around 1976–77 with the Colorado Rockies. In the 1979 expansion draft that supplied the four WHA teams joining the NHL, he was claimed by Edmonton, where his teammates included Gretzky, Messier, and Lowe. After a year with the Oilers he was claimed on waivers by Vancouver. He spent two seasons there, including 1981–82, when the Canucks under Neilson went to the Stanley Cup finals before being swept by the Islanders.

Campbell became a free agent, and was the first player signed by Jimmy Devellano after Jimmy D left the Islanders' scouting department in 1982 to become Detroit's GM. When Campbell retired in 1985 after three seasons with the Red Wings, he had played in 636 NHL games. He never scored more than seven goals in a season, never more than 20 points. He hit, he fought, he survived. But he never won.

"There were times I said to myself, 'Maybe I'm not a winner.' And I know that's not true. A lot of it is being in the right place at the right time. I believe that when a team wins, every single man on that team contributes, no matter how small or what his contribution is. Gord Lane was the sixth defenseman on the Islanders, a team that won four Cups. I could have been that guy."

Although the Red Wings missed the playoffs his first year and got knocked out in the first round of his last two, Detroit was the right place at the right time. He moved directly from the ice to the bench, as an assistant coach under Harry Neale, then Brad Park, and finally Jacques Demers. People liked his earthiness and his commonsense intelligence. Players liked his pedigree, for he related equally well to superstars and scrubs. His bosses liked his dedication and allegiance.

The complicated Devellano-Demers-Campbell relationship deteriorated over their five years together. The Red Wings were a dysfunctional franchise, erratic and uncontrollable. While they groomed a future superstar in Steve Yzerman and baby-sat an immature Czech defector Petr Klima, they struggled to cope with Bob Probert's drug and alcohol abuse. Campbell was Probert's on-ice guidance counselor. He paid regular visits to Probert's mother across the border in Windsor. He patted the confused young winger on the back when everyone else criticized him, but one day at practice he offered to fight him straight up with boxing gloves when Probert's behavior threatened to upset the team.

Throughout their Red Wings tenure, Campbell and Neil Smith saw each other only at Detroit's annual staff meetings and the draft, but they grew to like and respect each other. When Smith got the Rangers' GM job and hired Neilson as head coach in the summer of 1989, he tried to hire Campbell as an assistant, although Campbell had one year left on his $65,000 deal. Devellano wouldn't let him go.

"I can't stay, Jimmy," Campbell pleaded. "It's time for me to move on. But if you won't let me leave, give me a raise."

"No, I won't give you a raise," Devellano stubbornly replied. "I'll give you another year on your contract."

"I don't want another year."

"Well, I'm not letting you leave."

The 1989–90 season was the most awkward of Campbell's career. Devellano and Smith, two of Campbell's closest friends, became estranged. Detroit sank while the Rangers rose, which made the jealous Devellano sick. That convinced Campbell he had to get out.

"Our satellite dish used to be hooked into the feed in Jimmy D's office. He could change it whenever he wanted to. I'd set it up at night to tape a game to prescout, like if we were playing St. Louis in our division in a few nights. I'd come in the next morning and the satellite would have been changed to the Ranger game. We'd be standing there together lots of times, watching a Ranger game, and he'd be hoping they'd lose. He and Neil were lifelong friends. It was strange."

Detroit missed the playoffs in 1989–90. Campbell sold his house, let his contract expire, and prepared to move his wife, daughters Lauren and

Courtney, and son Gregory to New York. Before he left, however, he agreed to speak with Mike Ilitch when the Detroit owner asked for a confidential meeting. Campbell calls it one of his biggest regrets in hockey.

"He asked what was in store for my life, what I wanted to do. I should have told him, 'Hey, if I were Jimmy D or Jacques I wouldn't want one of my people talking to you, even though he was leaving.'"

Instead, Campbell outlined his plans, bantered briefly with his ex-boss, and said goodbye. When Ilitch fired Demers and demoted Devellano later that summer, Jimmy D blamed Campbell for undermining them, and accused Campbell of trying to get Demers's job. Every accusation was false, but it still hurt to be publicly labeled disloyal. Five years later, it still stung.

Early in the dismal 1992–93 season, Campbell got stuck in the middle of a growing rift between Neilson and Messier. The fatherly coach believed in a specific role for every player. He wanted scorers in his lineup to score, checkers to check, fighters to fight. He distributed ice time accordingly. His perfect hockey game was a mistake-free defensive 1–0 gem in which his leading scorer tallied on a power play generated by his grinding forechecking line. Neilson did not mind playing his checking line thirty minutes a game if his opponent played its scoring line thirty minutes a game. His chess match centered on his ability to teach his players whatever role was necessary to counter the other team. You wanted to skate? He had his mobile defensemen ready. You wanted to fight? He had his punchers prepared.

He compartmentalized the Rangers in 1991–92 well enough to win the Presidents' Trophy, but he collected too many role players along the way. When the playoff marathon arrived, the Rangers were understaffed. They were out after two rounds.

Messier knew that the team he came to in 1991–92 was good enough to win games, but far from strong enough to win the Cup unless changes were made. He believed the best teams, Stanley Cup–winning teams, loaded up on size and speed, and forced their foes to worry about them instead of their worrying about the opponents. Messier's idea of a perfect hockey game was one in which the top players got the majority of ice time, played the opponents' top players head-to-head, and beat them. Messier knew how to score. He knew how to check. He knew how to kill penalties and he knew how to battle. He wanted the Rangers' stars on ice protecting a one-goal lead in the final seconds, not a trio of fourth-line waiver pickups whose specialty was clutching and grabbing around the crease.

Both men were headstrong, stubborn individuals. Campbell hoped that after the disappointing defeat to Pittsburgh in the 1992 playoffs, both would compromise, but neither did. Messier publicly criticized Neilson's methods, and prodded the meticulous, organized instructor to loosen up the system. Neilson wouldn't. So Messier backed him into a corner by withholding his allegiance.

The feud came to a head on January 1 when Neilson excluded Messier from a meeting in Pittsburgh with the team's other leaders—Lowe, Graves, and Gartner—in which Neilson criticized Messier for failing to lead and asked the others to pick up the slack. Three days later, Smith reluctantly fired Neilson and expressed disappointment at Messier for creating the discord. (Smith's current punchline: "But I forgave him when he handed me the Cup.")

"I had to speak out against Roger Neilson and be willing to take the lumps as a coach killer, a spoiled athlete, and to take the blame for that season coming apart," Messier said thirteen months later. "I really had no choice. I couldn't just shut up and finish my career; nice try, Mark. I had to stand up, almost cross that line of what a captain is about. It was my obligation."

Campbell saw the merits of both men's positions, but his vocal support for Neilson never wavered. He defended him during the feud and he defended him afterward. He did so out of loyalty to the dear friend who had helped bring him to New York and out of respect for the authority Neilson had as the head coach.

Neil Smith promoted Ron Smith, who was coaching the Rangers' AHL team in Binghamton, to replace Neilson on an interim basis. Ron Smith had been one of Neilson's assistants the previous two seasons. To take his place in Binghamton, Neil Smith asked Campbell to take the first head coaching job of his career, convincing him to accept the reassignment by stressing the importance of head coaching experience. He promised Campbell he could walk away from the final two years of his contract after the season if he didn't like the reshuffling of the coaching staff.

When Smith hired Keenan three months later, Campbell took advantage of his free-agent window. He had an offer from Neilson to assist in Miami, where Neilson had been hired by the expansion Florida Panthers. But Campbell wanted to stay in New York. The tough choice was accepting a job in Keenan's world, which he knew would be chaotic.

"I had to have leverage," Campbell explained. "I knew [the Smith-Keenan marriage] was going to be tough. Mike demanded you take a stand at times. I knew it was going to be a challenge."

Campbell asked Neilson's longtime friend and agent Rob Campbell to help him negotiate a deal that would protect against a disastrous end to the

Smith-Keenan regime. Rob Campbell wrangled Colin a new four-year contract, a length virtually unprecedented for an assistant.

A year later, Colin Campbell's foresight proved prophetic. He reaped the joyous double benefit of a Stanley Cup and Keenan's subsequent exit, but he had his loyalty tested again. There was no way Rob Campbell could represent Colin in his negotiations, not after the summer he and Smith had endured. So he asked a friend, former NHL head coach Gary Green, for advice. And then the new head coach, with three years left on his contract, negotiated a raise from $160,000 to $425,000, and he got Smith to agree to a unique clause: the three years left prior to the 1994–95 season would remain three years after the 1994–95 season if Campbell survived his first year. The clause offered Smith protection in case Campbell proved to be an inadequate NHL head coach. It offered Campbell security once he proved he could do the job.

Campbell and his assistants, holdover Dick Todd and newly hired Mike Murphy, had braced themselves for a slow start. Graves, Lowe, Kocur, and Zubov were all returning from significant injuries that necessitated rehab during the lockout, when their minds were distracted by the season's uncertainty. Messier's ongoing negotiations provided a steady stream of speculation and lively conversation in the dressing room. The Banner Night revelry, the first four games at home in front of a populace still partying from 1994, and the team's adjustment to Campbell's methods and personality all added up to an early-season hangover that figured to have the Rangers stagger into February.

Messier was concerned, too. In each of his five seasons that followed Cups in Edmonton, the Oilers' nucleus had stayed virtually intact. A group secure in its personality and confident in its ability spent the first 30 or 40 games of the next season working out the kinks, building its identity, and gearing for the second half, a stretch run, and the playoff marathon. Although the biggest names on the 1994–95 roster were the same, the Rangers had to assimilate three new faces, speedy center Petr Nedved, defensive left wing Mark Osborne, and utility defenseman Glen Featherstone, and the compressed 48-game schedule took away their breaking-in period.

More important, the team had to compensate for its formidable losses: role players Gilbert and Hudson were lost in the waiver draft; Glenn Anderson left to play for Team Canada until February, and then joined Keenan in St. Louis; Craig MacTavish took advantage of unrestricted free agency early in the summer and signed with Philadelphia, where he was promised far more ice time than he figured to get in New York; Esa Tikkanen and Doug Lidster were in St. Louis, exchanged for Nedved to resolve the Keenan debacle.

Most important, there was no Keenan prodding, no Keenan pushing, no Keenan enraging the players enough to prevent a pro champion's understandable complacency early in the season after.

Keenan has never returned to a team he led to a title. He left Peterborough for the AHL in 1980, the year after he won the Memorial Cup. He left Rochester in 1983 for the University of Toronto, the year after he won the Calder Cup. He left the University of Toronto in 1984, the year after he won the Canadian Collegiate championship. His Canada Cup crowns came four years apart, in 1987 and 1991. And he didn't spend one moment over the summer of 1994 plotting a Stanley Cup defense for New York.

"I didn't have to," he said a month into his St. Louis tenure. "I knew I was gone. You know, though, Pat Riley did it the best."

The Knicks' head coach, with whom Keenan shared an attitude, an arena, and a slicked-back hairdo in 1993–94, won the NBA Championship with the Los Angeles Lakers in 1986–87 and established a mind-set for 1987–88 before his players even got the corks popped off the champagne bottles.

"He got up there at the podium, they didn't have the trophy thirty minutes, and he said they were going to do it again," Keenan marveled. "His players didn't know he was going to say that. He didn't tell them. But he set the challenge almost from the moment they won the first one."

Campbell decided soon after he got the job that he was not going to try to be Mike Keenan. Loyalty meant too much to him. He owed the people who won him a ring the time and space to win another.

Human nature being what it is, and professional athletes being who they are, the players took advantage of that space. And as Messier learned before the Rangers were eight games into their season, this mutation of a season offered no time for space. Not when the 1995 Rangers still lacked their personality.

"We can't say we did this, or we did that last year," was his early February reminder. "Every year is different, every team is different. We and we are two different entities."

- The 1994 Stephane Matteau who scored the biggest goal in Ranger history reported for the January training camp depressingly out of shape.
- The 1994 Adam Graves who scored a team-record 52 goals rushed back from back surgery and was clearly not the same battering power forward.

- The 1994 Sergei Zubov who led the Rangers in scoring during the regular season and teamed with Brian Leetch to form the NHL's most dangerous power-play point men recovered from his knee injury, but he began complaining when the season began about a left hand he had hurt six years ago in Russia. It bothered him terribly in Quebec on January 28, when the Rangers fell to 1-4 after a 2–0 loss to goalie Stephane Fiset and the Nordiques. He complained and requested an operation the next day. "I won't let him have it," Smith told Campbell. "Not now."
- The 1994 Brian Leetch who spent an entire year proving he was among the NHL's elite had nothing to prove.
- The 1994 Kevin Lowe who quietly served as Messier's source of advice and support spent the first ten days of the season renegotiating his contract, which was in its final year. Although Lowe's skills were slipping, he still was a reliable fifth or sixth defenseman, although paired with Zubov he was slotted as the number four.

Defense wasn't the Rangers' problem the first two weeks of the season. Richter started the first four games as if they were Games 8 through 11 of the Stanley Cup finals. He allowed only nine goals and was terrific but he was 1-3 because the Rangers lost three at the Garden by a single goal.

When Glenn Healy got his first start of the year and lost 2–0 in the road opener at Quebec, Campbell's anticipated hangover began to feel more like a pounding headache in his skull. Already he had benched Alexei Kovalev for an eight-minute stretch of the home loss to Boston after Kovalev's inexplicable giveaway led to Boston's first goal forty-one seconds into the game. Already he had lost a center, Ed Olczyk, who was hospitalized with a kidney stone. He was experiencing the effects of a team that hadn't found its edge.

"Because of the success we had here last year, you have to have some patience," Campbell insisted. "But patience is an easy word to say in an 84-game season. It's not easy in a 48-game season. Patience is not a word we can throw around lightly."

Patience, however, was one of Neil Smith's favorite words. He knew that the Rangers didn't have the team to win another Cup, not yet: "That team was built for last year's Stanley Cup, it wasn't built for the 1995 Stanley Cup. We'll do what we have to do in April to win again. Am I worried I won't be able to? No. With this many championship-caliber players, I can add some pieces around them. I still think we can do it."

His belief rested with the roster he regularly jotted on napkins, scrap paper, or whatever else he could find. The GM assessed the Rangers by slot: if he couldn't scribble three powerful lines, a fourth line of dependable role players, three sets of capable defensemen, and one goalie, he didn't have a team that could even fool itself into thinking it had a shot at a playoff run.

The Rangers had eight forwards whom Smith would compare to the league's most talented: Graves and Matteau on left wing; Messier, Nedved, Nemchinov at center; Larmer, Kovalev, and Noonan on right wing. He was content with a defense of Leetch-Beukeboom, Lowe-Zubov, Karpovtsev-Wells, backed by Featherstone and Joby Messier (Mark's distant cousin), and Mattias Norstrom in the minors. Richter and Healy were a perfect goaltending tandem. From among Osborne, Olczyk, Kypreos, Kocur, and Hartman, Smith believed Campbell could complement the scorers with muscle and grit.

"I'm just thinking maybe we need one more dependable checker, maybe a center. I just want to make sure I have enough checkers, because the games are going to be tight and you always need those kinds of players in the playoffs. That's one thing I learned last year."

Yet he had sacrificed Tikkanen to get Nedved, lost Gilbert to protect Osborne, failed to re-sign MacTavish, and was having trouble convincing Anderson to return to the Rangers after he finished a stint with the Canadian National Team.

"I couldn't have done the St. Louis deal without giving up something. I'll get someone to irritate. You can get guys to check in this league, they're available without paying too high a price. You just can't get players like Petr Nedved. One of the things I have to do here is win today, but still keep turning over the talent for tomorrow. I'm all about adding youthful talent that'll be here for the next five, six years. Nedved is one of those guys.

"I will say, though, Tikkanen added to the character in the room because he was nuts. He added to the atmosphere because when you wanted to ease the tension, there he was willing to do something dopey. And you need that."

He found it easy to be patient with a 1-4-0 record when the problem was a dearth of goals. "It's the one thing I know we have a lot of. Messier, Graves, Larmer, Leetch, Kovalev, Zubov, Nedved. We've got plenty of guys who can score. So I know it's a matter of time. Now if we weren't playing good defense or getting good goaltending, I'd be more worried."

On January 30, the Rangers feasted on an NHL patsy, the Ottawa Senators, to temporarily salve their offensive wounds. Graves scored a hat trick in the first thirty-one minutes, and Nedved scored his first two goals as a Ranger late in the third period of a 6–2 rout.

Nedved and Kovalev, the two speedy young offensive stylists, started the year together on a line with either the reliably defense-minded Sergei Nemchinov or the workmanlike Brian Noonan. Nedved had two assists in his first four games, but hadn't scored until late in Game 5 after failing on an astounding 24 straight shots on goal. Nedved and Kovalev were generating a slew of scoring chances, but Campbell had a nagging suspicion that Nedved preferred the perimeter of the ice to the slots; he appeared allergic to the corners, and seemed to want no part of the Eastern Conference's reputation for nightly physical punishment.

The Rangers dropped a 4–3 decision at Pittsburgh on February 1 and stunk out the Garden the following night with a 3–3 tie against Tampa Bay. Cup or no Cup, their record was worse than all but five NHL teams. After eight games the Rangers were 2-5-1, even though six of the eight were at home. Leetch didn't have a goal yet. Messier had only two.

"The urgency really hasn't swept over everybody yet," admitted Healy, who gave Richter a night off against the Lightning. "But I think it will in time."

The Rangers nipped the Senators in Ottawa two days later, 2–1, and then beat Washington at the Garden in a tight, emotional game. The schedule next brought Messier back to the scene of his guarantee for the first time since his phenomenal Game 6 hat trick against the Devils. In a bizarre coincidence, Scott Niedermayer and Claude Lemieux gave the Devils a 2–0 lead, just as they had nine months earlier; then Messier assisted on the goal that cut the Devils' late lead to 2–1, just as he had in that epic playoff encounter. But reality intervened, as the Devils outplayed the Rangers in the third period to cement a 4–1 triumph.

(Just ninety miles down the New Jersey Turnpike, the Flyers dropped a 3–0 decision to the Florida Panthers that lowered their record to 3-7-1. But this was the day that ultimately changed the balance of power in the Atlantic Division. That morning, Flyers GM Bob Clarke closed a fabulous trade with Montreal: he sent high-scoring right wing Mark Recchi and a third-round pick to the Canadiens for defenseman Eric Desjardins and left wings John LeClair and Gilbert Dionne. In the game that night, Flyers coach Terry Murray sent the 6-2, 220-pound LeClair out with his top two forwards, the 6-4, 229-pound center Eric Lindros and the 6-1, 218-pound right wing Mikael Renberg. "I think that looks pretty nice, those two big guys beside each other standing in their faceoff dots," Murray said. "The more power-forward kind of guys you can have in this league today, the more it's going to allow you to have success." A monster had been born; Murray had created a line that would soon be undoubtedly the league's best.)

The Rangers flew from New Jersey to Tampa that night. The coaches huddled as usual in the first-class section of their spacious charter. The topic was Nedved. Not only hadn't he scored a goal in five games, but he wasn't generating much offense. He was getting manhandled defensively. Worst of all, he lacked the competitive fire necessary to win his share of the one-on-one battles that mark every game. While assistants Murphy and Todd noted his deficiencies, Campbell realized he was becoming reluctant to play the talented center in critical situations because he didn't know if he could count on him.

Messier had meanwhile noticed a more critical problem: Nedved didn't act like he was a part of the team. So, after the Rangers' practice in Florida to prepare for the Lightning, Messier remained on the ice while most everybody skated off. A few of the guys were still fooling around on the ice, so the captain asked Petr to join him at the far bench.

"Petr, we want you to just play your game, to keep doing the things you know," Messier said. "But you have to show the guys you want to play."

"What do you mean?" Nedved asked.

"If you have to go in the corners for a loose puck, go. If you have to fight off a guy in front of the net, fight him off. If you have to take a punch in the face, that's what you have to be willing to do. I don't care if you score one goal or 40 goals. If you concentrate on one thing, make sure you get the respect of your teammates. If you do that, everything else will be fine."

Nedved listened. Messier remained positive, but he spoke bluntly. He told him that the Rangers won a Stanley Cup by sacrificing and relying on one another. He used as an example a former Oiler teammate who made a successful transition from the European game. "Jari Kurri, he never fought in the NHL. He was tough in a different way. He'd take his abuse, keep going, and he got respect for that."

Nedved told Messier he was still adjusting to the more physical brand of hockey played in the Eastern Conference. He assured him he was not making an excuse, and he would apply Messier's suggestions immediately. As Nedved skated away, he wondered if the Rangers doubted his courage, or his mental toughness.

Nobody who truly knew Petr Nedved had to question his courage or his mental toughness.

Petr Nedved was born on December 9, 1971, in Liberec, Czechoslovakia, fifty-five miles north of Prague on the nation's northern border, just south of the boundary between Germany and Poland. He grew up sixty-five miles west of his birthplace in Litvinov, an industrial city of two hundred thousand in which most of the population were employed by Chemical Works, the chemical manufacturing factory that sponsored local hockey teams. His father, Jaroslav, was a civil engineer who played hockey as a young adult and now coached in the Czech Elite League. His mother, Sonja, was a nurse.

This college-educated couple raised their two sons, Jaroslav and Petr, to be thinkers. Despite living under an oppressive communist regime, Petr in the mid-1980s daydreamed as often about freedom as he did about one day playing in the NHL.

Petr Nedved was a phenomenal hockey player as a youth. Tall and lean, he possessed explosive speed, smooth hands, and crafty moves. A few weeks before his seventeenth birthday, he accompanied the Czech National midget team to the Mac's Midget Tournament in Calgary. Six weeks before he departed Prague airport with his teammates, coaches, and government-employed chaperones, he began fantasizing about a life in the free world.

"I was fifteen, sixteen, seventeen, so I didn't have any problems with the government. Well, I had certain problems at school, but it wasn't anything that would have put me in jail. Just little things that I disagreed with. They didn't like it and they made it tougher for me, but that was okay."

Young Petr remembered how in 1984 his parents planned a family vacation to Italy and applied for four travel visas. Three were approved, but his mother's was not. "They were always afraid we wouldn't come back. But we didn't have any plans to stay there, even if my mom went."

Oppression irked the mature teenager. He didn't want to be afraid to speak his mind. He wanted the right to live without fear of reprisal. More than that, he wanted to play on hockey's greatest stage. So on January 2, 1989, less than twenty-four hours after the Czechs won this midget tournament five thousand miles from home, a skinny seventeen-year-old with twenty Canadian dollars in his pocket who spoke no English made an irrevocable decision.

"Nothing in my life will ever come close to that decision. I still remember pretty much everything about that day. The feeling that I felt."

Until the day of the finals, his plan to defect was a dream. The magnitude of the decision was far too great for a seventeen-year-old to understand. All Nedved knew was, as the tournament progressed, he couldn't stop thinking about doing it. Or not doing it. He couldn't tell if he was a fool fantasizing about the impossible, or a man about to overcome a herculean obstacle to fulfill one of his life's ambitions.

"The decision was too huge for me to make. It came down to the last minute, two o'clock in the morning. We won the tournament in the afternoon. I shook everybody's hand after the game and I said, 'Hey, I might not be in the airport tomorrow.' I just kind of said it in a funny way, but I was pretty much—not pretty much, I was serious. But at that time, I wasn't 100 percent sure if I was gonna do it, but I felt I couldn't tell the guys for sure I was gonna stay."

Wary of the chaperones, Nedved said very little. He returned to the home of the Canadian family with whom he had boarded during the tournament, and enjoyed the farewell dinner party they threw. The team was scheduled to depart Calgary airport early the next morning for Prague, so Nedved excused himself from the party early. He lied and said he needed to go to sleep.

He didn't sleep.

"I couldn't stop thinking. I couldn't make my mind up. So many things were going through my mind. Because I knew I was too young to be drafted into the NHL, I did a little scouting thing, what I would have to go through. I didn't want to jump and stay, and not know what was up."

Nedved sought the advice of only one person, a fellow Czech living in Calgary, a friend whose identity he still protects. The friend made sure Nedved had considered all the pros and cons, for there were many a seventeen-year-old could not imagine.

"I didn't know if I was going to see my parents. Some other people who were in Calgary, other defectors, hadn't seen their families in ten, fifteen years. Our country wouldn't let their parents come over here. I was really afraid, because I was so close with my parents and my older brother.

"Two A.M., I was shaking. Wow. I've gotta do it. It's an opportunity for me. I knew it was gonna be tough, but I wanted to. This is my kind of life. Whatever I have to go through, I'll accept that. At that point, I was positive, although I knew it wasn't going to be easy."

Nedved quietly phoned his Czech friend. "I want to do it. Come pick me up," he whispered.

His friend was groggy from being awakened. As he tried to clear his head, he thought Petr was playing a prank.

"No, no. Come over here. The family I'm here with is supposed to drive me to the airport at 7:30 in the morning. If I don't leave before then, that's it."

"Are you sure? Make sure. Be sure. Once you do it, there's no turning back."

Nedved knew he had to do it. At that moment he realized he would never see his homeland again. His friend arrived at 2:30 A.M. Nedved sneaked out of the house and returned to his friend's, where he tried unsuccessfully to sleep. When dawn broke, the two men drove fifty miles into the Alberta countryside to avoid being found when the authorities began looking for him. Nedved by now had missed his flight.

Little was said in the car. Nedved was too scared. He didn't sleep. There were so many things going through his mind, he couldn't focus on any one. Fear briefly paralyzed his objectivity. He waited for his plane to leave, waited an extra hour, and then called his father, who had planned to pick him up at the airport in Prague.

"I'm still here, Dad," Petr said.

"At the airport already?"

"No, no. I'm still in Calgary."

"What happened?"

"I just stayed here."

"What do you mean you stayed there?"

As soon as his father grasped what his son had done, he began yelling furiously. "You're making a big mistake. Come home at once."

Nedved began to cry. He loved and respected his father. He felt pain in his voice, and he didn't know if he would ever talk to his father again. But he recognized that his father did not understand that there no longer was any question about him coming home. He had defected. He was free.

And so Petr hung up.

"I had to. I didn't have the answers to his questions. 'What are you going to do? Where are you going to get money?' I didn't know. But I was really surprised about the way . . . for the first time in my life, at that point in my life I was surprised at how I handled it. Mature. I felt kind of alone, stuck with all this. And it wasn't getting easier."

When he was certain his countrymen had departed, Nedved returned to Calgary, found a police station, and through his friend's translation, asked about political asylum.

"We were expecting you," the officer said.

Because he was under eighteen, it took several months for the Canadian government to confirm his defector status. Nedved moved in with another friend, his future agent, Tony Kondel. He started skating again, just for something to do, since his hockey season was over. He called his mother and brother a few weeks later and eventually spoke on the phone again with his father. Jaroslav Sr. finally accepted his son's decision.

"I started feeling comfortable two months after I defected. I trust people. I never had a bad experience with people. At that time, I just couldn't.

I didn't know who I should trust. I was surrounded by a few people I knew were good people, but I didn't go outside of them for a month, two months. Then I started getting my feelings back."

That spring, he was the first player selected in the Western Hockey League's entry draft, by Moose Jaw. His rights were soon traded to Seattle. A strapping 6-3 and 185 pounds, he enjoyed a phenomenal 1989–90 junior season; he scored 65 goals and 80 assists in 71 games and was named the WHL's Rookie of the Year. That spring, with his parents sitting in the B.C. Place seats thanks to Czechoslovakia's Velvet Revolution that overthrew the communist regime in December 1989, he became the second player selected in the 1990 NHL entry draft, by the host Vancouver Canucks.

As most underaged rookies and foreign-born players do, Nedved adapted slowly to NHL life. He scored only 10 and 15 goals in his first two seasons, but emerged in his third year—the option year of his contract—as a future star by scoring 38 goals and 33 assists, with 96 penalty minutes. He and Kondel demanded a huge new contract that the Canucks refused to tender.

So Nedved held out. He had become a Canadian citizen in 1993, and when negotiations stalled with the frugal Canucks, he took a popular route for holdouts and joined the Canadian National Team preparing for the 1994 Olympic games at Lillehammer, Norway. As one of Canada's best players, his was a season-long audition for twenty-five NHL GMs acutely aware of Vancouver's unwillingness to meet Nedved's astronomical demands and their eagerness to trade him.

Smith wanted Nedved to fill a gaping hole in Keenan's lineup, a number two center. Smith attempted to work a contingency deal with Vancouver, to agree in principle to a contract with Nedved once permission was granted by the Canucks to talk to Kondel, make the trade, and sign him. He wanted Nedved badly enough to offer GM Pat Quinn his own Eastern European prodigy, Kovalev. Quinn would have been happy to trade his major problem for the Rangers' young forward, whose inconsistency frustrated Keenan. Smith was actually less certain; he figured he could at least agree in theory to the deal to gain sole permission to deal with Kondel and buy time to further evaluate Kovalev. If the Russian's undisciplined play continued to infuriate Keenan, and if Nedved continued to impress in international competition, they had the deal already done; if they finally decided not to give up on Kovalev, they could opt out by claiming they couldn't make a deal with Kondel.

That's exactly what happened. Nedved's asking price remained ridiculous, Keenan got through to Kovalev, and Nedved remained a holdout until March, when the Blues signed him as a free agent and worked out compensation with the Canucks.

Four months later, after he scored 20 points in 19 games for St. Louis but had only one assist in four straight playoff losses, Nedved became a Ranger. Now, 11 games into his Ranger career, he sat on a cold bench with Messier and heard his character being questioned. The lopsided deal looked very lopsided—in St. Louis's favor.

It did not get Nedved down.

"I've been through a lot of things," he said. "And sometimes I do look back at the things I went through. I don't want to use that as motivation, but sometimes when things don't go the way you want them to, I say, 'Look, I did tougher things in my life. I can battle through this.'"

A dozen games into the season, Campbell was fighting too many battles. The Rangers beat the Lightning that night, 3–2, but two games later, Campbell benched Nedved for nearly half the third period of a 2–2 Garden tie with Montreal because he had overstayed his shift by more than thirty seconds and got burned at the end of it when the Canadiens scored the tying goal.

A 6-6-2 record after 14 games was good enough for first place in the Atlantic Division only because the Rangers' rivals were struggling more than they were. Mediocrity, warnings from Campbell, and grumbles from the fans all failed to generate a sense of urgency in the champions. Throughout the final two weeks of February, even the most reasonable Rangers maintained a state of denial. They lost sloppily to Montreal 5–2, edged Florida 5–3, lost at home to Hartford 2–1, tied the Panthers 0–0 despite peppering John Vanbiesbrouck with 44 shots, and still tried to convince themselves they were playing well enough to win.

They were 20 games into the season, almost halfway to the playoffs and their defense of the Cup, and already they had lost sight of the big picture. They were not playing like defending champions using the first half to find their identity, not acting like experienced veterans who knew how to coast through the boring segments of the schedule without losing their edge. They were playing like a team split between hungover champions overstaying their honeymoon and newcomers who didn't feel they belonged.

Campbell was forced to overplay Messier because he couldn't rely on Nedved, who hadn't scored a goal since the two against Ottawa 15 games ago. He couldn't give Graves adequate rest for his recovering back because Matteau was providing nothing. Leetch had spent the last few weeks trying to shake a season-long flu, but Zubov's hand had gotten so bad that the Rangers finally relented and scheduled surgery for February 27, which increased Leetch's workload despite his questionable health. And one day after Dr. Martin Posner removed a bone chip from Zubov's left hand, just above the wrist, an MRI detected an inflammation in Nedved's abdominal muscles, which sidelined him for two games, a 5–2 win at Hartford and a 5–3 triumph over Philly.

Despite their imperfect play, the Rangers were 11-8-3 and fifth overall in the NHL. On the morning of March 5 they awoke in Landover, Maryland, with a four-point lead over the Flyers and a five-point edge over the Devils. With a 9-3-2 record since their 2-5-1 start, they believed their troubles were over.

But Smith wasn't fooled. Although the trade deadline was six weeks away, he began browsing the market. Two checking centers interested him: Florida's Brian Skrudland and Buffalo's Bob Sweeney. Three two-way wingers with skill, strength, and character also piqued his interest: Edmonton's Shayne Corson, Hartford's Pat Verbeek, and Montreal's Kirk Muller.

"It's early, things are still cold," Smith said when asked if any talks had heated. "In two weeks, that's when it gets hot."

On the cold, gray morning of March 6, a thick mist floated ashore off Long Island Sound as Campbell hopped out of his 4x4 and fumbled for the keys to his office door. It was 8:10 A.M., the time Campbell started work. As he did every weekday morning before practices at Rye, he drove his son, Gregory, to school and then headed directly to the rink. Two hours before the prepractice stretch, equipment manager Mike Folga had already made the coffee, hung the proper colored practice jerseys in the dressing stalls, and stocked the food counter of the players' lounge with the daily supply of fresh fruit, muffins, and bagels.

This was a game day, so the players had to be on the ice for an 11 A.M. skate. Campbell wasn't thinking about the night's opponent, Ottawa, at that moment. He was still thinking about Nedved. On the charter flight home from the previous night's 4–2 loss to the Capitals, Campbell had mapped in his mind yet another private pep talk with the center, buried deep in a goal-scoring drought and totally ineffective at both ends of the ice.

The head coach had cued up on video a simple play he wanted Nedved to review. It was a three-on-three battle for the puck along the boards in the Caps' zone. Nedved found himself one-on-one with Dimitri Khristich when the puck squirted to the two forwards. Khristich, a stylistic winger from Russia hardly known for his cornerwork, easily won it from Nedved and swept it to a teammate. One pass later, the Caps escaped their zone. The Rangers scrambled to defend the transitional attack.

Growing up playing hockey in Czechoslovakia, Nedved rarely found himself in situations like these. The European game on its larger ice surface is played primarily away from the boards; the confrontations along the borders of the larger European rinks determine puck possession, but they do not create scoring situations as quickly because of the added distance to the nets. Even among the NHL's Western teams, who countered the Oilers' dominance in the 1980s by building sleek teams of their own, thankless cornerwork was overshadowed by speed and flashy passwork.

"I could have shown you a play like this from four games ago, or six games ago, or eight games ago," Campbell told Nedved, who listened quietly and nodded repeatedly. "Any of our players could have been in this situation. It's what happens in Game 49 and Game 85. You could have won the puck, and you would have been one of the forwards who could have scored off that play. And in a 2–2 game, it could have won us a game we lost. But you're not going to get us to that point unless you battle and compete. Battle and compete."

Nedved left Campbell's office a few minutes later. Campbell showered, finished some paperwork, and reflected on the chat.

"I don't know if I'm reaching him," he said. "I have to find out if he's getting it. It's not coaching, it's teaching. It's part of being a parent. Petr Nedved could have won that game for us. What scares me is, maybe Esa Tikkanen would have. But that's behind us, that's done."

What scared Campbell even more was that on March 6, with the playoffs only two months away, he was close to concluding that Nedved simply couldn't do it. Each time he tried to delay that conclusion, the rookie head coach reminded himself of the Cup.

"I have to admit, my judgments are flavored by what I went through the last six months of last year. That's one of the things I learned from Mike. I'm here to win. I don't have time to wait and make assessments. I don't know if you can teach a player to compete."

Keenan would have banished Nedved by now, a thought that evoked Campbell's hearty laugh. Campbell knew he'd never have a team of twenty players who all competed like Graves or Messier—or Campbell. He held off asking Smith to trade Nedved only because he knew giving up on a talented young player after only twenty games was tantamount to admitting he couldn't do what Smith had hired him to do.

"I can't be wanting to trade every young guy who hasn't arrived yet for an older guy who's there," Campbell says. "I know that. But I'm hanging on the edge. We're in the middle of a five [games] in seven [days] stretch, I've got the whole picture to figure out, and I've got to deal with Petr . . ."

That night, Nedved finally scored a goal, his first in 16 games and thirty-six days. It came against Ottawa, but it won the game. Nedved won a race to a loose puck, broke in alone on Don Beaupre, and lifted a break-away forehand over the goalie to break a 3–3 tie at 5:29 of the third period. The 4–3 win was the Rangers' third in four games.

The Devils were next on the schedule, forty-eight hours later, for their first Garden date since Game 7. At 10:45 A.M. on game day, Smith's palms were sweaty. His smile was forced. He nervously fingered the pocket of his baggy suit, the slacks cuffs of which were fitted in typical hockey-player fashion—a few inches too long.

Nervous small talk kept the Rangers' GM from obsessing over the fact that in a few minutes he would step out from the dressing room runway underneath the stands and speak to a few thousand Ranger fans who came to watch the team's only open-to-the-public morning skate. The players hated it because it meant an early-morning trek through rush-hour traffic to Manhattan instead of their usual game-day routine at Rye. The coaches hated it because they couldn't get much accomplished. But the marketing department loved it. American Express sponsored this event, and it ran smoothly.

After addressing the crowd, discussing the Cup, and answering a few questions, Smith meandered back toward the dressing room, immediately assuming a more relaxed posture. In public situations at the Garden he is the Rangers' Godfather: schmoozing, gossiping, consulting, confiding, mediating, solving. He couldn't move five feet without somebody—an NHL executive, a beat writer, a player, a friend—pulling him two feet from the crowd and requesting a private moment. There could be a hundred people around, many eavesdropping, but to the person who got to corner Smith for as little as thirty seconds, it meant a moment for which he or she had been preparing for days.

Of course, some requests got higher priority than others. As the players trudged off after practice, Graves needed a moment of Smith's time. So did Wells. And then a solemn-faced Messier angled Smith to a larger corner of the runway. Even the rudest interlopers respected this conversation, so Smith and Messier got a piece of the hallway to themselves. They didn't have to whisper.

Messier delivered a complaint. A few of the ex-Rangers who received their Stanley Cup rings learned that each of the players still on the team also received an expensive diamond pendant—which replicated the ring—for a wife, mother, or significant other. The ex-Rangers—Anderson, Gilbert, Hudson, Lidster, MacTavish, and Tikkanen—wanted their pendants.

"What do you think we should do?" Smith asked Messier. "I don't want this to come out any way but classy."

"Well, the players could kick in some money," Messier suggested.

Smith shook his head. The Rangers ordered one pendant for every ring, so there had to be more around. Smith realized he had presented the pendants to the players during Ring Night, but forgot to add the pendants to the ring packages sent to the players who had left. The solution was to give each married ex-Ranger a pendant; letting Messier help make the decision fostered goodwill between players and management. Messier smiled, thanked the GM, and headed for the dressing room to shower.

"You know what went through the pit of my stomach when Mess said he wanted to talk to me?" Smith said later. " 'Oh, oh. Did we do something wrong? Is he pissed at us? Is there trouble brewing?' That's one thing I have to work on. I'm always worrying."

No, not always. Not when he makes trades.

Smith that day got Buffalo GM John Muckler to agree to trade Sweeney to the Rangers for Kypreos. Campbell had hardly been playing Kypreos because a better fighter, rookie Darren Langdon, had been recalled in mid-February and had provided more spunk.

The trade took only two days to finalize. Muckler called, knowing Smith had been looking for a checking center, and Smith said he'd swap a draft pick for the thirty-one-year-old former Bruin. Muckler said he wanted Kypreos.

"I don't know if the coaches will let me get rid of him," Smith said, knowing full well they would. "I'll get back to you."

Smith planned to call in a day or two because he didn't want to seem overeager on the deal. He closed the Messier trade the same way. He is a complex jumble of contradictions, a supremely confident hockey man cloaked in a veil of insecurity and self-doubt. But he believes his deliberate style works in his favor. "I'm never afraid to lose the sale," he insisted. "If you lose the sale over waiting a day or two, the sale wasn't there to begin with." He didn't know then that the Kypreos deal would soon disappear.

Although he spent the morning on the Garden floor, he pushed plenty of paper off his desk that day. One reason he could was his supremely organized and efficient assistant, Barbara Dand. On game days, Smith is always running in sixty directions (as opposed to nongame days, when he's running in thirty). Dand knows how and where to point the GM. Her ability to organize his job and life enables him to juggle the dual roles of president and general manager. She reads the waiver wire most mornings, screens his calls, outlines his itinerary, and coordinates well with John Gentile, Smith's director of administration, and Nicole Wetzold, the team's senior secretary and Dand's backup. Today she completed the transaction that sent Mike Hartman on loan to the Detroit Vipers of the IHL, since he had been getting even less ice time than Kypreos and Olczyk, whose play had Campbell dissatisfied.

The defending Stanley Cup champion Rangers finally showed up that night. In an intense, angry, emotional sixty minutes, they defeated the Devils, 6–4, on Larmer's goal with 1:14 left in regulation and Messier's empty-netter thirty seconds later. The caliber of play in this game rose to a level comparable to the great semifinal series of the year before—not as high, but close enough to conjure memories of that classic.

On most nights, the spotlight would have belonged to Nedved. Forty-eight hours after snapping his drought, he scored a second-period goal and made the play that created Larmer's game-winner. Nedved used his speed to burst down right wing past Scott Stevens, the Devils' best defenseman. Nedved curled directly to the net—hard to the net, as he had been told—and took a good shot that Martin Brodeur stopped, but Nedved's rush to the goalmouth created the traffic that enabled Larmer to bury the rebound.

It would have been Nedved's night, except that Larmer's assist on Noonan's goal earlier in the third period was the 1,000th point of his career. He became the forty-third player in NHL history to reach 1,000 with the assist, but characteristically acted as if nothing special had occurred. In fact, the puck with which he registered the milestone was used for the ensuing faceoff before somebody remembered to collect the historic disc and present it to Larmer after the game.

The victory improved the Rangers' record to 13-9-3. It put them four games over .500 for the first time all season and padded their first-place lead over the Flyers to six points. The Rangers were 11-4-2 over the last five weeks. With 23 games to go, they looked like they were positioning themselves for a second-half launch into the playoffs, just as Messier said they needed to before the season. Richter was playing well, Healy was 4-0-1 in his last five starts, Noonan had six goals in his last five games, Messier had seven points in four, Nedved had finally contributed.

It was all a mirage.

On Thin Ice

8

The seven-game losing streak that nearly killed the Rangers' season began with a death in the family. On the morning of March 13, two nights after the Rangers fell 3–1 at Montreal, the telephone rang at Rye. Staff assistant Brad Kolodny answered a call from the Los Angeles coroner's office. The representative was looking for a Mr. Murphy. Kolodny thought the person meant assistant coach Mike Murphy, so he walked into the coaches' office, where he found Todd and explained who was calling. Todd told Campbell, who guessed something had happened to somebody close to Mike, since he had once coached in Los Angeles.

Campbell grabbed the telephone.

"Do you know a Joe Murphy, Jr.?" the coroner's clerk asked Campbell. "I'm sorry to inform you that a Joe Murphy, Jr., twenty-eight years old, was killed last night in a one-car accident."

Campbell felt numb. He hung up and slumped in his chair. Joe Jr. was the only son of Joe Murphy, the Rangers' longtime equipment trainer, who was in his office across the training facility fixing a pair of skates.

"What do I do?" Campbell asked himself. "Call him in, sit him down, and ruin his life?"

He knew he had to inform Murphy, of course. He asked him into his office and gently repeated the information. At about 2 A.M., the L.A. Police Department responded to an accident. Officers at the scene identified Joe Murphy, Jr., and contacted his ex-wife. She directed the coroner's office to the Rangers' Rye complex.

Murphy's first concerns were for his wife and daughter. He called his wife and his sister from Campbell's office and then went home to deal with the tragedy. The head coach walked into the dressing room, where the Rangers were five minutes from their prepractice stretch. He broke the sad news. Practice was delayed fifteen minutes, but it should have been canceled. The mood was gloomy. The players skated in a stupor.

Campbell had no choice but to shake his depression that morning. It was the day before the Rangers' first truly big game, the Flyers at the Garden. Philadelphia was 9-3-2 since the trade with Montreal. John LeClair, Eric Lindros, and Mikael Renberg were tearing up the NHL. The Flyers were only two points behind the Rangers, with two games in hand.

Who was going to check the Flyers' big line, aptly nicknamed the Legion of Doom?

Two weeks earlier, in the Rangers' 5–3 Garden victory, Campbell tried Kovalev at center between Matteau and Noonan. The young Russian loved the head-to-head challenge of Lindros, but the line yielded two even-strength goals to the Dooms. Campbell knew Messier wanted his line going straight up against Lindros's, but the head coach wanted to keep his top trio from having to concentrate more on defense than on offense. On the other hand, Lindros had idolized Messier; he had a poster of Messier on his bedroom wall when he was growing up. There was a chance he'd be slightly in awe of his hero if they spent the night in each other's face. However, if Lindros outplayed Messier, any psychological edge the Rangers' captain owned might be lost.

"The other question is, do you waste Leetch against that line?" Campbell mused. "I want my top defense pair against Lindros, and Beukeboom's a guy who can handle him physically. But do I want Leetch against those three studs, banging all night instead of skating and running things with the puck? If I don't, I'd have to break up my top defense pair."

Campbell also had the names Nedved and Olczyk on his mental list of players with whom to connect. He gave Nedved a little positive reinforcement for the manner in which he lifted his game against Ottawa and the Devils. "You made a key play at the right time, a play only a talented player could make. And you made it in a tough game, against a tough defenseman. That's what we're looking for, Petr. Keep it up."

The chat with Olczyk was not going to be as happy. The captain of the

1994 Black Aces, whom his mates last season had voted the Player's Player Award for his positive attitude, wanted out. He had been scratched for the last two games after missing three before that with back spasms. Olczyk was certain he didn't want to endure a second straight season of frustration. Campbell had no good news to give Olczyk; this was a part of the job that you can't learn as an assistant coach. "As an assistant, you can get a little more personal, closer, to the players," Campbell reflected. "You can't as a head coach.

"I don't want to have a thin skin. I don't want to go out there and candy-coat things and try to be nice to guys. I'd rather be hated for who I am than loved for what I'm not. It's a natural thing for people to shit on their boss. After a loss, critique the coach. 'I've got a sore ass, full of slivers, he kept my butt on the bench.'

"You can normally guess who's pissed at you just by looking at the ice time. The guys who aren't playing aren't going to like you. They may not hate you, but they're not going to like you because you're the one making the decision."

Campbell had to be careful. He had already spent an inordinate amount of time, "too much time," with Nedved, Kovalev, and Matteau. He had to be careful not to overcoach people to the point where he was tuned out. "And they will pretty soon, shut you out. Like with Matteau, I could imagine him thinking, 'Here I go, into the head coach's office again. First it was [Doug] Risebrough in Calgary, then it was Darryl Sutter in Chicago, now it's Campbell. They all say the same thing. Don't they know I'm not a fighter? I'm a player.' You've got to somehow put yourself in his position. He's a big guy, we want him to hit more. We just want him playing with more zest and zeal, and being a force every game. You can't abuse that ability to get to him and communicate with him."

Either Campbell did not properly communicate or the Rangers did not adequately hear their coach before the Flyer game. The first four and a half minutes rendered the question of matchups against Lindros and friends moot. The Rangers were totally unprepared. The Flyers stormed from the opening faceoff, taking an early 3–0 lead on goals eighty seconds apart by Renberg on a power play, Anatoli Semenov at even strength, and Lindros on a power play. A minute after that, Messier tried to ignite his dormant team and settle an eighteen-month score with one flurry of his fists. He picked a fight with Kevin Haller, a defenseman who nearly broke Messier's thumb with a vicious slash in October 1993.

Fighting in professional hockey has been the NHL's most controversial issue since the early 1970s, when the Big Bad Bruins and the Broad Street

Bullies transformed intimidation and physical retribution for clean hits—which was always a vital part of the game—into an on-ice strategy as important as skating and stickhandling. The issue became a hot potato in the late 1970s, when courageous superstars like Marcel Dionne of the Los Angeles Kings and Mike Bossy of the New York Islanders publicly said they would refuse to fight. Bossy was ridiculed mercilessly for his stance. He felt the league could eliminate fighting by throwing players out of the game for it, rather than assessing five-minute penalties that encouraged goons to pick on more talented players and get them off the ice.

But the NHL didn't want to eliminate fighting. The old governors grew up loving the bloodthirsty bouts where two tough guys would hold on to each other's jerseys with one hand and punch with the other until one fell to the ice, and they believed the fans wanted fights, too. The influx of European players who defended themselves subtly with their sticks because they grew up in a system where fighting was banned prompted the argument that fighting was less dangerous than stickwork, which was certain to increase if players didn't have the option of dropping their sticks and gloves and settling on-ice disputes one-on-one.

The league did, however, recognize that many people did not take the sport seriously because of the ridiculous spectacle of untalented players brawling until they were bloody and half-naked from having their jerseys pulled over their heads. They did admit that when the playoffs began, the thuggery generally stopped because the coaches would not risk putting their goons on the ice. And so over the last eighteen years they have legislated fighting down to a reasonable roar.

Since 1976, the NHL has instituted stricter penalties for players who instigate fights. It has virtually eliminated bench-clearing brawls by assessing suspensions for players who participate in them. It has fined and suspended players who did not cease and desist when linesmen and referees instructed them to stop. And the players themselves have left the fighting to the fighters—or to the players who needed to settle their own scores.

Messier's fight with Kevin Haller was intended to avenge a past wrong and to wake up his teammates. It was a conscious, deliberate act, and it worked. Messier started the comeback himself with a shorthanded goal early in the second period. Featherstone and Leetch scored later in the period and it was 3–3 after two. But the Legion of Doom won it with 3:38 left in the third. Matched against Matteau-Nemchinov-Kocur, Lindros fed LeClair for a slapper from the left circle that zipped through Richter's skates, a bad goal and a bad loss.

"We weren't ready and that's our fault," Campbell said of the early 3–0 deficit. "They jumped on us."

Despite having been caught and tied by the Flyers for the division lead, and having seen how Lindros's line had beaten them, the Rangers still were not ready to concede that Philadelphia was growing too strong for them to handle. "I don't know if they have the depth an up-and-coming team would like," Campbell said. "Obviously they're depending on one line. But it's not a bad line to depend on."

Two days later the Rangers left practice together to attend the wake of Joe Murphy, Jr. Before the somber event, Zubov practiced for the first time since his February 27 hand operation and the Rangers contemplated the Stanley Cup stop they were making the next day.

After several postponements prompted by the lockout, the shortened schedule, and diplomatic problems in the world, the Rangers and the president of the United States found a mutually agreeable date to invite the Cup to the White House and a Rose Garden ceremony with Bill Clinton: St. Patrick's Day, the day before their game with the Caps at USAir Arena. Even the Canadian-born Rangers were excited to be visiting the world's most important address.

"It's the most powerful office in the world," Healy said. "More decisions are made there than even in our coach's office."

"I've never met anybody of that power," one Ranger cracked. "Just Mess."

"I want to find out who this FICA guy is, and how come he's taking so much of my money," Kypreos said.

Forrest Gump had to share his nickname for a day, since Richter was visiting the White House for a fourth time, with a third president. He and Leetch met Ronald Reagan in 1988 with the U.S. Olympic Team ("He was like your grandfather. A great conversationalist."), and Richter met George Bush a few years later as one of the sports figures participating in a program called the Great American Workout.

Kovalev and Nemchinov, who were impressionable lads when Reagan called the Soviet Union the "evil empire," were overwhelmed by the chance to flank President Clinton for a picture. "It's very exciting," Nemchinov said. "As a young boy growing up in Russia, I never dreamed I'd get the opportunity to meet the president of the United States."

The entire team crowded around Clinton for photos. When he posed holding the Cup with Messier for a team shot, who was directly over his shoulder, grinning broadly with that Gumpian look in his eye? Who else but Kypreos?

The next night's 4–1 loss to the Capitals was the night Colin Campbell stopped playing nice guy.

At 3:07 of the second period, with the score 1–1, Kevin Kaminski, Washington's pesty little irritant, goaded Messier into reaching over linesman Ron Asselstine and walloping him with a right. That started a fight that degenerated into a ten-man brawl. Noonan, Kypreos, Featherstone, and Joby Messier for the Rangers, Mark Tinordi, Jim Johnson, Dale Hunter, and Sylvain Cote for the Caps were all banished by referee Don Van Massenhoven.

Campbell was angry behind the bench. He didn't think it too smart having his best player in the box for fighting for the second straight game, although he understood why his captain did what he did.

Midway through the third period, it was still 1–1 when Messier and Steve Konowalchuk began pushing and shoving. The Caps' winger grabbed the captain's face, so Leetch flew into a pileup that ended with Messier, Leetch, Olczyk, Konowalchuk, Pat Peake, and Joe Juneau all off with minor penalties.

Campbell grabbed a water bottle and flung it so hard at the bench he almost hit Kypreos in the head. It didn't help the coach's mood when, five minutes later, Konowalchuk broke the tie on a soft goal that Healy, who had played brilliantly for two periods, should have stopped.

When the game ended, the dressing room door was slammed closed.

"What are we doing? What are we doing?" Campbell yelled, the first tirade of his tenure. "Mark Messier's thirty-four. He's our leader, our leading scorer. He's thirty-four. He shouldn't have to be doing that. And why is Brian Leetch the alert guy jumping in for Mess? We should be aware, we should be alert. We should be doing that to [Michal] Pivonka, to [Peter] Bondra. We should be getting under their skin, bumping [goalie Jim] Carey. Do we have to spell it out? C'mon, it's something you guys should know."

Campbell wasn't angry at Messier for getting himself thrown in the penalty box two games in a row, because he knew the captain had a score to settle with Haller three days earlier and was simply trying to ignite his lethargic teammates this time by not ignoring Kaminski. He was ticked off at his bangers, Matteau and Beukeboom, Kypreos and Wells, for not dishing out more than the Rangers absorbed.

"The message was clear," Healy said. "Look, it's one thing to play well and lose. When you play poorly and beat yourself, like we did, that's another thing. This one we can correct."

Only 20 games remained. Smith decided he could no longer wait for corrections. The Stanley Cup champions no longer existed. Three straight losses had dropped the Rangers six points behind the torrid Flyers. The toasts of the town—they had yet another big party scheduled for a week later at the Auction House—were now fifth overall in the East, but only four points from falling below the eight-team playoff cutoff.

"I'm gonna do something," Smith said when he reported to work on Monday, March 20. "Soon. I've got irons in the fire. I'm going to get Sweeney for Kypreos and I'm getting Verbeek without taking anything away from our team. That's the only move I can make without taking something from Peter to pay Paul. Everybody else who has someone available wants somebody back off our team. I can't do that. We're not deep enough."

With three days between the ugly loss to Washington and a critical Garden joust with the Devils, who were one point behind the Caps and two behind the Rangers, Campbell ran a hard, spirited practice on Monday. Zubov pronounced his surgically repaired hand ready and said he hoped to help a power play that was 6-for-45 during his nine-game absence.

Playing for his option-year salary of $275,000, Zubov was the most underpaid Ranger. His agent, Jay Grossman, pestered Smith all year about a new deal. The supremely talented Muscovite was certain to eventually land a multiyear, multimillion-dollar deal, but Smith was in no hurry to do it. Not with the erratic year Zubov was having. And not with Zubov his prime trade bait.

The twenty-four-year-old felt vindicated by the necessary surgery, since he was stung by management's early-season implication that he was exaggerating his pain. They had approached him as they had in the finals, when Zubov had to be prodded to play through the pain. When his courage was tested, he responded. A day before his operation, Zubov scored a pretty goal, set up Messier's game-winner, and added an empty-netter—quite a sendoff to the hospital. Now he was back. But for good?

"I don't want to trade Zubie," Smith said. "I want teams to think I'll trade him, so they'll spend more time negotiating with me and not with other teams, so I'll have early dibs on players on the market."

Hartford GM Jim Rutherford was one salesman. Pat Verbeek, the one-time Devil and current Whaler captain, was going to be traded within seventy-two hours. Hartford wanted to part with Verbeek's $1.2 million salary, and to rebuild with fresh, young faces. Verbeek had grown tired of the team's perpetual losing atmosphere; both sides agreed a change was necessary.

Rutherford told Smith that two other teams were seriously bidding on Verbeek. He wouldn't say who, but Smith suspected one was Toronto. "[Hartford] wants a first-round pick and something else," he said. "We're going to talk again tonight and try to finish it tomorrow or the next day."

Early that evening, long after practice, weight training, medical treatments, and the hum of the vacuums dragged over the red carpet in Rye had stopped, Campbell faxed Smith his prospective playoff roster of forwards. It read like this:

Graves	Messier	Larmer
(Verbeek)	Kovalev	Noonan
Matteau	Nemchinov	
Langdon	(Sweeney)	Kocur

Nedved, Kypreos, Olczyk, Osborne

And underneath it read like this:

Graves	Messier	Larmer
(Corson)	Kovalev	Noonan
Matteau	Nemchinov	(Verbeek)
Langdon	(Sweeney)	Kocur

Olczyk, Osborne

The top list was the lineup Campbell expected to have after Smith completed the two trades he still hoped to make. The bottom roster was Campbell's wish list. In the coach's mind Smith would trade Nedved for Edmonton's Shayne Corson, Kypreos for Sweeney, and a first-round pick for Verbeek. Montreal's Kirk Muller was also on the market, but Campbell doubted the Rangers could get him for Nedved, even though the Canadiens were struggling, Muller was slumping, and GM Serge Savard was under intense pressure to shake up the Habs.

"Both Neil and I know we have to make a couple of key moves," Campbell said.

Campbell was on his office doorstep at 8:10 the next morning. He looked tired.

"[Montreal coach] Jacques Demers rear-ended somebody at a stop sign recently. He was focusing on his team's slump, what he could do, and he totally clicked out. One coach told me recently, 'It's terrible. I wake up in the middle of the night, in a cold sweat.' I told him, 'That's great. I don't even sleep.'"

Campbell felt pressure—not from ITT-Cablevision, Checketts, or Smith; not from the fans who said he was no Keenan and were deriding his team's embarrassing Cup defense. "It's not the eighteen thousand people in the Garden, it's the thirty people in Toronto. It's the friends, the relatives, the people you love. Pressure is self-inflicted, self-applied.

"Defensively we're not so bad. It's offensively, we're not creating pressure. Is that my problem? I have to look to myself, am I taking something away from us offensively? Why don't we have quick feet? Why are we not buzzing?"

Campbell and Messier had talked a few days earlier. They talked about team chemistry, and why it was lacking. They talked about players who were frustrated with others who weren't pulling their weight, like Nedved, who had played three utterly invisible games after the pat on the back from Campbell following his contributions against Ottawa and the Devils. They talked about the urgency to turn the season around.

"I think there's a touch of apathy," Campbell said after he digested Messier's views. "I think we're looking to Mark. I think we're sometimes a little self-enthused with Stanley Cupishness. I haven't liked any of the Cup things we've done. I thought it was over when the Cup left my house this summer. I know we should be proud of it, should think we're defending Stanley Cup champions. But I know the battle is tougher the second time around. We've got to win it again. Hopefully we're going through a very humbling period. Forget about repeating as Stanley Cup winners. We're on the verge of not making the playoffs. No one ever wants to say that: 'Aw, that can't happen.' Yeah, it can happen."

Campbell had already told his players that, but he wasn't sure if they listened. He had rewarded his returnees with the loyalty that was earned along with the Cup, but he was beginning to second-guess himself.

"I've got to be less sensitive. I can't give a crap about people's feelings anymore. Guys who want more ice time; I should never give them a sympathy shift. I have at times. I call it a sympathy shift. I shouldn't care about a guy's feelings . . . but we won the Cup together and I think they deserve that. But it's almost over with. They deserve the benefit of the doubt, every player on this team. Alex Kovalev deserves the benefit of the doubt, Matteau, Kocur, all the guys. But it's almost over with. Now we've got to stand up and be counted."

Campbell was on a therapeutic roll now, speaking out loud to unburden the weight on his shoulders.

"Like the other night in Washington, we were just shuffling along when Kaminski starts with our leader, our Mario Lemieux, our guy who's making $6 million. Mess said he started it, but he started it for a reason, to get the team going. When that happened, and Leetch had to fly in, I'd just about had it. It had just been happening too often to our team. We should be pushing Pivonka, not only grabbing and fighting. We've got Joey Kocur, the hardest puncher of all time, who throws the fear of permanent injury into people's souls. They're not going to fight him. No one wants to fight him, or have to challenge him. And Langdon, Graves. The Washington players weren't going to fight our guys. They were going to aggravate.

"But we had guys on the bench not into it. Eighty percent, 68 percent. We're not going to win like that. We've got guys going into the games thinking we're going to win, which is good. But when we're down 2–1 with a few minutes left, we're not thinking we're going to score a goal. We've got four or five guys like that, and four or five others who get down on the culprits. I'm upset at those guys, too, because it doesn't help the team concept. Don't be complaining or worried about other guys, just do your job. If we let this go on for too long, it's our fault.

"Whether Mike Keenan was here, Vince Lombardi was here, Toe Blake was here, Pat Riley was here, it happens to every team. I'm not making excuses. Those are my feelings."

A few hours later, Campbell called Smith. "Anything up?"

Smith told him Sather was willing to trade Corson, but wanted a number one draft pick and at least two of the Rangers' top prospects: defenseman Mattias Norstrom, center Niklas Sundstrom, and goalies Dan Cloutier or Corey Hirsch.

"I won't do that," Smith said before telling Campbell he was supposed to talk to Rutherford again about Verbeek. "I'll let you know what he says."

Smith was torn. It's his job to provide the coach with the tools the coach feels are necessary to win, but it's also his job to assess whether the coach is using the tools properly.

"He wants me to move Nedved because he and Mark don't think they can win with him," Smith said. "He can't count on him to be among his top nine forwards. How do you deal with this insanity? I can't. I don't like their attitude that you can't win with this guy, that they give up on him after two months. Colie wants twenty-two guys who will go through the wall every night. We all would, but it's not reasonable. There are twenty-six teams in the league and you're lucky if you get two players like that."

Smith thought he could acquire twenty-seven-year-old checking right wing Mike Keane from Montreal for Nedved, but he didn't want to. Keane for Nedved would've made Campbell happy and probably improved the Rangers for the very short term. "But it's not a GM's delight," Smith said. Keane has nowhere near the potential of Nedved. But if Smith got him, Campbell would play him, which was more than he was doing with Nedved, now relegated to fourth-line status behind Messier, Kovalev, and Nemchinov. "I've never told him to play Nedved," Smith says. "I never tell him to play anybody. I let the coach coach."

Smith had the chance to acquire Jari Kurri from the Kings without giving up too much, but he wanted Verbeek. "I can't take both. Kurri makes $2 million. I can't take on two big salaries. [St. Louis Blues checking center] Guy Carbonneau's out there and available, but one thing I've tried to tell Colie is, 'Focus on one thing. If you throw too many balls up there, you'll drop them all.'"

On March 22, the time had come to make something happen. Smith wanted to close the Sweeney and Verbeek deals before that night's game with the Devils, who were two points behind the Rangers.

Barbara Dand briefed him when he arrived in his office a few minutes before 10 A.M. She outlined the calls he needed to return, the memos he had to review, and the papers he had to sign. "And you have to tell me who's using your tickets tonight, so I can get them down to the box office in time," she reminded him.

The first item on Smith's agenda—the Kypreos-for-Sweeney deal—collapsed at 10:50 A.M. when Muckler called. Sweeney has a ruptured muscle in his right shoulder, he told Smith. The center had been complaining about a lack of strength in his arm for a while, so the Sabres had him undergo an MRI. It found a problem that only surgery will correct.

"We're going to continue to play him," Muckler said. "I don't want to trade him and then you get him and say damaged goods. If he can't stand the pain, and requests surgery, the doctor said he'll operate on him. And then he's done for the year."

"I appreciate your honesty," Smith replied. "A lot of guys would hope that you didn't ask for a physical before making the trade, and would try to get away with not telling you."

Smith asked Muckler if there was anyone else he could offer for Kypreos. Muckler said no. When they hung up Smith banged his desk. "Damn," he said. "That's how quickly your plans get screwed up."

Smith pulled out his skinny blue spiral notebook, his trade book. He thumbed to the Buffalo page, jotted down the notes of his conversation with Muckler, turned to Hartford's page, and asked Dand to dial Rutherford. He needed to do the Verbeek deal that day.

They began with some small talk. Rutherford asked Smith about Daniel Lacroix, the center whom the Rangers traded to Boston last summer for Featherstone. The Bruins had put Lacroix on waivers and Rutherford said he was interested. Smith admitted the Rangers were thinking about claiming the physical center as insurance against injury. Rutherford then asked if Smith had formulated a firm proposal for Verbeek.

"I really haven't," he said. "The way I like to do it is, I like to know what you need, because I want Verbeek. I'd prefer if you tell me what you need, and how I can give it to you. Because I know you want to get as much as you can, and I want to give you as little as I can."

Rutherford liked Featherstone, because he was looking for a strong defensive defenseman who didn't earn much. At 6-4, 212, and $373,850, Featherstone fit. The first-year GM then told Smith he had a "standing offer on the table" from another team. Smith knew it was Toronto, and had to be careful not to get into an auction. On the one hand, he had to give Rutherford enough to close a deal quickly. On the other, he couldn't offer too much too soon.

"Obviously, we need the pick," Rutherford said, referring to a first-round pick in the 1995 draft. "We want a player who can play for us, and a prospect. That's what I have on the table right now."

Rutherford, who played goal for Detroit, Pittsburgh, Toronto, and Los Angeles in his thirteen NHL seasons, loved Dan Cloutier, the Rangers' 1994 number one pick. The Rangers' reports on their prospect were excellent, too. Smith would have rather dealt a yet-to-be-used pick, than a known quantity, even if that quantity is a young prospect who had yet to develop.

"Does Cloutier become part of your proposal?" Rutherford asked.

"Not if I can help it," was the reply.

Smith told Rutherford that in his pitch to Checketts he told the Garden president that in order to win the Cup again they'd have to mortgage part of their future by making a big trade or two that added to their current roster without deleting from it. Smith couldn't trade Verbeek for a regular because then he would have to replace the regular.

They dickered for several minutes. Rutherford asked about Michael Stewart, the Rangers' 1990 first-round pick, a defenseman playing in Binghamton who was below Norstrom and another minor-leaguer, Eric Cairns, on the depth chart. Smith said he was willing to trade Stewart or Barry Richter, the former Whaler who arrived a year earlier in the three-way Larmer trade and was in Binghamton with Stewart.

"I'd like to make a decision so I can firm this up within the next forty-eight hours," Rutherford concluded. "So I think we've got two options for Verbeek: a first [round pick], Featherstone, and Stewart. Or Cloutier, Featherstone, and Stewart."

Smith told Rutherford he needed to talk to Campbell and mull his options. They agreed to talk again later in the afternoon. "One more thing," Smith asked. "What about Jocelyn Lemieux or Geoff Sanderson?"

Rutherford said he was not trading Sanderson, one of his better scorers, but said Lemieux, a feisty winger, was a possible bargaining chip. Before he hung up Smith asked Rutherford where he stood with Verbeek.

"I'm fifty-fifty. I won't do anything before I talk to you."

By the time they talked again, Smith's blue trade book was filled with a few more interesting nuggets. When he called Campbell to update him on the Verbeek talks, the coach said Keenan had called offering Brendan Shanahan for Kovalev, or Kevin Miller for a third-round pick. Smith didn't ask why Keenan had called Campbell; ever since the combatants shook hands at the GMs meetings in California months earlier and agreed to put the summertime battle behind them, Smith didn't care how Keenan went about his business. "He's not my problem anymore," he said.

Smith also spoke to Calgary GM Doug Risebrough, who fished for Graves, expressed no interest in Nedved, and asked if the Rangers would trade Kovalev. When Smith started throwing out names like star center Theo Fleury, the two GMs realized they were wasting each other's time.

At 4:45, Smith called Rutherford again.

"I'm ready to make my offer," Smith stated. "The first [round draft pick], Featherstone, and Stewart rather than Cloutier, Featherstone, and Stewart."

"I'd rather have Option B, with Cloutier," Rutherford replied. "If you said you would take that deal, I won't go back to the other team I'm talking to. If you say I have to take Option A, the first rather than Cloutier, I'll go back to the other team and see what they'll do. I want to get this finished up within the next forty-eight hours, so if I get the deal I want to make, I won't call you back. And that's the same thing I'm telling the other team."

"Can I sweeten it up?" Smith asked.

"Well, if you do, just tell me your sweetener, I'll call [VP of hockey operations] Terry McDonnell, and I'll call you back in five minutes with an answer."

"Option A is Cloutier, Featherstone, and Stewart. That's the one you prefer. Option B, I'll make a first in 1995, Featherstone, and Stewart. And I'll throw in an extra fourth-round pick to keep Cloutier. But I also want to call Larry Pleau, to get his assessment of Cloutier, because we may want to give you him instead of the first-rounder."

At 5:15 P.M., Rutherford hung up and promised a response in five minutes. Smith didn't know if he was being truthful, or if he was hurrying to call Toronto GM Cliff Fletcher. Smith believed Rutherford was asking the Maple Leafs for top goalie prospect Eric Fichaud in whatever deal they were considering for Verbeek. He tried to reach Pleau, but the assistant GM was on a scouting trip and wasn't in his hotel room.

Rutherford called back at 5:40 P.M., apologized for the delay and insisted he hadn't called any other team. Smith said the fourth-round pick was on the table only until the end of that conversation.

"I added that because you're saying you won't go back to the other team," Smith said. "I trust your word that you didn't go back, that you only called to talk to your people. I couldn't reach Pleau."

"Well, Neil, we'll leave it up to you," Rutherford said. "We'll take one of the options, either Cloutier, Featherstone, and Stewart, or a first in 1995, a fourth in 1996, Featherstone, and Stewart. It'll be your choice. We have a deal, is that right?"

"Yes, we do. It's my option," Smith confirmed. "I'll make a decision as soon as I possibly can, definitely by noon tomorrow."

It was 6:05 P.M. when the GMs hung up. Hartford and the Rangers both had games that night, and the GMs agreed the traded players would play since the deal was not going to be finalized or reported to NHL Central Registry until the morning, after Smith talked to Pleau.

Smith spoke to Pleau after he hung up with Rutherford, and they decided Cloutier was worth keeping. So for two draft picks, the Rangers' seventh defenseman and a minor leaguer they did not think would ever play for their club, the Rangers acquired a feisty thirty-year-old, 35-goal scorer who packed 190 pounds into a barrel-chested 5-9 frame.

"I'm thrilled," the GM said minutes before he climbed to his perch atop the Garden. "We need somebody like Verbeek, a guy who's not afraid to get in people's faces, who's going to be hungry getting away from a young team like Hartford and in with our experienced group. He's gonna fit perfectly. And he didn't cost us anybody off our team."

Only Campbell knew the Verbeek deal had been made before the Rangers stunk out the Garden again. The 5–2 loss, in which the Devils scored three second-period goals and kayoed Richter, was the second straight game in which the Rangers failed to compete.

The next morning, the trade was officially made. After getting the good news, Verbeek hopped in his car for the three-hour trip to Long Island, where the Rangers were hoping to stop their four-game skid.

Verbeek was ecstatic to be going to a powerful team like the Rangers. Campbell was delighted to add a Tikkanen-type agitator to the core of his lineup without losing anybody in return. He didn't mind that Smith had also claimed Lacroix off waivers and recalled Norstrom. Since Larmer missed the game with back spasms, Verbeek was immediately inserted into Larmer's spot with Graves and Messier.

The line meshed well. The Rangers were terrific. They outshot the Islanders 37–15, outplayed them even more than the shots indicated, and spent sixty minutes around goalie Tommy Soderstrom's net.

Yet they lost, 1–0. Soderstrom played the game of his life. He stopped breakaways, rebounds, tip-ins. The game was scoreless until 9:55 remained, when Steve Thomas flipped his own rebound behind Richter to drop the Rangers under .500 for the first time since February 18. Their 13-14-3 mark left them tied with the Devils for seventh overall in the East, just two points ahead of Florida and Montreal.

Two nights later, it got worse. The Rangers staggered into Quebec and played their worst period of the season. The first period at Le Colisée was a humiliating twenty minutes in which the Rangers were outshot 16–5, outscored 2–0, and terribly outclassed.

"What do we need, another savior?" Campbell yelled in the cramped visitor's dressing room of the antiquated arena. "There ain't no trade in the world that's going to help that period."

As if they were telepathically connected, Smith spat out virtually the same angry words as he paced in the press box before the second period of the Rangers' eventual 2–1 loss. "I could get Mario Lemieux and Wayne Gretzky for Mike Hartman, and it wouldn't have helped us that period. And this team, the one on paper that everyone's going gaga over, I'm just sitting up here, swallowing my anger. It's The Curse. I'm cursed. It's off the franchise and it's on me now."

It was on everybody. Kovalev scored the third-period goal that made the Quebec game close. It was his first goal in the six-game losing streak. Graves didn't have a point. Nemchinov didn't have a point. Matteau didn't have a goal or an assist in his last 17 games. Nedved had one assist. Leetch had two goals, Messier a goal and an assist.

On the somber plane ride home late Saturday night, Campbell decided to keep the Rangers off the ice Sunday and Monday. A quirk in the schedule gave the Rangers four idle days before their next game, a rematch with the Nordiques. So Sunday became a full off-day in which the Rangers were told not to think about hockey. A team party was Monday night, so Campbell scheduled a 4 P.M. film session followed by a weightlifting and stationary bike workout. He chose to skate the team hard on Tuesday, taper off on Wednesday, and be ready to try and break the six-game skid on Thursday, which marked the final block of their season, 17 games in thirty-three days.

Campbell couldn't not think about hockey, though. Here he was, an NHL head coach for the first time in his life, watching his dream turn into a nightmare. He was screwing up a Stanley Cup champion.

"I know I can't compare myself to Mike. Firstly because of his experi-

204 / BARRY MEISEL

ence, and secondly, because I'm not him. But Mike would have had a hard time following Mike. And all I have to do is look across the river and look to see the [Devils' Jacques Lemaire, last year's] Coach of the Year with the same record as me. It's a toilet seat business. Up and down. Up and down. And if you're not careful, when it's down they'll flush you away quickly."

Campbell was asked if he doubted his ability. He closed his eyes, leaned back on his chair, sighed. "In a quiet moment, never around people, you question, 'Can I do it? I'm a rookie, too.' I want to prove to all the doubters."

He knew the season had changed him when he recently found himself questioning the value of loyalty, the trait his parents had taught him mattered more than anything.

"I have trouble now playing Mike Richter every game. I know I have to, but Glenn Healy's such a good man. He works hard, he's a good person. And it's not fair that he can't play, but who from sports said life is fair?

"Loyalty can bury you, too. And I don't say this lightly at all, and I don't mean to pull this into hockey because it has no place in hockey, it's much bigger than that, but if I can bring Joe Murphy in here, and tell a man the worst news he's ever going to hear in his life, then I have no problem after that telling anybody in that room anything about their business. You're not supposed to tell someone that his only son has just died. And when you do that, hey, loyalty, whatever, I have no problem telling someone you're not playing."

Keenan's loyalty was to the mandate, never to the man. It was to the group, not the individual. It gave him the freedom to do whatever he wanted. With 17 games left and a playoff berth very much in question, Campbell was asked if the Rangers had shown him, or each other, the loyalty he had shown them.

"That was my question back in August. That was my first question. How are they going to deal with the next guy, whether it's me or whoever? How would they have dealt with Mike Keenan? And how would Mike have dealt with Mike?"

Smith didn't get four days off that week. With the trade deadline approaching on April 7, he still wanted to find a checking center and another tough winger. Since Kypreos hadn't dressed for the last three games, Smith hardly blinked when he got a call from Harry Francis, Kypreos's agent, requesting a trade. Smith had little patience with Francis. "Call everybody, try to make a deal," he said. "There isn't any place I wouldn't trade him."

When a team has lost six straight, the vultures arrive. GMs call, looking to pick its carcass, hoping the GMs'll make a desperate move. Smith did not. He listened to every call, jotted every offer in his trade book, and moved on. He tried to not think that the six-game losing streak, the standings that showed the Rangers tenth in the eight-team Eastern playoff hunt, were a reflection of the work he has done.

"I can't personalize it. If I did, I'd have to jump off a bridge."

With the deadline less than two weeks away, Smith got a few nibbles. Quebec GM Pierre Lacroix wanted Zubov for hard-nosed center Mike Ricci, but Smith wouldn't do it. Lacroix then offered flashy winger Valeri Kamensky for Matteau, but Smith wouldn't do that, either. He thought he might be able to get center Dean Evason from Dallas for Osborne; Messier had told Campbell that Osborne was not fitting in off the ice or helping on it.

Smith shopped Nedved, but there was little interest. He was still praying Savard in Montreal would make a desperate move, but he was not counting on Muller arriving neatly wrapped to cure the Rangers' woes. He shopped for a defensive center, but they were impossible to find at a fair price.

For the first time all year, Smith told Campbell to make up his mind on Nedved, to stop putting him in the lineup, sticking him on the fourth line, and ensuring yet another ineffective game by playing him two shifts with guys like Langdon and Kocur. "We're bastardizing him," Smith said. "Either put him in a role that makes sense, or put him in the stands. Let's get down to reality, Colie. Let's stop this. You won't hurt my ability to deal him by sitting him out."

Campbell then told Smith that Messier had turned up the pressure to get rid of Osborne. "I'll try," Smith said.

Later, the GM reminded himself that Messier's input was not only desired but necessary. "Colie and I are both cringing when he talks to us with stuff like that, but what can you do? If you have a superstar, you have to let him have a voice. He proved he deserves one, and we trust him. It'd be foolish not to talk to him about stuff like that. He's usually right."

With Smith in Buffalo scouting Sweeney, who was playing hurt, the Rangers ran their losing streak to seven with a 5–4 defeat at home to Quebec. Nine teams were still ahead of them in the East, including Florida. Two days later, they finally won a game, their first victory since March 8, edging the Bruins, 3–2, in a matinee at Boston Garden. Healy got the victory, which raised his record to 5-3-1, compared to Richter's 9-13-2. It gave him a 2.34 goals-against average, compared to Richter's 2.78. It gave him a .904 save percentage, compared to Richter's .895.

It gave Campbell a problem. The number one goaltender wasn't playing better than Healy. The number one goaltender wasn't winning as consistently as Healy. Yet the number one goaltender had won a Cup and had established himself as a team's workhorse, while Healy had done a magnificent job as Keenan's forgotten number two.

A number two must be humble enough to accept a supporting role, mentally prepared enough to jump off the bench in relief when the starter bombs or the coach wants to shake up the team, physically talented enough to win playing a game only every seven to ten days. Healy was. That's why, when asked about the goaltending after the Boston game, Campbell simply said, "It was time to start Healy. Time to make changes."

Lost in the victory was a superb game by the soon-to-be Sabre Kypreos, who got a rare opportunity to play on a solid line, with Nedved and Kovalev. He responded with a dynamic two-way game. He crushed every Boston defenseman who came near the puck in his path, he dumped the puck in just as he was instructed, he forechecked aggressively, and he earned his first point in nearly two months by assisting on Kovalev's first goal. He was trying to stay in New York. Meanwhile, all Sweeney did on Long Island that day was score two shorthanded goals (he had one goal in his first twenty-nine games) and lead the Sabres to a 5–1 rout of the Islanders.

The Boston victory didn't ease the Rangers' problems, for twenty-six hours later they were in Philadelphia trying to cope with Lindros's Legion of Doom. This was the feature game on the premiere of Fox's five-year, $155 million TV gamble on the NHL: the reigning Stanley Cup champs against the league's future kings.

Campbell chose Richter, who usually played well in his hometown, and also because Healy often slipped when playing the second of consecutive games on successive days. The coach scratched Matteau for the second straight game. He kept Kypreos on the Nedved-Kovalev line. He pitted Messier against Lindros, but because he lost that matchup, the Rangers lost the game. Messier took nine shots on goal to Lindros's seven, but Lindros scored twice and set up one by LeClair in the Flyers' 4–2 victory.

Their next game three days later was now a must game: they had to beat Florida, who jumped one point ahead of them into the eighth playoff spot. Smith had barricaded himself in his Key West condominium since Sunday night so he could focus on the trade deadline without interruptions, but he lost one option on Wednesday. The Canadiens sent Muller to the Islanders in a blockbuster trade. For Muller, defenseman Mathieu Schneider and prospect Craig Darby, Isles GM Don Maloney shipped center Pierre Turgeon and defenseman Vladimir Malakhov to Montreal.

"I knew I was never going to get Muller for Nedved when I heard Serge had that going with Donny," Smith said.

The Rangers won their crucial game with Florida, 5–0. Vanbiesbrouck and Neilson's neutral-zone trap kept the game scoreless until Larmer scored at 18:25 of the second period. Richter, who only had to make 17 saves, silenced Florida's already quiet offense until the Rangers broke it open on third-period goals by Messier, Verbeek, and two late ones by Kovalev.

Back in eighth place for the moment, the Rangers' flight north was upbeat. Kypreos gave it to Graves, who had spent too much time in the Miami sun the day before the game and suffered a painfully sunburned face.

"What were you doing, Gravy?" Kypreos warbled. "Bobbing for french fries?"

Smith made the trip back with the team. He barricaded himself in his Manhattan office on Thursday and huddled at Rye with Pleau, Campbell, Murphy, and Todd until 3 P.M. on Friday, four and a half hours before the Islander game that night. He talked to every GM. He explored trades involving every player on a list of a dozen realistic possibilities Campbell had provided.

But the Rangers didn't get Corson from Edmonton. They didn't get Sweeney from Buffalo. They didn't get Florida's Brian Skrudland or Quebec's Ricci or any other impact center. All Smith managed to obtain before the 3 P.M. deadline was speedy twenty-two-year-old center Nathan LaFayette, the Vancouver Canuck who nearly precipitated an epidemic of coronaries ten months earlier when his shot hit the post in the final minutes of Game 7 of the finals. In fact, after trading for him, Smith was asked by a writer what he liked most about LaFayette. "That he hit the post," Smith cracked.

The GM also traded Olczyk, who had requested a trade, to Winnipeg for a fifth-round pick. And he claimed journeyman left wing Troy Loney from the Islanders on waivers.

"It's always the same, it comes down to the last two hours, when the GMs are forced to shit or get off the pot. Last year we had the bullets to fire and people to fire them at. This year, I was ready to make a move, but there were no moves to be made."

The Corson deal died because Sather asked for Kovalev and Norstrom after Smith told him he couldn't have three prospects. Corson stayed with Edmonton. The Skrudland deal died because Florida had hopes for the playoffs and certainly didn't want to strengthen the team they had to beat. Florida GM Bryan Murray said he would trade Skrudland for Cloutier, but when Smith offered Hirsch, the Panthers said no.

Kypreos-for-Sweeney fell apart because Muckler failed to complete a deal he thought he had with Pittsburgh. The Sabres were going to get crafty Czech center Martin Straka, which would have given them the depth in the middle to deal Sweeney. When the Penguins sent Straka to Ottawa, Muckler decided not to trade Sweeney. "I think Sweeney played too well for them," said Smith, who could only wonder if Muckler would have pulled the trigger three weeks earlier if he tried to close the deal. "Muck got cold feet."

The consolation prize to the trade deadline's disappointing conclusion was a gimme against the reeling Islanders, who limped into the Garden 1-10-1 in their previous 12 games, but without Muller, who was shocked by the trade and initially refused to report, without Benoit Hogue, traded for a prospect, and without goalie Jamie McLennan, who was demoted the day before.

Campbell, Murphy, and Todd warned their players that morning at Rye not to let down. They implored them in the dressing room after the warm-up not to let down. They said it again after a first period in which they led, 2–1.

But the Rangers let down. With a patchwork lineup that lacked the talent to beat an American Hockey League team, the Islanders rallied from an early 2–0 deficit and shocked the Rangers, 4–3. Richter yielded three poor goals before he was yanked at 1:59 of the third period. Nemchinov, Kovalev, and Loney failed to communicate on a faceoff in the Rangers' zone, which allowed Travis Green to tie it 2–2 on a shot directly off the draw late in the second period.

If anyone on the team still harbored the illusion that they were a championship-caliber squad coasting into position, this game should have shattered it. Good teams simply do not lose games by making fundamental errors.

The door to the Rangers' dressing room remained tightly shut for nearly fifteen minutes. After most games, players amble out of the dressing room and through the hall in their sweaty, long underwear to the exercise room for their postgame stints on the stationary bikes. Not this night. The bikes sat empty. Usually, the stereo could be heard. Not this night. The first sound emanating from the room was the slam of the door behind the jacketless Campbell, who emerged with eyes glazed and teeth clenched.

Campbell was infuriated by the Green goal. Peewee players know that when a centerman is thrown from a faceoff, the next player to jump in should be a guy who knows how to take faceoffs. Kovalev had spent half the year at center, so he was the natural second choice when Nemchinov was waved off by the official. But Loney, new to the club, wanted to accept the responsibility. He didn't know Kovalev was a center. It was Nemchinov's job to wave Kovalev in, or Kovalev's job to wave Loney out.

"Before the game I said, 'Make sure your responsibilities are right on the faceoffs,'" Campbell explained. "Now it's my responsibility. I said it, they didn't execute it. It's still my responsibility. There has to be a reason why they didn't listen."

After the game, Leetch was asked by a reporter how the Rangers planned to deal with their predicament. "Your choice is to quit and decide in this short season we're not going to do it, but I don't think there's anyone in that locker room like that," he said. "So we've just got to fight through it. There are no other choices. The trading deadline is gone. The guys who are here have to get it done. There are no other options."

While Richter accepted responsibility for the loss, an angry Messier showered, dressed, and found Smith. Messier, who had been carrying his weight on the ice and off, pulled the GM aside and told him that Zubov had spent the afternoon worrying and chain-smoking cigarettes in his day room at the Southgate Hotel on Seventh Avenue across the street from the Garden after getting a call from his agent, Jay Grossman. Messier said the agent had called Zubov to ask him if he would sign a long-term contract with Quebec if the Nordiques traded for him that day. Messier said Grossman had gotten a call from Quebec GM Pierre Lacroix, who said he and Smith were discussing a trade for Zubov.

"I'm gonna slap a tampering charge on that bastard," Smith fumed.

Smith had spoken to Lacroix that day, but had rejected Lacroix's offer of Ricci-for-Zubov. The GMs had spoken in generalities the day before, when Smith said Zubov was not untouchable. Smith had told him he was having trouble working out a new deal with Zubov, but he never gave him permission to talk to the player or the player's agent about a possible trade.

After thanking Messier for the information, Smith called NHL director of hockey operations Brian Burke at home. It was approximately 11:30 P.M. "I've got enough problems without a rookie GM pulling this shit on me, Burky," yelled Smith, who met with Zubov the next day to assure him he didn't want to trade him. "What the fuck is going on? I want the league to investigate."

Smith didn't find out until months later that another of his players was also badly shaken that afternoon. Matteau had checked into his day room at the Southgate for his pregame nap to find the message light in his room lit. He called the operator.

"Message from Neil Smith," the operator said. "Call Neil Smith."

Matteau panicked. He had heard rumors he was going to be traded again, and they bothered him. He loved playing for the Rangers, he loved

New York, he didn't want to leave. He didn't sleep the night before either, after having received a call from a reporter who told him he was headed to Montreal or St. Louis.

"I called my wife. I called my agent and said, 'I'm going somewhere. I don't know where, but I'm going.' He said, 'We haven't heard anything. Give Neil a call.'"

Matteau didn't. He sat up that day and waited for the bad news to reach him. None came, because Smith hadn't called and didn't trade him. Somebody had played a callous joke.

"I never found out who did it," Matteau said. "It wasn't funny."

A year ago at the trade deadline, Smith and Keenan shuffled the deck and drew an ace. This time, Smith expressed relief that he did not panic by gambling on a long shot.

"First of all, just because we didn't do a deal at the deadline doesn't mean we didn't do a deal. We got Verbeek, who replaces and is better than Tikkanen. Yeah, I could have gotten Skrudland for Cloutier, and Skrudland would have been this year's MacTavish. Yeah, I could have gotten Corson for our three best prospects, and he would have been this year's Glenn Anderson and Gilbert combined.

"That would have been the selfish thing. The owners might have loved the deals now, and the fans would have loved the deals now, the media would have said Neil Smith's a genius again. But I'm not going to cripple the Rangers' franchise like some of my predecessors did. Trading Cloutier for Skrudland, or Norstrom and Sundstrom for Corson, would have been great for Neil Smith and horrible for the franchise two or three years down the road.

"I don't know if we'll win the Cup without those guys, but I'm not sure we would have won the Cup if I traded for all those guys. Because the guys who are going to win us the Cup if we win it—Messier, Leetch, Richter, Graves, Kovalev, Zubov, Matteau, Noonan—have to start playing better, or we're not going to win no matter who I would have gotten."

Smith and Campbell had a long talk that night. With their next game Sunday afternoon at the Meadowlands, they considered ripping the players at a scheduled team dinner Saturday night. They quickly realized that was their own frustration surfacing, and opted to take a more positive approach.

"We're all bruised," Campbell said. "We're all afraid of missing the playoffs."

"You're right," Smith replied. "I just want to say something to them,

Colie, because I feel so helpless. I think I want to remind them that we're good."

So simple a statement was necessary because from top to bottom the organization had lost its confidence. Smith gave Campbell a public vote of support, although he detested an environment that demanded one just thirty-six games into a first-year head coach's career, especially a coach who walked into the situation Campbell had. Smith also gave his coach a private reassurance that no matter what happened, he was not going to be pressured into doing so foolish a thing as firing him. Not if the fans demanded it. Not if the media demanded it. Not even if his own bosses demanded it.

"Thanks, Neil. That helps," Campbell said. "This is the toughest thing I've ever been through in my life."

The Devils didn't make it any easier on Sunday. In front of another Fox audience, the Rangers spent all day trying to score a goal. Martin Brodeur stopped 32 shots, the Devils' defense was brilliant, and the Rangers fell, 2–0. Hartford, Montreal, and Florida all sat above the Rangers in the scramble for the eighth and final playoff berth. The Devils, Buffalo, and Washington were comfortably ahead in fifth, sixth, and seventh.

The Rangers were 2-10-0 in their last 12 games. With 11 to go, they sat eighteenth overall with a 15-19-3 record. They needed to go 7-3-1 just to finish .500, and they figured they needed seven or eight victories to assure themselves a playoff spot. They were trying not to become the first team since the 1970 Montreal Canadiens to miss the playoffs the year after winning the Cup.

Messier, Lowe, and Leetch dressed very slowly in the off-limits medical area of the visiting room at the Meadowlands. Before the door separating the main locker room closed to protect their privacy, fear and concern reflected off their faces. Leetch, though, refused to drop his guard.

"We will get through this," he promised.

But to what end? The team that had raised the Cup back in June now had eighth place as its goal. The edge that had made them champions was nowhere to be seen.

The Push

9

With two days between the deflating loss at New Jersey and Game 1 of his team's 11-game playoff push, and with the call for Campbell's head starting to surface on talk radio, Smith chose to combat the noise. The last 11 games were going to be nerve-racking enough without the head coach having to hear the rumors and innuendo, the GM figured. It was time to stamp out the speculation so the 1994–95 Rangers could live or die in peace.

"The less you're able to analyze the sport, the quicker you'll come up with the conclusion that it's the coach's fault, because you don't have the ability to look at things deeply," Smith said publicly. "If I allow myself or the people above me to react to that nonsense—which is exactly what it is, nonsense—then shame on me."

Smith asked three crucial questions: Had Campbell altered the system of aggressive puck pursuit that he, as Keenan's assistant coach, implemented the year before? Did Campbell anger or upset Messier, Leetch, Graves, or Richter, the four most critical Rangers? Were the Rangers speaking negatively about their coach, on or off the record? The answer to all three was no.

Smith then outlined the areas where Campbell excelled, areas even the most informed reporter or perceptive fan could not readily assess: Campbell worked long hours studying film and prescouting opponents; he communicated productively with the players; he had a network of league sources on whom he relied for tidbits of information that occasionally helped him prepare for opponents; he ran a tight bench; and he properly handled a delicate relationship with Messier.

"The coach will always be an easy target—especially when it's hard to say this team doesn't have talent. So it must be, 'He isn't getting it out of them.' But these are not circus bears who can't think for themselves and whom we don't have respect for. These are, for the most part, seasoned professionals."

Having made his public posture clear, the GM went to work on the team's fragile psyche. He had a forty-minute chat on the phone that night with Graves, who had scored one goal in 13 games, but who wouldn't admit that his surgically repaired back was not yet 100 percent for fear of anyone thinking he was looking for an excuse.

"Adam, try not to press," Smith said. "Nobody knows you better than I do. You're putting the weight of the world on your shoulders. You're not going to get us out of this all by yourself, you're going to be a part of the solution. Just do your part. Don't try to score, pass, protect Mess, forecheck, back-check, and fight all at once."

The players, coaches, and management assembled at Rye after practice the next day for the annual team picture. Smith made sure to be upbeat, a deliberate attempt to show his players he wasn't worried about the team's dilemma.

"Where's the Cup, Mess?" he cracked.

"What are circus bears?" Kocur ribbed back.

Pierre Lacroix invited Smith to breakfast in Manhattan the following morning. Quebec's rookie GM made a special trip to apologize for calling Grossman and asking about Zubov, and for misleading the agent enough so that Grossman called the defenseman on the afternoon of a game. Smith agreed to drop the tampering allegation.

"I get more for letting him off the hook," he reasoned. "If they're found guilty of tampering, we'd get half the fine . . . and no satisfaction. Now Pierre owes me one."

While the GMs dined, Campbell pored over the Rangers' game sheets from the 2-10-0 slide. He wanted to find some explanation for the slump before the Rangers played the Sabres later that night.

"We're not fighting enough around the net, along the wall. Here's the stats from the last 12 games. We never get killed in a game. We do a meticulous job of keeping [track of] each team's scoring chances. We were 5-5-2 in who has more chances those last 12 games. When you have more chances, you should win, so let's be tough and say with 5-5-2 in chances we should go 5-7. Okay, it's a tough year, so make it 4-8. But never would you think we'd go 2-10."

The stats couldn't explain the losses. Last year, they couldn't explain the wins.

"The day I was named, I knew it would be a difficult year to match, only because of all the great things that happened to click. We weren't a Montreal Canadiens, a New York Islanders, an Edmonton Oilers, teams that dominated and won the Stanley Cup. We just went into each game last year and found a way to win. And then we lost some key elements. When you scraped by like we did, right to the seventh game, right to the last face-off with a second and a half left, you needed all the elements to win.

"Mike's a master at formulating and diverting pressures. We had internal pressures, whether they were there or they were formulated by Mike. But it worked. Don't ask me how, but it worked, because we won. I don't think Mike had a master plan. He just took it hour-by-hour. Mike's been there before. Three times in the finals. I wasn't going to argue with him, Dick Todd wasn't going to argue. Dick and I would question, what the hell's going on here? But Mike was unwavering. And it's not easy to be unwavering as a head coach, I'm finding out now. Because in those toughest times, you make those decisions in solitude. You have to."

Campbell stopped. He had the Sabres' last game on his office TV, and he paused to watch a Buffalo goal. It was by Sweeney. Campbell shook his head. "It keeps haunting us. It never stops."

Campbell turned back to Richter, and the number one goalie responded with a brilliant 22-save effort in a 3–1 Ranger win that snapped a four-game Garden losing steak. Verbeek, now a fixture on the top line with Graves and Messier, scored his fifth goal in nine games as a Ranger. Sweeney, naturally, scored Buffalo's only goal, at 1:03 of the third period, but the defense stiffened until Larmer scored an empty-netter at 19:40.

The most encouraging aspect of the game was the Rangers' 15–3 shots advantage in the first period and their ability to carry that momentum deep into the game. "We maintained the forechecking and the attack we were known for last year," he said.

Two mornings later, Leetch asked Messier if he thought it would be a good idea to request a greater workload from Campbell. "I've been feeling really good the last few weeks and I can handle more ice, Mess," he said. "Should I do it?"

"Absolutely," Messier replied.

It wasn't as if Leetch wasn't already playing a lot. He was getting his regular shifts, anchoring the power plays, and killing penalties. He simply wanted Campbell to know that if Campbell wanted to play him thirty minutes a game, he was prepared to accept the responsibility. "I just know I can play a lot more if you need me," Leetch told Campbell. "I feel really good, Colie."

"You know, we'd been talking about that, Brian," Campbell replied. "We know you can handle it."

The Rangers won their second straight that night, the first time they had linked victories since March 6 and 8. They jumped to a 4–1 lead over Boston on goals by Nedved and Leetch and two by Verbeek. The Bruins closed to 4–3, but Leetch's second goal late in the third period iced a second straight win for Richter, who was 1–7 in his previous nine starts. Messier had four assists.

Two nights later, the captain's contributions were not limited to the arena. Two putrid periods against the Islanders at the Nassau Coliseum threatened to undo the two previous solid wins. The Rangers trudged off for the second intermission trailing 2–1 after a lethargic forty minutes, and found themselves staring into the scary eyes of an angry Messier.

He shut the door. No trainers, no equipment guys, no coaches. For the first time all year, Messier's teammates saw the fury opponents see in his eyes on the ice. He stared people down.

"He blew a gasket," one Ranger said.

"So how much longer are we gonna bullshit ourselves?" Messier bellowed, his deep voice piercing utter silence. "This is not good enough. It's just not. We're not playing with any heart, we've gotta start playing with more intensity. No more excuses. You can only make excuses for so long. We started the year poorly, we just lost seven straight games, we gave ourselves no more room for error.

"Do you understand? How can we play two periods like we just played? It's not good enough. Now either we go out and win this game and go on, or we pack it in. I'm not packing it in."

It was a tongue-lashing. There was no response needed or possible. When Messier finished, the meeting was over.

"It was pretty awesome," said Verbeek, who had never heard a Messier lecture before.

"It was controlled, but very much from the heart," Lowe described. "It was emotional, but that's the way he is. It was probably one of his best. And I've heard a lot of good ones."

The Rangers launched themselves out of the dressing room. They took the first 11 shots of the third period and starting throwing the Isles around like they had in the playoffs the spring before. Messier, who assisted on Lowe's first-period goal, set up Zubov's power-play tally that made it 2–2 at 9:45. Two minutes later, Nedved deflected in Zubov's slapper. Two minutes after that, Richter made the save of the season on Steve Thomas's point-blank one-timer. The Rangers held the Isles to three third-period shots, won their third straight game for the first time all season, and ended the day in eighth place after Hartford lost that night.

Messier said he chose that moment to erupt because "we just had to win that game. Sometimes you've got to get mad to get things going. Quit thinking about consequences, or the good things or the bad things. Don't think. Just get out there and get mad and play by instinct."

The Rangers went from Long Island to Pittsburgh, where they instinctively got into a shootout with the Penguins. Bad move. Four times the Rangers replied to a Pittsburgh goal, but the Penguins grabbed five one-goal leads.

Leetch from his left defense flank was assigned the job of neutralizing Jaromir Jagr, the phenomenal Czech right wing who was battling Lindros for the scoring title. Jagr had four assists, but Leetch had five. He set up every Ranger goal, by Zubov, Graves, Nedved, Graves again, and Kovalev, who tied it 5–5 with 5:29 left.

But Jagr made a terrific move to beat Leetch cleanly out of the corner, and fed Ron Francis alone in front of the helpless Richter for the 6–5 win that snapped the Rangers' three-game winning streak. It was not a demoralizing loss, because the Rangers had significantly lifted their intensity level and fought it out with a team that was second overall in the East, and was in a heated fight for first in the Northeast Division. But moral victories would be worthless come playoff time.

The loss also rendered their next game, April 20 against Hartford at a nervous Garden, absolutely imperative. The Rangers were now 18-20-3, two points out of a playoff spot with seven games to go.

The overachieving Whalers were loose; they were in a no-lose situation. Rutherford's trade of Verbeek signaled the start of a rebuilding job, but his team refused to fade away. The Whalers had 41 points, tied for sixth with the Caps, but just one more than eighth-place Buffalo.

After two periods at the Garden, the Whalers led 2–1. This time Messier didn't slam the door. No speeches were necessary. There comes a point in every team's season when every man in the room understands what needs to be done.

Zubov tied the game at 4:41 of the third period. He took a pass from Messier on a power play, stickhandled down the slot, and lifted a gorgeous shot over goalie Sean Burke's glove. Six minutes later, the creative Russian tried a very Neanderthal North American move: he dumped the puck in. Larmer, in his 1,000th NHL game, had a step on his man. Zubov read the play impeccably, as Larmer corraled the puck in the corner and fired it toward the goalmouth, where Nedved burst in like he had been told to do for months. He fanned on the hard pass with his stick, but it deflected off his skate and slid behind Burke with 9:01 left.

"Two months ago he'd have followed that play wide," Campbell said. "Tonight he went where you get slashed, where you get high-sticked. He went where you score goals."

The goal wasn't what impressed Messier. It was the sacrifice Nedved made in getting to the net. Maybe Messier and Campbell had been too hasty in their assessment of the young Czech, or perhaps their harsh judgments had forced Nedved to look honestly at himself and decide what he wanted to be.

"Until you have to play in that environment or are forced to play in that environment where pressure's on every day, you don't get a sense of what it really means to have the respect of your teammates," Messier said. "It doesn't come with one game. It comes over a gradual amount of time. In fairness to Petr, he hadn't played in the NHL in a year and he hadn't played in this conference his entire life. It's a completely different ballgame over here. Plus he comes to a Stanley Cup champion team.

"Because Petr Nedved got traded to the Rangers and was living in New York—or any player, I'm only using Petr as an example—a player getting traded to New York isn't automatically a Ranger, so to speak. A true Ranger in his blood who deeply cares about the organization, if we win. Is he going to really feel the consequences in himself if we lose? You only get that over time. You have to have a deep, deep, deep sense of loyalty and commitment and bleed red, white, and blue. Now Petr's starting to feel important, responsible. And he's seeing the effects of those things in a city where if you do do it, how great it is."

Campbell's choice of Healy over Richter for the Hartford game was not a signal that the coach's loyalty had at last run out. Campbell wanted to start Richter, but for the last few weeks he had been quietly nursing a sore shoulder and slightly sprained knee. He wasn't 100 percent, yet he insisted he was fine and ready to play whenever his coach asked.

Richter's physical condition and Healy's huge win made Campbell's choice for a goalie three days later at Boston an easy one. For the first thirty-seven minutes of their last regular-season visit to Boston Garden, the Rangers' big guns controlled the game. Leetch, who took Messier's prodding to heart and had an April to remember, scored just 1:10 into the game. Messier and Verbeek set up Zubov's power-play slapper late in the period.

Healy protected the 2–0 lead until three minutes remained in the second period, when Cam Neely poked in a power-play rebound. Seconds later, Wells took a high-sticking penalty. With eight seconds left in the period, Neely deflected a weak point shot over Healy's glove with 7.4 seconds left.

Leetch, Zubov, Messier, Verbeek, and Graves were at their best, but the rest of the team did not respond. Early in the third period, Glen Murray tipped a shot off Healy's shoulder, off the crossbar, off the goalie's back, and into the net. Boston scored again midway through the period, before Verbeek (from Zubov and Leetch) narrowed the Bruins' lead to 4–3. But Neely completed his hat trick on a power rush after a Zubov turnover with 2:28 left, a goal that rendered Kovalev's with 0:16 left meaningless.

"We're all right," Graves insisted after the loss dropped the Rangers' into a three-way tie with Montreal and Hartford for the final slot, one point behind seventh-place Buffalo, but only two ahead of Florida in eleventh. "We have four games left at home and one on the road. And of all the locker rooms in the league, there's only one I'd want to be in."

The Rangers won their next two, both at the Garden, 5–4 over Washington on the twenty-fourth and 6–4 over Tampa Bay on the twenty-sixth. The victories moved them into sole possession of eighth place, and they seemed a lock for the playoffs since they next played the Islanders at home, and they had a two-point cushion over Hartford, which only had two games left, a three-point lead over Montreal (three games left), and a five-point bulge over Florida (four games left). None of this made Campbell any less worried or angry.

"This is hell," he said, almost spilling his coffee on the game reports sitting on his desk. "I'm almost done now with this crap of loyalty. I've gone too far. The Stanley Cup is light years away. The mistakes these guys are making . . ."

In the 5–4 victory over the Capitals, Messier got stuck in a tangle of players near Washington's bench during a line change in the second period. The captain didn't know who hit him, but he was bent backward over the low boards by a check that hyperextended his back. And Campbell was absolutely hysterical when Tampa Bay jumped to a 3–1 lead after twenty-four minutes two nights later. In Keenanesque fashion, he yanked Richter, although the goalie hadn't played badly, and inserted Healy. He never had to say a word, though, because Messier started screaming at his teammates on the bench. Again, it worked; Beukeboom, Verbeek, and Nedved scored in the third period, Tampa Bay tied it early in the third, but Graves scored at 8:07 and added an empty-netter to avoid disaster.

"Mark Messier could hardly get out of bed the other day because of his back. It's crazy. I've got to play him every other shift. And he's the only guy getting mad on the bench. He's saying what I want to say, but I don't want to sound like a rookie coach who's losing his composure. But I'm fuckin' mad."

The Rangers were in a life-or-death struggle to make the playoffs, and Campbell couldn't forget that in his 1995 blueprint, this was supposed to be the time to gear up for the postseason. He didn't want Messier playing twenty-five minutes a game, taking every crucial faceoff, drawing on the reserves of mental strength and physical stamina he'd need in May and June. He didn't want to wring every ounce of offensive thrust from Zubov and Leetch. He didn't want to have Beukeboom and Graves and Lowe physically punishing themselves every shift now, against the Hartfords and Floridas of the world. But he had to. Larmer was hurt, Matteau and Noonan were ineffective, Kovalev was unreliable. Campbell never dreamed he'd be searching for his playoff goalie three games before the end of the regular season, but Richter hadn't lived up to his number one status and Healy hadn't completely stolen the job. The playoff marathon was looming, and Campbell's club was in an all-out sprint just to reach the starting line.

"When I came into New York, as a player and as a coach, I always looked at the New York players as being cocky, overpaid, pompous players. Now that I'm one of these cocky, overpaid, pompous guys, I see that's wrong. These guys are humble, quiet guys. They were traded here, acquired here, or drafted here. I came here because it was a job, not because I liked the city routine, or the Hollywood people in the seats, or the limo scene. The only time I ever rode in a limo before I came here was at my wedding.

"But I'm starting to wonder. Are we caught up in it? Is this why we've developed our bad habits? And I don't mean to paint everybody with the same brush."

Messier, Leetch, and Richter lived in Manhattan the last few years. Lowe moved his family in this year. Noonan and Kypreos then made it five bachelors downtown.

"That bothers me, too. Some guys can handle it. I talked to Noonan, he hasn't been playing well. I've given these guys the benefit of the doubt. Totally. Because they won the Cup. Now I'm just full of it. The mistakes we're making. I've read before about where I'm a quiet, nice guy. I'm not. I've fuckin' had it.

"But at this stage of the season, I've been around long enough to know that if you do go bombastic, players have the tendency—I've seen it before with guys—to just say, 'Hey, it's a nice day out. The leaves are coming out. I can write this off.' There are many built-in excuses here. We've got a free year [because of the lockout]. Reporters know it, they've said to us before, it's a crazy season. We can come back next year and do it."

The one Ranger Campbell totally exonerated was Messier. Incredibly, considering the esteem with which he was held when the year began, the captain had actually gained more of the coach's respect. At the age of thirty-four, after cashing a check for $3.65 million and after signing a contract that guaranteed him $11.9 million and a lavish rest of his life, Messier was trying harder than anyone. He was taking the season as hard as Campbell was.

"He's probably more dejected than I am, in the sense that he's supported some of these guys that I questioned earlier. These guys are letting him down. He's a great promoter of Stephane Matteau. He's a great promoter of Alex Kovalev. He can't understand what's going on. I put Alex Kovalev with Mess last night in the second period to get us going. Going into the third I said, 'I can't do that. I've been trying to get these guys going too much by putting them with other people.' Am I going to wreck one good line to get guys going? He doesn't understand why these guys are playing the way they are.

"I don't want to be a Mark Messier follower saying, 'Oh, he's the guru.' But he's done everything. He's helped me all along. We discuss a lot of things. It's been great. When things have gotten tough, he's gone out and played great games. And last night, he was the only one who got mad!

"For anyone who's accusing Mike Keenan of being too hard last year, bullshit. I'd like to rent Mike Keenan right now for a day, bring him back in here. I should. Because his attitude is right. What Mike did was he went to the very heart and soul of these players and challenged them. I've got to now."

Can you do it, Campbell was asked.

"Yes I can."

Will they buy it?

"I don't give a fuck if they don't buy it. I can present it technically. I can go to the video and I can ask questions. Mike would ask questions if you had a bad game like, 'Where were you last night? What did you do? You just don't have it.' I understand him more and more. His attitude was when the owners come to him and put the gun to his head, he turns the gun on his players. Mike, he manufactures chaos and pressure within our room. If you can handle that, then you can handle the opposition very easily. I understand it entirely.

"I'm a competitive guy. I want to win a coin toss. Sports has been my chosen path my whole life. I have to win at sports or I look at myself as a failure. I look back at scenes I've been in, and I can only remember when I lost, not when I won.

"The worst part for me in sports is the feeling when your eyes open the next morning, if you ever get them closed the night before. The hangover that you produce from losing is so awful. And the ecstasy from winning is so great the next morning that it permeates me totally. I've got to somehow figure out how to handle it. Because this is crazy. Yesterday [my son] Gregory told me he got a 95 on his project. One traffic light later on the road I said, 'A 95, great.' He said, 'What were you thinking about, Dad?' Lauren and Courtney have been excellent. Whether they're keeping it in, I don't know. My wife's been through everything with me. All hockey wives, particularly after the game, they're the sounding boards all the way home. They just sit there and nod and go, 'Uh, huh.' And when they do say something, you snap at them and say, 'What do you know?' So they do the right thing. 'Uh, huh, you're right. I agree.' And they listen to you harp and harp and harp all the way home."

Two hours later, Campbell's message to his team was blunt and brief: "We won last night, but I'm not gonna come in here and kiss everybody's hand and say you did a great job. There are fundamental things that have to be changed if we're gonna be successful later on. We may be able to get into the playoffs, but how successful are we gonna be when the stakes get higher and teams play more disciplined? If we don't clean up our act, we're gonna be in trouble. I'm getting tired of hearing this crap about 'I'd rather be in this room than the other room because we're Stanley Cup winners.' We've got to quit fooling ourselves, stop shooting ourselves in the foot."

Campbell didn't end up showing the team its mistakes on video. "Instead, we talked about it. 'Adam, you can't pass the puck across and give it away with thirty seconds left. Jeff, you can't play with a lack of confidence. Brian, you can't run over there. Mess, you can't give the puck away.' We picked on the big guys. They needed it. They wanted to hear that."

For Campbell, the idea that the regular season meant nothing more than a 48-game warm-up was an exasperating one. But for the players, whose belief in themselves was essential to their ability to prepare for the next stage, it was a necessary fiction. Their side of the issue was eloquently expressed that night by Messier, as he stretched himself flat on his aching back and contemplated the question: through all the ups and downs, with all the awful games, how have the players remained united?

"Because of the experiences you go through when you win a championship together," he said. "Any other year, any other time, if we wouldn't have shared the experiences of last year, perhaps we would have come unraveled by now. It's so important when you have a good team like we are. You're not always going to have a good year like last year, I don't care how many good players you have. Some people are going to have off-years. That's just the way it is. This year seems to be one of those years when a lot of things, the schedule's been against us, teams are obviously prepared for us, we're having off-years. Through all that, we have remained united. We really believe in each other.

"When you win together, it becomes so deeply ingrained. The old saying, 'Win today and walk together forever.' Now, the guys probably don't even realize it because they haven't been in the game long enough, but it's so true. Right now I see it as clear as ever. I see it as one of the reasons we haven't become unraveled, and why we still are quite capable of winning the Stanley Cup again, and why we are going to be quite dangerous."

To be dangerous, the Rangers needed one hot goalie on a roll. But for the last four games, Richter-or-Healy had become a hard question for Campbell. Richter was the obvious answer, of course; he was the guy who had won a Cup. He was the more talented goalie on the scouting sheets. He was the safe choice. But Healy was currently playing better. The unorthodox flopper with the goofy old helmet who stopped pucks with every part of his body had climbed beside Richter on the depth chart.

Both exuded an air of supreme confidence when asked about Campbell's goaltending question.

Richter: "Why is there a question? How has there become a question? Have I not played well the last few games? I think it's an easy thing to say I'm not playing well. I think I've played more consistently than I did last year, for sure."

Healy: "As difficult as it is, it's a good position for him to be in. All coaches would like to have a team where they can look down the bench and all the players are playing well."

On the night before the Islander game, neither goalie knew who was going to play. Well after midnight, Campbell paced the darkened streets of Rye with his golden Labrador retriever, Oliver, still uncertain what to do. Finally, he chose Richter.

"The fact has always remained, Richter took us to the promised land last year and we expected him to take us to the promised land this year," Campbell said. "I talked to enough people, assistant coaches, and Neil. I got some good feedback."

He could have chosen Healy, because it made no difference which goalie got the word at the morning skate. The Rangers stunk again. Matteau scored his first goal in 26 games, but Soderstrom stopped 20 of the Rangers' 21 first-period shots and 46 overall. Messier played in pain and was ineffective. Ray Ferraro scored two goals in a 4–2 Islander victory that extended the Rangers' agony for two more days.

Hartford eliminated itself by losing that night, but Montreal and Florida were still hanging on. The Rangers needed to win one of their last two games, either Sunday afternoon at the Spectrum against the Atlantic Division champion Flyers, who were the Rangers' possible first-round playoff foe, or Tuesday against Florida at the Garden.

Campbell's choice of goalie for Philly was easy. He told Healy before the team left on Saturday that it was his game.

"I've got to," Campbell later explained. "Healy came in and won [against the Lightning]. We came back with Richter. He didn't win. I've got to base it on winning."

The bus pulled out of Rye for the three-hour trip down the Jersey Turnpike without Messier. His back simply needed a break. He and Campbell knew how important the game was, but they considered the consequences of Messier playing and ruining himself before the playoffs even began. "If you sit out Philly and we win, you can sit out the Florida game, too," Campbell told him. "That'll give your back a week to rest. If we have to win the Florida game, and your back feels well enough to play, at least you'll have had a few days off."

In the dressing room before the game, Lowe reminded his teammates of their disabled captain. The team's pregame chat became a sermon on Messier's influence.

"Mark did it for us all year," Lowe said. "Let's do this for him. If we're going to do anything special for Mess, it's have a gutsy performance. We have to show that we're determined to win."

On this day, they were. Beukeboom hit every attacking Flyer in sight. Leetch scored two goals. Healy stopped 24 shots. Graves, Verbeek, and Larmer led a band of forechecking wingers in working over the Flyers, who had nothing at stake. Centers Nedved, Nemchinov, and LaFayette stepped up and did their part to fill the huge hole left by Messier's absence.

The 2–0 clincher was probably assured 4:25 into the game, sixteen seconds into the game's first power play. Lindros took a shot that hit a sliding Beukeboom in the pants. Strangely, the puck took an acute path back toward the shooter and struck the mammoth center under the left eye. Lindros crumpled to the ice and lay in the left circle for several minutes while a trainer tried to stop the flow of blood from the cut under his eye.

The scary injury—Lindros developed a blood clot in his eye that temporarily blurred his vision and sidelined him for ten days, through Game 3 of the playoffs' first round—emotionally drained the Flyers and flattened the atmosphere of this potential playoff preview.

Instead of drooping with their opponents, the Rangers surged. Leetch scored on a power play at 8:21. The Rangers carefully protected that slim lead until 16:27 of the second, when their superstar defenseman instinctively stepped up to intercept a pass in the Flyers' zone and rifled a slapper through Dominic Roussel's pads.

From his brownstone, Messier watched the Rangers nurse their lead through the entire third period—while undergoing acupuncture. Messier hated the needles poking through his skin the first time, but he liked the effect. So after a battery of diagnostic tests taken earlier in the week showed no disc or other structural problems, the Rangers and Messier agreed to try the unconventional treatment to prepare him for Game 1.

The bus ride home from Philadelphia was the Rangers' best all year, despite the bumper-to-bumper Jersey Shore traffic that turned the trip into a four-hour odyssey. The Rangers were in no rush. The season finale meant nothing now. The playoff-pressure atmosphere that had gripped the club for nearly a month was now loosened for a week.

Messier reported to practice the next day smiling. A few pinpricks, a playoff berth, and a great night's sleep made May 1 one of the most relaxing days at Rye all year. Checketts called to congratulate Campbell. Messier didn't practice. While his teammates did, medical trainer Jim Ramsay slapped heat, ice, and electrostimulation treatments on his back.

After the dressing room cleared, Messier admitted that he had not been and would not be consulted on the new biggest question of Campbell's brief coaching career: who starts Game 1 of the playoffs, Healy or Richter? Since the Rangers' final seeding and playoff opponent had yet to be determined, the final factors that weigh in every goaltending decision were not yet there for Campbell.

"It gets too complicated if there are too many ideas in his head," said Messier, explaining why he planned to stay out of Campbell's office on this one. "He'll go with Ricky. It's the way it's gone all year. If it doesn't go our way with Ricky, he can always come back with Healy, who has played that role tremendously. It's the way we've done it all year. You don't change now."

But in the days that followed, Campbell did change. Twice.

A False Spring

10

The season finale against Florida on Tuesday, May 2, meant little to the Rangers after Buffalo won the night before, virtually assuring the Rangers of the eighth playoff seed and a series against Quebec or Pittsburgh, the still-to-be determined winner of a fierce fight for first place. The Rangers were 22-22-3, so there was the minor matter of dressing up their poor regular season by finishing above .500.

The game was supposed to be nothing more than a tune-up, another chance for Messier to rest his back and for Lowe to rest a sprained neck that had bothered him for weeks. Except it cost Glenn Healy his Game 1 playoff start.

In a surprise to virtually everyone in and around the organization, Campbell started Healy against the Panthers, fully intending to start him in the playoff opener as well. "The mind-set we'd had for over a month now was winning the next game, just the next game," Campbell told himself. "And that's what we'd be trying to do now."

But the Rangers lost to Florida, 4–3. Healy played poorly. And Campbell found himself second-guessing his choice. "It was kind of a nothing game, but we went out trying to win it," he said. "He let some soft goals in. I said, 'Gee. But he won such a big game in Philly.' I was really in a bind who to start. I really didn't know."

Healy's loss gave Campbell a reason to return to the preseason blueprint and start Richter. It enabled him to re-create the 1994 championship attitude, which Messier helped establish on Thursday when he said, "For us, anything short of winning the Stanley Cup again this year can't be considered a good year."

Since the Nordiques and Penguins had one more game left on their schedules to determine first and second in the Northeast, Campbell contemplated his goalie choice on Wednesday and planned a general practice. Before the players arrived, he moved Nedved's locker across the room, placing the young center between Messier and Lowe.

Reasoned Campbell, "Mark and Kevin are so intense during the playoffs, that if he's between them physically . . . all year long he sat across from them. Now he's sitting with them, just to hear things they say to each other when they're talking across him."

Messier felt great after his second and third session with the acupuncturist, but he went for another MRI exam Wednesday just to reconfirm that his back was as close to 100 percent as it was going to get before the 1995 marathon began. He reported to Rye Thursday morning prepared to ready his mates for the Quebec Nordiques.

Privately, the Rangers were delighted when they drew Quebec instead of Pittsburgh. The Nordiques were a young club directed by a rookie GM, Pierre Lacroix, and coached by another rookie, Marc Crawford. After missing the playoffs the year before, they rebuilt their team at the 1994 draft in Hartford with stunning success. They traded smooth center Mats Sundin and rugged defenseman Garth Butcher to Toronto for rugged left wing Wendel Clark and defenseman Sylvain Lefebvre. That same day they sent center Ron Sutter and the ninth overall pick in the draft to the Islanders for defenseman Uwe Krupp and the Isles' tenth overall pick.

Quebec enjoyed a fabulous 30-13-5 season in which it scored an NHL-high 185 goals. Joe Sakic finished fourth in scoring, centering a line with the intense Clark and the crafty Andrei Kovalenko. Rookie Peter Forsberg, one of the blue chips acquired in the bombshell trade for Eric Lindros at the 1992 draft, cracked the Top 15 in points with a Calder Trophy–winning season centering the second line with right wing Owen Nolan, who finished tied for third in the NHL with 30 goals, and defensive-minded Claude Lapointe. Even Quebec's third line, Valeri Kamensky–Mike Ricci–Scott Young, was a dangerous offensive trio. And when the Nords threw Chris Simon, Bob Bassen, and Adam Deadmarsh on the ice, their opponents were forced to face a buzzing, forechecking unit that could skate, hit, and fight.

Goaltending and defense were the areas the Rangers hoped to exploit. Stephane Fiset was twenty-four and had never started a Stanley Cup playoff game in his four-year career. His backup, Jocelyn Thibault, was twenty and only an NHL sophomore.

Krupp and ex-Devil Craig Wolanin were formidably sized and skilled defensemen, but neither possessed great speed. Wolanin played with Lefebvre. Krupp paired with Steven Finn, a plodding banger. Adam Foote and Janne Laukkanen were the third defensive duo.

Quebec's terrific 1995 regular season was compensation for five miserable years in which Quebec City became Siberia for the NHL's English-speaking players because of its high taxes and predominantly French culture. After a league-worst record in 1990–91 won the Nords the right to select Lindros first overall in the amateur draft, he refused to play there. A year later, at the 1992 draft, owner Marcel Aubut doublecrossed the Rangers by agreeing to trade Lindros to New York minutes after he had permitted Philadelphia to work out a contract pending a trade with the Flyers. One messy arbitration later, Smith was deprived of a fabulous deal when the Flyers were awarded Lindros, and Quebec received $15 million, Steve Duchesne, Peter Forsberg, Ron Hextall, Kerry Huffman, Mike Ricci, Chris Simon, and the Flyers' first-round draft picks in 1993 and 1994. (The Rangers were prepared to send $12 million, John Vanbiesbrouck, Doug Weight, Alexei Kovalev, Tony Amonte, and first-round picks in 1993 and 1995.) Four years later, the ransom money was gone, but the flock of players stockpiled directly or indirectly via the assets acquired for Lindros included Forsberg, Ricci, Simon, Bassen, and Deadmarsh.

Despite a year-long race with Pittsburgh, the Nordiques had endured very few bumps and felt very little pressure in the shortened season. Messier knew from the Oilers' early years that the transition from regular-season joy ride to playoff pressure cooker was difficult to make, especially against a veteran team that knew what Stanley Cup expectations did to one's psyche.

"If we can get on them fast, take a game up there, put them under the gun," Messier said, "we'll be in good shape."

The Nordiques already had been tentatively sold for $75 million to a Denver-based communications group, COMSAT, and the provincial government was embroiled in desperate negotiations to keep them in Quebec. Quebec City viewed the playoffs as the Nordiques' chance to provide the fondest of farewells, a Cup parade. The Rangers wanted to raise the fearful possibility of a disastrous first-round defeat as soon as possible by taking control of what they knew would be a long series.

Lowe and Messier went to work on the Rangers' psyche, just as they had a year ago. Back then home-ice advantage meant everything because they owned it. Now it meant little. A year ago the dominant regular season forecast Stanley Cup success; now Lowe wanted his teammates to buy into the notion that the slates were wiped clean when the regular season ended.

Campbell did his part to rekindle 1994. On Friday, he skated over to Richter during practice and said, "You're going tomorrow." Just as Messier had predicted.

MSG Network did its part, too. It produced a highlight film of the 22-23-3 season that somehow made the Rangers look like defending Stanley Cup champions. The day before Game 1, with the song "Desire" accompanying the film clips, the Rangers watched themselves score big goals, make big hits. Messier beat up Haller. Kypreos bombed Washington's Calle Johansson. Beukeboom dropped half the NHL. Leetch dazzled and Kovalev dangled, Zubov scored and Nedved scored and the video opened with the banner going up and closed with the Cup shining in their eyes.

The next night, the Rangers burst out of their dressing room for the legitimate start of their Stanley Cup defense. They found a lounge singer badly brutalizing Elvis Presley's "Hunka Hunka Burning Love" with a guitar, an amp, and a microphone, sitting on a string of hideous burgundy carpet runners stretched across the Rangers' zone. Richter had to roll one carpet aside just to scrape up the smooth ice in his crease. The Rangers couldn't circle around in their end to loosen up without stopping to leap over the runners. Smith fumed, complained to the league that night, and got a weak note of apology after the first period from Lacroix. "I'm sorry," he wrote. "It won't happen again."

"But that's like saying, 'I won't tamper anymore,'" Smith muttered.

Yet it was neither the lousy lounge act, the Rangers' Stanley Cup wisdom, nor the young Nordiques' vastly superior firepower that decided Game 1. It was a pocket-sized camera, one of the Canadian Broadcasting Company's two tiny mechanical eyewitnesses strapped to the roof of each net for Hockey Night in Canada's coverage, that played the deciding role in the game.

Video helped kill the Rangers, 5–4, in Game 1 because the tiny recorder detected what referee Don Koharski could not possibly see: Richter's glove a scant few inches behind the goal line when it snapped Joe Sakic's shot out of the air and slapped it down a few inches in front of the goal line midway through the third period.

Until then, the Rangers were in control of a game that contradicted their regular season. They grabbed a two-goal lead because their underachieving supporting cast backed the usual domination of Graves, Messier, and Verbeek. Kovalev played as if he was still the blossoming superstar who helped bury New Jersey and Vancouver a year ago and this was Game 8 of the 1994 finals. Nemchinov and Kypreos skated and forechecked as if they had been magically dipped in the Stanley Cup itself. Two power-play goals by Graves, a slap shot through traffic by Karpovtsev directly off Nemchinov's winning faceoff, and Kovalev's dunk off a slick Zubov feed gave the Rangers a 4–2 lead going into the third period.

The building where the Nords had gone 19-1-4 over the regular season was all but silent nine minutes into the third period as the Rangers blanketed Quebec's forwards. Although the Rangers had lost quite a few games when they were tied or behind after two periods, they were 15-0-1 in games where they led going into the third; the lead that yielded the tie was just one goal.

But Quebec's comeback began when Simon unleashed a high bullet from inside the blue line that caromed off the glass behind the net. Sakic at the doorstep batted it off Richter's mask, into the air, and into the goalie's glove. Koharski couldn't tell that the puck had fluttered in the air behind the goal line. Neither could two of the usual camera angles. Only the mechanical moving video camera taped to the top back piece of the net iron spotted the goal. It took several minutes to watch the replays, while both sides held their breath.

"If they tell me it's inconclusive, I've got to call it no goal, Joe," Koharski told Sakic, Quebec's captain. "I never saw it go in. The goal judge said it didn't go in. If they look at it upstairs and tell me it's inconclusive, then I've got to call it no goal."

Koharski held the phone linking the scorer's table and the replay booth to his ear. Finally, video official Jim Christison relayed the news. "It went in," Christison said. "The camera in the net got it right. If we didn't have that camera, Don, we never would have been able to call it. You couldn't tell from the other angles. But there's no doubt it was in."

The Rangers were obviously unnerved by the fluke goal, because they suddenly could not repel the energetic thrust unleashed by the Nords. Bassen tied the game at 14:07 when he knocked Larmer down in the corner, moved alone to the front of the net, and buried Nolan's feed behind Richter. And Sakic won it with 0:37.7 seconds remaining in regulation. Leetch gambled deep in Quebec's zone, but Sakic got the puck from Krupp and countered one-on-one against Beukeboom. The left-handed shooter from high in the slot used the big defenseman as a screen and snapped a perfect low dart off the right post to complete a personal hat trick and a stunning comeback for the Nords.

Yet Messier's postgame sermon instructed his disciples to feel confidence, not disappointment—to be angry, not frustrated. "First of all, we had 'em. We just didn't finish 'em," Messier said with a gleam, not a glare, in his eyes. "If we execute and do the things we should be able to, we'll beat them."

Later that night, Lowe acknowledged that letting Quebec get off to such a thrilling start was no way to apply pressure to a young team. But "after the way that game went, the way we played, I knew we would beat them," Messier said. "And I think they knew we would."

Brian Noonan suffered a severely pulled groin in Game 1, so Matteau returned to the lineup for Game 2 after being unceremoniously scratched for the opener. Osborne for Loney was the second of Campbell's three lineup changes. The third was Healy for Richter.

After the opening loss, Lowe offered the most astute assessment, although he was again putting a necessary spin on the situation with which he was presented. When asked why the Rangers' experience couldn't prevent the third-period collapse, he said, "You show your experience not so much from the loss, but how you regroup for the next game."

On Monday May 8, the edge returned. Their championship form flickered back to life as they played like the skilled, deep, tough team Smith and Campbell thought they had. They rendered the goaltending question moot, blowing the Nordiques out of Le Colisée, 8–3. The game wasn't even that close.

Nemchinov scored two goals, the first off the kind of work by Matteau that was last seen in the Devils series. Nedved took seven shots and scored two goals. Messier notched the 100th goal of his Stanley Cup career, assisted on Larmer's game-opening shorthanded goal, won a thousand face-offs, and ignored his ailing back. Kovalev assisted on three goals and absorbed a vicious elbow from Clark without stopping. Leetch took a punch from Owen Nolan, one of the few times a Nordique got close to him. Clark speared Verbeek, who simply continued to pepper the Nordiques with hard hits all over the ice.

"We're not blind," Quebec coach Marc Crawford said between Games 2 and 3. "We know they outplayed us in two games except for the third period of the first game."

The Nordiques weren't blind, just dumb. In Game 3 they elected to invade New York by trying to intimidate the Rangers. They foolishly attempted to turn the series into a Cold War in which they targeted the Rangers' three most dangerous Russians, Zubov, Kovalev, and Nemchinov.

They sat one of their own Russians, Kamensky, who might have been injured but was definitely contributing little, and dressed Bill Huard, a goon.

Misguided as the strategy would have been in Games 1 and 2 at home, it was a ridiculous tactic to employ at the Garden, where the Monster was sure to make an emotional playoff return. They quickly targeted Clark as the main villain.

Although the NHL had fined Clark $1,000 for his unpenalized Game 2 elbow on Kovalev, the Nords again unleashed the muscular Saskatchewan farm boy against the baby-faced star. Instead of working the corners to make room for Sakic, Clark looked like a buffoon chasing Kovalev around the rink. For every check he delivered, Kovalev shook free to make a play.

The Garden erupted late in the first period only a few seconds after Kovalev lifted himself off the ice following a Clark wallop. Clark had taken off with the puck, but Zubov stopped him with a poke check just inside the blue line. Kovalev grabbed the turnover and countered crisply; he sped deep, feathered a pass back into the slot, and watched Zubov bury it behind Fiset. He then taunted the Nordiques' bench by pointing to Quebec's net with his stick.

"I showed them, 'Maybe you can hurt us, but we'll score goals,'" Kovalev said. "I don't think, 'You hurt me this time, next time I'll hurt you.' I just think I want to score a goal and win the game."

"When somebody scores," Zubov said, "that hurts worse than a hit."

The Rangers took a 3–1 lead on goals by Zubov and Nemchinov. But the Nordiques rallied—not behind the Clark-Sakic-Kovalenko line, which was shut out for the second straight game, but on goals past Healy by Forsberg and Nolan, now playing with Bassen instead of Lapointe.

And then Ricci roughed Nedved, who had learned enough all season and in this round to know this was the time to show toughness not by retaliating, but by walking away. Two seconds after the power play expired, with 7:18 left in the game, Nedved's discipline paid off. Leetch backhanded a puck that plopped off the mesh atop the net and into the crease past Fiset's right skate for the 4–3 victory that gave the Rangers command of the series.

Brian Burke, the NHL's czar of discipline, summoned Smith and Lacroix to his Sixth Avenue office on the day of Game 4. He didn't like having to fine Clark $1,000 for the Game 2 elbow. He didn't like having to review Clark's slash of Kovalev in Game 3, an overt act that prompted Campbell to send his enforcer, Kocur, over the boards for a brief chat with the Nordiques' incorrigible Clark and the gifted Sakic.

"Boys, if it's going to be like this, I'm just going to start swinging my stick as hard as I've seen you swing your sticks," Kocur had warned. "I don't know where it's gonna hit and when it's gonna hit."

Burke met with the two GMs for thirty minutes. "Both of you stop bitching about the officiating. Watch your team's cheap shots and head-hunting. Make sure they cut out all the bullshit after the whistles. Keep it clean."

The Rangers had not been choirboys, either, but they had restricted their conduct to heavy hits while the puck was in play. Beukeboom was the one Ranger to pound Clark; he also bombed Nolan and Huard. Verbeek continued to poke and jab, to pester and irritate in the manner that had made Tikkanen so valuable the spring before.

"You're just not going to go out and say, 'Go out and beat that guy up,'" Campbell admitted. "Fighting is not the answer. Especially in this position."

Joey Kocur understood that fully. At the age of thirty, despite a right hand that had been surgically repaired four times, he was still one of the NHL's most feared punchers. In 1989 he shattered the face of the Is-landers' Brad Dalgarno, a punch so thunderous that Dalgarno quit hockey for a year to recuperate and reconsider if playing tough guy in the NHL was worth it.

Kocur played all 48 regular-season games, but scored only one goal. He has played 640 games over an eleven-year NHL career and scored just 69 goals. He has, however, amassed 2,202 penalty minutes. He has had several hundred fights, most with the other team's fighter. It's part of hockey's unwritten rule: intimidate the other guys.

But in the playoffs, intimidation tactics often fail. They certainly weren't bothering the Rangers. Kocur knew he was Campbell's holstered weapon, to be fired if the Rangers got desperate, but not before. Certainly not with the series going their way.

"Yeah, we talked about how we don't want to retaliate," Kocur said. "But nobody's ever come up and told me not to fight. It never has happened in my career and never will happen. They may say something like, 'It might be in the team's better interest not to when the game starts.' But as the game goes on, you don't know what's going to happen. I've got to go out there and make sure guys like Wendel [Clark] know that at some point, at some point it's enough."

And did Quebec cross that line?

"Absolutely. They crossed the line in the first game with the cheap shots. But at this point, we have to turn the other cheek. We're winning.

The league has to look into this a little closer. It is not the players' job to police the other team. It's the referee's."

If 1994 was the bountiful payback for a franchise's fifty-four years of bad luck, Game 4 was one final dividend. One of the wackiest possible interpretations of a weird play cost Quebec a first-period goal that probably would have buried the Rangers for the night and evened this best-of-seven series.

The Nordiques were as smart in Game 4 as they were stupid in Game 3, but the Rangers escaped a terrible first period trailing only 2–0. Healy was awful; the score could easily have been 5–0. It would have been 3–0 were it not for the insanity that started with a swat.

The Rangers were on a power play in the final minute of the period. Kovalev had the puck along the boards when Wolanin, using his stick like a whip, whacked Kovalev in the middle of the back. Kovalev collapsed to the ice as if he were shot. Sakic, the closest Nordique to the fallen Ranger, took the puck and headed up ice.

Referee Andy van Hellemond did not see Wolanin's swat. He noticed Kovalev motionless on the ice a few seconds later, but correctly allowed Sakic to complete his rush down right wing. Sakic fanned on his first shot, but then recaptured the puck before Zubov could collect it and sent a backhander from an acute angle past Healy, who had lost his balance on Sakic's first attempt and was stumbling badly around the crease when the second shot got by him.

Amazingly, van Hellemond disallowed the goal.

"There was a whistle," he told an enraged Crawford. "I did blow it before Sakic went in and before the goal was scored."

"There was no whistle," Crawford screamed back. "How could you call that?"

While the Nordiques ranted and raved, Kovalev was helped to his feet and escorted into the dressing room. Ranger team doctor Bart Nisonson, summoning the latest advances in modern sports medicine, applied a bag of ice to the welt. When the intermission ended, the Russian was back from the dead.

So was Richter. Campbell pulled Healy after his dreadful performance. Richter steadied the game while the Rangers came to life. Kovalev burned the Nordiques in the second period's fifth minute, when he read Matteau's excellent checking pressure (yes, Matteau, another regular-season dud who became a born-again playoff producer once he got back into the lineup following his Game 1 benching) and stole a Kovalenko pass. He fed

Nemchinov, who found Leetch high in the slot. With Matteau screening young Thibault, Leetch's shot whizzed past Matteau's left hip and under the goalie's glove and arm at 4:28.

Leetch returned Kovalev's assist at 2:03 of the third. From the left point he threaded a long diagonal pass to the lower right circle. Kovalev's series-leading seventh point was a dart before Thibault could slide across. It tied it 2–2 as Madison Square Garden went wild.

Richter was sensational. He saved the game with 5:30 left, when Sakic broke in alone and made two breakaway moves before Richter turned aside his backhander to force overtime. But the Rangers lost Beukeboom with 1:43 left in regulation. He went to blast Nolan at center ice, but the Nordiques' winger saw the hit in time and got his shoulder and elbow into Beukeboom's face just as the defenseman hit him. Beukeboom caught the worst of it, suffering a concussion.

Quebec dominated the overtime, outshooting the Rangers 5–2, but Richter dominated the shooters. He kept the game alive by stopping Clark's point-blank wrist shot from the slot at 2:27 and smothering Clark's tap-in try with the rebound. Thibault replied three minutes later when he caught Nedved's breakaway wrist shot in the chest.

Eight minutes in, Richter skated out to control a dump-in. From the outer rim of the left circle he wound the puck behind his net to Karpovtsev, who chipped it off the boards to Leetch. The Nordiques, sensing they had the Rangers on their heels, forechecked hard. Too hard. Leetch ricocheted a long diagonal pass off the right-wing boards that caught Quebec's three forwards, Sakic, Bassen, and Young, in the Rangers' zone below the circles.

The pass found Larmer just short of the red line. He fed a short pass to Nedved, who attacked with speed down right wing. Nedved's burst forced defenseman Janne Laukkanen to back off, which bought Nedved time and open ice. He dished the puck back to Larmer at the top rim of the right circle. Larmer cut toward the middle, dipped his shoulder as if to shoot, kept cutting around the sliding Laukkanen, and fired a wrist shot that Adam Foote went down to block.

All five Nordiques were out of position, the two defensemen on the ice trying to block Larmer's shot, the three forwards hustling to get back into the play. Thibault stopped Larmer's wrist shot, but Larmer grabbed his own rebound and snapped it behind the helpless goaltender to complete the comeback.

"Here We Go Again" was how one banner put it as the Garden rocked.

In the bowels of the building, Lacroix and Crawford were apoplectic. They brandished a videotape that clearly produced the sounds of Sakic's puck entering the net before van Hellemond blew his whistle so the trainers could attend to Kovalev. Shrieking that he had the evidence to overturn the verdict, Lacroix vowed to protest the game in a sport that has no provision for protest.

"A protest?" Burke asked. "That's a new one on me."

The NHL executive did admit that van Hellemond's call, while technically correct, was an error in judgment. The ref might have wanted to blow his whistle after Sakic fanned on his first shot, and he might have thought he blew his whistle before the puck entered the net, but as Burke said on reviewing the tape immediately after the game, "It was troubling to reconcile the sound of the tape. It's clear you hear the whistle after the puck's in the net."

About an hour later, on the short drive from the Garden to his apartment, Smith's portable phone rang. It was Checketts, as pumped up about the overtime win as was Smith.

"Thank God we didn't trade Nedved," Checketts said. "He's going to be a great player."

"Dave, we should remember this call when we're in the dead of winter and things are going wrong. It's why we have to be patient sometimes, even when everybody's at our throats."

So it was back to Quebec, and back to Richter for Game 5. Ignored for three games, aware that his season might be over if Healy stayed hot and kept winning, Richter had not fallen apart. He did not sit in the corner and sulk while Healy won Games 2 and 3. For relaxation he was reading the biography of Japanese home run king Sadaharu Oh. For concentration he stayed out late after practice and drilled himself on not overplaying shots by coming too far out of his net. And he tried not to guess when his next game would be.

"That only gets you into trouble," he said.

What Campbell didn't know then, but soon deduced, was how angry Healy was. The good-natured backup goalie, who is never at a loss for words, did not speak to his coach again all series.

The NHL spoke up regarding Lacroix's protest, promptly rejecting it. "Results are not subject to protest," public relations VP Arthur Pincus announced to nobody's surprise.

The Rangers played the fifth game without Beukeboom, still woozy from his collision with Nolan. The Nordiques played with a sense of urgency shared by a city fearing this could be its last NHL game. Both teams played under the watchful whistle of sheriff Kerry Fraser, who promised to call every slash, hook, hold, and cross-check.

For the third straight game, Quebec scored the first goal. They staved off elimination in the first uneventful game of the series by capturing the first period 3–2 and protecting that edge until Young's empty-net goal with 32.1 seconds left. The 4–2 loss sent the Rangers home to clinch, and ensured they would face a better-rested opponent in the second round if they got there, because the second-seeded Flyers finished Buffalo in five, and were poised to inherit the top seed if the Rangers ousted Quebec.

The Rangers scored their two goals in Game 5 on power plays. Their power play was 6-for-22 in the series compared to Quebec's 1-for-21. But as good as the Rangers' power play was, it paled in comparison to the power play Zubov's agent tried to pull a few days before Game 6.

Jay Grossman had gotten nowhere with Smith regarding his client's new contract. He had grown impatient, so he told his boss, Art Kaminsky, to intercede. Kaminsky was once one of the top hockey agents, but his company, Athletes and Artists, also represented a slew of TV news and sports personalities and Kaminsky had moved on to more lucrative matters.

When Grossman complained to him about Smith, Kaminsky agreed to call Checketts and see if he could help get the negotiations moving. It was a foolish maneuver under normal circumstances, but with this timing it was a colossal mistake. Checketts, naturally, told Smith, "You handle it," which meant that Grossman was going to have a harder time than ever.

"I know why he did it," Smith said. "He's afraid of losing Zubie as a client. It was an ignorant, disrespectful thing to do."

If Zubov's contract was bothering him, he certainly didn't show it in Game 6. He only showed why the Nordiques wanted him so badly, and why Lacroix had tried so hard to persuade Smith to trade him for Ricci. All series long the Nordiques lacked an offensive defenseman who could quarterback a power play. All series long Leetch, Zubov, Kovalev, and Nedved had used their quickness to exploit Quebec's relatively immobile defense.

First seed or not, the Nordiques by this point were obviously over-matched. Verbeek flung a power-play goal into the unguarded side of Thibault's net 2:11 into the game after tic-tac-toe passes from Messier and Leetch. Kovalev's masterful breakaway moves made it 2–0 after the Rangers caught Quebec on a line change. Nemchinov scored his fourth goal of the series (he had seven in 47 games during the season) on a rebound of Leetch's shot. Fiset replaced Thibault for the second period, but the Rangers kept coming. Kovalev's fourth goal and ninth point (which tied Leetch for the series high) made it 4–0 at 10:18.

The romp came to a halt at 15:56. With the Rangers on a power play,

Sakic grabbed a loose puck and broke in alone on Richter for a short-handed goal. When Forsberg scored at 5:34 of the third the Garden party stopped. But two minutes later, referee Dan Marouelli banished Simon for ramming Kypreos into the boards from behind. It was an illegal check that got Simon a five-minute major and a game misconduct. The Rangers didn't score on the power play, but the momentum-draining penalty effectively ended the Nordiques' season and, as it turned out, their franchise's twenty-three-year Quebec City history in the WHA and NHL.

It hardly helped Quebec that before the game, the NHL fined and criticized van Hellemond for "a glaring error in judgment" in his Game 4 mistake. Bettman issued a statement after reviewing the videotape and interviewing the veteran official in which he said "van Hellemond said he did not see the puck enter the net and when he blew the whistle, he was not aware that the goal had been scored. He thought, erroneously, that he was blowing the whistle to stop play. It should be noted that an NHL referee does not blow his whistle with the scoring of a goal. The videotapes show that he was wrong."

Beukeboom made it through the game despite his headache, but Messier finished with a massive toothache that required medical attention after he took a Wolanin shot in the left side of the jaw with 4:50 left. He finished the game, taking the final faceoff through clenched teeth, but needed nine stitches to close the wound.

When it was over, when the Rangers and Nordiques shook hands at center ice, the Monster started cranking itself up for Round Two. "We want Hextall," it roared.

The Rangers were in no mood to look ahead to the Flyers so quickly. Messier's mouth was stuffed with gauze, so Lowe took it upon himself to verbally stroke the supporting cast that awoke so dramatically. Nedved, Nemchinov, and Matteau each had an excellent series, which nobody could have predicted. And Kovalev was the big story of the series. He outscored Clark, the forward with whom he was most often matched, 4–1 in goals and 9–2 in points. He outclassed Quebec's plodding defense and infuriated the entire Nordiques organization by absorbing the cheap shots without retaliation, taunting them after key goals, and unwittingly starting the controversy that they believed cost them Game 4.

"Clark did in three games," Campbell said, "what I couldn't do in four months."

Kovalev's reply spoke for the team, the fans, and all who hoped that it was the struggles of the first four months of the year that were a mirage, not the last six games. "It's the playoffs," he said. "Because the team played better, that's why I played better."

Skating on Empty

11

Messier began preparing for Eric Lindros by slurping soup and sipping Gatorade. It was not what he had in mind the day after the Rangers vanquished Quebec, but his mouth was too sore from a painful, sleepless night and an afternoon in the dentist's chair. He required X-rays of his badly bruised jaw (they were negative), root canal to clean up the mess made by Wolanin's deflected shot, and the restoration of four chipped teeth. "And they were all originals," Mess mumbled that night at home, where he spent the evening drinking dinner through a straw. "Chewing's still a problem."

Relaxing was Campbell's problem. He caught a stomach virus from someone in his family the day of Game 6 and couldn't keep food down all night. The emotional high of the Rangers' playoff success did not mix well with the nausea and indigestion that hit full blast over the next twenty-four hours. He finally fell asleep at four o'clock, awoke a few hours later, and dragged himself to Rye.

The players got Wednesday, May 17, off. The coach told his players after Game 6 to "savor the accomplishment for a day, enjoy what you've done, and work it out of your system. Come back Thursday ready for work."

Game 1 was scheduled for Sunday afternoon on Fox, so Campbell used Thursday to let the team collect itself, work up a light sweat during a forty-five-minute practice and scrimmage, then train hard on the exercise bikes. Friday was Flyer Day.

Campbell's problem was deciding how to neutralize the Legion of Doom. Not counting the 2–0 playoff clincher on April 1 when Lindros got hurt early, the Flyers' incomparable first unit scored nine goals and 10 assists in winning two of three regular-season games against the Rangers. A Matteau-Kovalev-Noonan checking line didn't work. A strength versus strength matchup with Graves-Messier-Larmer and later Graves-Messier-Verbeek didn't work either.

Campbell really only had one choice: it had to be Messier against Lindros with Leetch and Beukeboom behind the number one line whenever the Legion hit the ice.

At 6–1 and 205, Messier yielded three inches and twenty-four pounds to the talented behemoth. At thirty-four, he yielded twelve years of NHL mileage. Most significantly, he was about to play with a back that his chiropractor had just realigned, with a mouth that was killing him, and after a regular season in which Campbell used and needed every ounce of his physical and mental strength.

Lindros, conversely, was well rested. Once the blood clot in his eye cleared and doctors assured him no permanent damage had been done, the injury proved to be the best thing that could have happened to him. After playing thirty minutes a game throughout the regular season, he got to take ten days off while his team won without him. They took two of the first three from the Sabres, welcomed their captain's return in Game 4 at Buffalo, and behind Lindros's five points bounced the Sabres out quickly enough to earn a week's rest before facing the Rangers.

Messier chose for a variety of good reasons to downplay his personal duel with Lindros. "I don't need that motivation," he said. "Winning is enough for me."

The Flyers' season-long roll troubled Messier, too. All year he had talked about the "snowball that has to build as you get to the playoffs. It grows as you start winning, it grows as you gain confidence and it starts generating its own momentum." The Rangers' 7-4-0 playoff push hardly qualified as a hot streak compared to the Flyers' 25-9-3 run that started the game after GM Bob Clarke acquired LeClair and coach Terry Murray fit him with Lindros and Renberg.

Worse still for the Rangers, Buffalo wasn't buried by the Legion alone. Lindros scored five points in the two games he played, but Renberg and

LeClair combined for only five themselves in the five games. Number two center Rod Brind'Amour scored eight points in the five games. He, left wing Brent Fedyk, and right wing Kevin Dineen lacked the firepower of Quebec's second or third lines, but this trio relied on a persistence that wore down opponents.

After them, the Flyers dressed two adequate lines: Shjon Podein–Craig MacTavish–Patrik Juhlin and Shawn Antoski–Anatoli Semenov–Rob Di-Maio. The wily MacTavish gave the Flyers what he gave the Rangers a year ago, a dependable checker and faceoff man.

Philly's defense lacked a dominant thirty-minute man. Their three units were (in order): Kevin Haller–Eric Desjardins, Petr Svoboda–Karl Dykhuis, Chris Therien–Dimitri Yushkevich. They were, however, physical enough, mobile enough, and offensive-minded enough to give solid two-way support behind the top-heavy top line.

The Rangers' relentless two-man forechecking system was designed to pin the Flyers' young defense in its zone. Throughout Friday's detailed practice, the coaching staff reminded the forecheckers to attack smartly, because Philly's defense loved to jump into the play.

"Don't get caught," Campbell said. "Even if our third guy back has their third guy, don't relax. They'll burn you with their fourth guy. Dykhuis, Desjardins, Haller, Svoboda . . . they all like to follow the play. Don't forget."

And then there was Hextall, strafed by the Rangers the previous spring as an Islander and cruelly demeaned by the Monster. Although his skills were considerably diminished by a string of serious groin injuries, he was as mentally tough a goalie as there was in the NHL. He had been traded by the Flyers to Quebec in the Lindros deal, by Quebec to the Isles in 1993, and by the Isles back to the Flyers a week before the lockout in exchange for Tommy Soderstrom. He bounced back from his horrid 1994 playoff against the Rangers to go 17-9-4, with a 2.89 goals-against average and .890 save percentage.

"I'm not a different goalie," he explained. "Just because you don't play well in a series doesn't mean you're a bad goalie."

Neither Campbell nor Murray backed off on the opening faceoff. It was Messier versus Lindros, strength versus strength. Lindros batted the opening draw to his left, and after only five seconds LeClair had rifled a dangerous, rising bullet high and wide of Richter's glove. Twenty-five seconds later, Lindros slid a low wrist shot from between the circles that Richter kicked aside.

Vancouver won Games 5 and 6 in the 1994 finals by pounding and harassing Leetch. That was Philadelphia's strategy, but it backfired immediately. At 2:57, Koharski penalized Lindros for needlessly cross-checking Leetch in open ice well after Leetch had delivered a pass. Just eleven seconds later, Messier won a faceoff from MacTavish in the circle to Hextall's left. He sent it back to Leetch at the blue line in the middle of the ice. Leetch didn't hesitate; he fired a low slapper that easily sailed past Hextall's glove at 3:08.

Midway through the period, the Flyers still had put only Lindros's one shot on goal. With under a minute to go and the score still 1–0 but the Rangers in control, Dineen elbowed Leetch against the glass at the left point. Koharski caught it. Seconds later Nedved lined up against Lindros in the circle to Hextall's right. Lindros butted his helmet into Nedved's upper chest as the puck was dropped and steamrolled the skinny centerman to the ice. But as he did, Larmer swatted the loose puck back to Leetch. And Nedved, doing just as Campbell and Messier and half the hockey world had told him all year, picked himself off the ice and headed directly for the net. While he did, Lindros coasted high toward Leetch, who slid a quick pass across the ice to Zubov.

Nedved was open. Zubov got the puck past MacTavish. Nedved, still covered with ice shavings, made a nifty move to his backhand and lifted the puck over Hextall with 14.7 seconds left in an eye-popping first period for the Rangers.

For twenty minutes, the blueprint was perfect: Leetch and Beukeboom on defense against the Legion of Doom, Graves-Messier-Verbeek on whenever possible considering the Flyers owned the last line change at home, but Kovalev-Nemchinov-Noonan (back from his groin pull) or Kypreos-Nemchinov-Kovalev leaning on the Flyers' top line whenever Messier's line couldn't get out.

Kovalev and Larmer took hooking penalties a minute apart in the second period, and LeClair's power-play goal at 2:57 of the second made it 2–1. After needing only eleven and sixteen seconds to score on their first two power plays, the Rangers failed on their third midway through the period. But on their fourth, with 4:56 left, it took just thirteen seconds to score. Messier set up along the right boards and flicked a long pass through the slot to Verbeek, who one-timed it from the weak side past Hextall at 15:17.

Messier celebrated the goal with his mates, but when he returned to the bench he felt troubled. He wasn't able to crystallize why he began to worry until ninety-two seconds later, when the Rangers' 1994–95 season began to die.

What looked like an innocuous faceoff to Richter's left between Lindros and Nemchinov turned the period, the game, and the series around. Murray had managed to get his top trio on the ice against the Rangers' weakest defense pair, Wells and Karpovtsev. Alertly, Lindros deliberately batted the puck into the corner, where Nemchinov tried to win it toward Karpovtsev.

Lindros jumped past Nemchinov and bumped Karpovtsev. The massive Flyer positioned his No. 88 jersey in front of both Russians, one 8 for each Ranger as Renberg skated into the corner for the puck and then out with it. As Wells went to the front of the net to neutralize LeClair, Renberg took a shot from the right circle that hit the far post past Richter's left pad.

The red light flashed. Renberg lifted his arms in celebration, but play continued as Koharski waved his arms to signal no goal. Lindros, who had knocked Karpovtsev's stick out of his hands and one of his gloves off, held off Nemchinov with one arm and shoved the rebound back toward the short side with the other. Richter made the save and pressed his body against the post to prevent LeClair from shoving the puck in from the crease. Instead, LeClair poked the puck behind the net and headed for the far post. Richter was flat on his back when he blindly flung his right arm toward the open half of the net. LeClair hoped for something good to happen when he flicked the puck back into the scramble. What happened was, the puck hit Richter, came back to him, and he jammed the puck under the goalie with a helpless Karpovtsev on his knees trying to push LeClair away.

Skill, size, and brute strength had made it 3–2. While the Flyers hugged, the Rangers slumped, and Karpovtsev collected the articles of his equipment strewn on the ice, Messier looked left and right on the bench. He looked at Lowe. Then he looked down and said nothing.

"We don't have what it takes to win this series," he told himself.

He didn't tell anybody else, not even Lowe. But he suspected Lowe was feeling the same dreadful thoughts. He and Messier knew how to read body language on the bench and they knew their own limitations. At the age of thirty-six, with a neck that was killing him, Lowe couldn't handle Lindros, Renberg, or LeClair. Messier was going to lose his battle with No. 88, too.

Suddenly, ominous signs sprouted everywhere: Zubov's fear of Flyers, the defenseman's inability or unwillingness to pay the physical price he had gladly paid against Quebec. How easily the Flyers started to bounce Nedved, Kovalev, and Nemchinov to the ice. Matteau's lethargy. Aches and injuries that rendered Graves, Noonan, and Larmer unproductive.

"I know when you're in a playoff series in the second round, and you're up 3–1, it should almost be a lock on the game," said Messier later. "Our power play was sizzling, they only had 12 shots midway through the game, we were completely dominating. That's when you've gotta be able to start throwing the troops over the boards and not only think about winning this game, but start grinding them down for later in the series. Start punishing their defensemen, start grinding away at Lindros, LeClair, and Renberg, start wearing on them.

"Instead, it was vice versa. We got weaker and they got stronger. We had no gas left in the tanks. And not enough gas tanks."

The Flyers only took three shots at Richter in the third period, but they were by far the better team. With 8:05 left, LeClair split Leetch and Beukeboom and appeared to tie it off another scrum in front, but the goal was disallowed because Koharski blew his whistle after losing sight of the puck an instant before it crossed the line.

Just forty seconds later, Svoboda from the right point wound the puck behind the net, where Lindros waited. Not with size or strength, but with delicate skill he feathered a backhanded pass between Beukeboom's skates for LeClair, who boxed out Leetch, accepted the pass, and from twenty feet whipped the puck past Richter to make it 3–3.

Just over two minutes after that, an errant pass allowed the Rangers a chance to touch up for an icing. But when Richter detected Lindros chasing Leetch, he chose to play the puck rather than make his teammate try to win the race, touch for the icing, and get battered into the glass.

Richter: "Worst-case scenario: Leetchie gets crushed and Eric centers the puck. Second-worst: I pass the puck to the Flyers."

Richter passed the puck to the Flyers. His awful clearing attempt was intercepted by Renberg, who fed Desjardins trailing the play. Desjardins had position on Messier when he took the pass and flung a wrist shot between Richter's pads. It was 4–3 with 4:49 left.

All Campbell could do was put his hands on his hips and glare at his goalie.

Messier might have known the series was over, but he refused to allow the game to end. With twenty seconds to go and Richter off for a sixth attacker, Kovalev shoved him the puck behind the net. He got it to Verbeek, who sent the game into overtime with a backhander over the stunned Hextall with 19.1 seconds left. It was the first time all year the Rangers scored with their goalie pulled in the final seconds.

In the first seven minutes of overtime, the Flyers took six shots on goal to the Rangers' three. Lindros dominated Messier on a shift that ended at

6:58 with a faceoff to Richter's left. MacTavish won the draw from Nedved back to Desjardins at the right point. Matteau's job was to fight through the traffic and not give Desjardins a lane to shoot, but Matteau, who had angered Campbell all year by being out of shape and unwilling to exhibit the drive and effort the team demanded, did not fight through the pick set by Shjon Podein. Matteau gave a halfhearted effort, then allowed Podein to briefly grab his stick. It gave Desjardins time to skate to the top rim of the right circle. He waited until the Nedved-MacTavish duel screened Richter in front of the net before wristing in the goal that won Game 1 at 7:03.

As the Spectrum roared, a fan doused Campbell with beer as he stood helplessly on the bench. The frustrated coach threw a towel, grabbed a player's stick and swung it in the fan's direction, banging the plexiglass behind the bench. Campbell was assessed a gross misconduct and automatically fined $200. He calmed down a day later and joked about it when he said, "A $2,000 Armani suit. Wait till Checketts gets the bill."

What he didn't know was that his captain believed the players were unwilling to pay a far higher price.

Messier might have sensed an inevitable end, but Leetch did not. The defending Conn Smythe Trophy winner was easily the best player on the ice in Game 2. He scored the Rangers' first goal, on a power play 7:35 into the game. He scored the Rangers' second goal, also on a power play, 12:46 into the game. He scored the Rangers' third goal, too, with 8:41 left in regulation, to force another overtime.

But Game 2 was a carbon copy of Game 1, and not only because the Rangers lost in OT again. The Rangers took 2–0 leads out of the first period in both games at the Spectrum, but both were mirages forged by their crisp power play. At even strength, where the contest pitted size, strength, and depth, it was no contest. It wasn't only the Legion of Doom pounding the Rangers into the boards and establishing territorial domination; it was Brind'Amour and Dineen, Therien and Haller, Yushkevich and DiMaio.

The Rangers squandered third-period leads in both games, something they didn't do once during the regular season. Even before Leetch became the first Ranger defenseman to notch a playoff hat trick, and even before Haller won the game by lifting a two-on-one wrist shot over Richter's glove twenty-five seconds into overtime, they were skating on empty.

On the morning after Game 2, Smith didn't believe it possible that his team was down two games to none. "At two o'clock Sunday I was so pumped," the GM said, sounding more like a fan. "Now it's only thirty-six hours later and we're in a hole. It goes to show you how quick things change. A few days ago we beat Quebec and we're on top of the world, we've got Philly worried. Now we lose two games in overtime, and we're in a must-win. If one of the overtimes goes our way, we're in great shape. And we could have won both." He sighed.

"I'm never going to forget something Bobby Clarke told me about this job. He was comparing it to being a player. He said it was a brutal job because the highs weren't high enough, but the lows were too low."

Smith and Clarke got into a light tiff the afternoon before Game 3. The Flyers suspected Richter's leg pads were illegal and asked Burke to inspect them. Rule 22(b) limits a goalie's pads to twelve inches at their extreme width. Richter's pads probably were too wide; most goalie pads expand and shrink over the course of a season, as the material inside the leather casing absorbs ice and sweat and moisture.

When a member of Burke's staff called Smith to tell him Burke decided to measure the pads of Richter and Hextall, Smith called Joe Murphy, who told him, yes, Richter's pads were an inch too wide.

"Don't let Richter know this is happening," Smith told Murphy. "I don't want to upset him."

Murphy instructed equipment manager Mike Folga to tie and compress Richter's pads tightly enough for them to pass inspection. And they did. Not that it mattered; Richter's pads could have each measured three feet wide by four feet high and the Rangers would not have won Game 3.

The series' third game in four days was played in front of the loyalists, who tried desperately to summon the dragon-slayers of last year. But what Messier detected late in Game 1 became painfully obvious before the first period was ten minutes old: this was going to be a short series.

The crowd heckled Hextall, but the goalie was hardly a factor. Two mistakes by Beukeboom helped the Flyers build a 2–0 lead after one period on goals by Dineen and Renberg. On the first, the Rangers' giant defenseman threw the puck up the middle of the ice; Dineen intercepted and fired a forty-five-footer that Richter should have stopped. On the second, Beukeboom tried to dish out a little of what the Rangers were taking. He stretched his 6-5, 230-body and plastered Lindros into the sideboards at the Flyer bench. The only problem was, Beukeboom went too far out of his way to stir up the crowd and his team; he left LeClair and Renberg two-on-one against Leetch. LeClair held the puck long enough to draw Leetch and Richter toward him, and then in textbook two-on-one fashion slid the puck across the ice for Renberg to throw it into the empty half of the net.

A giveaway by Messier led to Dineen's soft goal at 3:07 of the second, a floater between the legs of Lowe and Richter. When Brind'Amour tipped Yushkevich's shot behind the goalie on a power play at 10:23, a helpless Campbell did the only thing he could: he replaced Richter with Healy.

The final was 5–2. The Legion of Doom had a hand in only one goal. Fifteen other Flyers were killing the Rangers, too.

"We obviously had a stinker," Campbell said in a hoarse voice after the game. "It was totally disheartening."

For the first time all season, Messier declined to answer questions when he met the media. "I'm going to make this pretty quick," he said. "We didn't get the job done tonight. We got beat. Now it's just getting ready for Friday. I don't think there's anything to talk about or any reason to analyze it. Now, we just have to get ready for Friday."

On the one-year anniversary of Messier's guarantee, the Rangers were assured of a Game 4. Nothing more.

Only two teams in NHL history have ever rebounded from a three-games-to-none deficit. The first was the 1942 Toronto Maple Leafs, who swept the final four from the Detroit Red Wings to win the Stanley Cup. The second was the 1975 Islanders, who rallied to shock the Pittsburgh Penguins, including a defenseman named Colin Campbell.

"It's the opportunity to do something great," Campbell told his skeptical team at its noon meeting before an optional practice. "I was as scared and afraid as at any time in the playoffs last year when we went up 3–0 on Washington and lost Game 4 down there. But before we get to that point, we have to win the first period next game. We need twenty guys playing flawless hockey. It's like tennis. Just hit the ball over the net."

The Flyers broke the Rangers' serve again. Two goals by Dykhuis gave them the same 2–0 lead they took out of the first period of Game 3. When Renberg made it 3–0 at 12:29 of the second, Elton John's "Funeral for a Friend" floated over the loudspeakers.

Campbell tried using left wing Mark Osborne, who didn't play in Games 1 and 2, to shadow Lindros. That's how desperate Campbell was to find a Ranger with a pulse and an ounce of adrenaline left. Semenov made it 4–0 at 14:22 of the second period, before Osborne provided faint hope with a goal thirty-nine seconds before the second intermission.

Messier hardly played in the third period after taking a slash on the wrist. Lindros, LeClair, and Renberg eased up on their beleaguered foes, which rendered the scoreless third period meaningless. The half-empty Garden sat silent until 2:30 remained when a chant of "Let's Go, Rangers" started in the blue seats and floated down toward the ice. For thirty seconds it built, then quieted.

Play stopped with 44.3 seconds left, and the ten thousand fans remaining in the arena stood and cheered. The swift and painful sweep ended with a 4–1 Flyer verdict as decisive as the 5–2 result two days earlier.

When it ended, Messier was the first to line up and congratulate the victorious Flyers. Lowe was the second. Messier shook hands with every Flyer, waved to the crowd a step before he left the ice, strode down the runway to the dressing room, and was gone. The Stanley Cup champion Rangers were through.

Aftermath

12

The 1994 Rangers won their Cup and earned their banner on Flag Day. The 1995 Rangers said goodbye at Rye on Memorial Day.

The players all took physicals. They stuffed shirts, hats, and pucks into huge black garbage bags. They packed full sets of gear into square blue equipment bags. They taped six or ten sticks into manageable stacks and threw them into the back of their sport-utility vehicles for the long rides home to Ontario, Quebec, or Saskatchewan.

Those who had homes in New York, or those who were staying behind for surgery or more medical tests, moved at a more leisurely pace. They autographed sticks for each other, exchanged phone numbers and addresses. Messier hid his bloodshot eyes behind dark, dark glasses and tried not to fall over. He was drunk, too drunk to talk to reporters that day.

His teammates were left to explain why they didn't keep their end of a hoped-for semifinal rematch with the Devils, why it was harder to defend the Stanley Cup than it was to win it the first time.

Leetch: "I don't think it was any harder to defend. Certainly no harder than winning it the first time."

Healy: "During the course of the season, we had difficulty in dealing with the success of winning the Stanley Cup. Mike would have had the exact same difficulties with this team as Colie did. Pat Riley talks about it in his book, the team covenant, the commitment. When you have success like we had last year, sometimes maybe you don't deal with that success effectively. Last year, a player might be willing to dump the puck in, have no turnovers. With the success of winning the Cup, a player might not dump the puck in. 'Hey, we won the Cup. I'm going to carry it in.' You sometimes forget what hard work—not forget, but you're constantly being challenged by personal agendas and team agendas. Sometimes they conflict. Life has a way of reaching out and biting you in the ass."

Richter: "I don't think there's one reason. It's a lot of things that cause you to fall short. Ultimately you have to come to battle and play a little harder than we did. Play more as a group. I fell short of what I had hoped for, what I expected out of myself."

Graves: "Anytime you get through being successful, you have to go back to the drawing board. Personally, and as a team, we didn't achieve the level we had set for ourselves. We had high expectations. When you factor in that other teams are ready for you when you're the champions, it's that much harder. Teams are using you as their measuring stick."

Beukeboom: "Who knows? You can start by saying there were changes in personnel. You could say there were too many distractions. Maybe we got ourselves in a hole and before we knew it, we couldn't get out. To be successful in the playoffs, it's hard to be the eighth seed, always playing the top seed of whoever's remaining. In general, we just didn't play well as a team."

Kovalev: "I don't know. It just happened. Another team is better than us, that's all."

Nedved: "Our playoffs started much earlier than a lot of teams' did. Our last 10, 12 games, every game was like a playoff game. We played well in the first round, but our gas tanks kind of ran out in the second round."

Matteau: "Any excuses are good now. Every time I look at my ring, I feel proud that I helped the team win one series. But to feel a part of [Ranger history], no. It's all over. I'm glad it happened. But what I'm thinking about now is the shitty year I've had and the tough playoffs. After being a hero—I don't want to say I've become a zero, but not being effective out there really hurt. I'm very pissed off at myself. I wanted to have the best year of my career. I played my option year. Everybody was kissing my ass, almost. And it was the most disappointing year of my career."

Sufficiently sober two afternoons after Breakup Day, Messier sat at a corner table at one of his favorite Upper West Side restaurants, Isabella's.

He sipped iced tea with lemon from a tall glass and explained why the tanks were empty before the Flyer series began.

"The Quebec series took a lot out of us. I don't think we were a better team, I think we just used all our resources by then. They were inexperienced. They got into the macho thing, which is the worst thing a team can do in the playoffs. Without the experience of last year, I don't think we would have even beaten Quebec in the first round. When you can play the kind of hockey every other day like we played last year to win the Cup, you get yourself mentally ready for a two-month grind.

"But five months of playing that kind of hockey—no way. But that's what happened to us. The second half of the year is when your conditioning, and—mentally, you get geared up for the playoffs. You get to rest, not by sitting out, but by lightening the load. We weren't geared up for the playoffs this year, we were just surviving to make the playoffs. So we went into the playoffs with a whole other mind-set."

By the 1996 All-Star Game in January, the Rangers will have to decide whether to exercise the $6 million option for 1996–97 on Messier's contract. He ended the 1995 season as he started it: the Rangers' best forward, their leader, their nucleus. Could he anchor another Cup run next year or the year after, or will Smith have to rebuild?

"They can win the Cup without me. And that's what they have to start thinking about. This team has the best nucleus in the whole friggin' league. I've been trying to get that across to people, and that's what I'm doing now with Leetch and Richter, Zubov and Kovalev. Gravy has to lead, Leetchie, [they're] the nucleus of the team. Sooner or later they're gonna have to look past me. They have to be confident that they can win a Stanley Cup here in five years, or whatever. And they can. I'm telling you, I've been around the league, I've seen a lot. The players they have here not only are great hockey players, but they have quality guys who love to play and want to win."

Messier admitted to one more dream: playing again beside his best friend.

In 1987, Ranger GM Phil Esposito offered Pocklington an ungodly sum—it was rumored to be as high as $25 million—for Gretzky. A year later, Gretzky became a King. Three years later, Messier became a Ranger. It taught both superstars that anything can happen.

"The way the cards were played out, I was meant to come to L.A.," said Gretzky, who has publicly stated he wants to finish his career with the Kings. "I was meant to do what I could do to help this organization. Obviously it was meant for Mark to go to New York. In a lot of ways, he was better for New York than I would have been, because Mark wears his heart on his sleeve and people in New York love that. I'm not saying I don't; I'm as honest as I can be. But there's something really special about Mark, and New York's a special place. Not that I wouldn't have fit in, but he was the right guy for that city and I think I'm the right guy for L.A., for some strange reason. We're proud that we're at opposite ends of the country to try and help sell the sport."

Messier discussed what Gretzky can't, that Gretzky's competitive fire needs rekindling. If the Kings don't rebuild, and they are one of the league's weakest franchises on and off the ice, will Gretzky remain content after his contract expires following the 1995–96 season? Messier chuckled.

"If you think he's done playing unbelievable hockey you're crazy," Messier said. "He needs to be with players who can do something, and do things for him like in Edmonton."

Messier knows the Rangers haven't considered the possibility, and he hasn't brought it up. Fitting another multimillion-dollar contract into a budget already bulging with a $6 million deal on a team that doesn't have any extra seats to sell won't be easy. Messier knows that. "But there's always ways to do things," he said.

For a full week after his first season as an NHL head coach ended, the same pitiless nightmare shook Campbell from his sleep. "I've got to somehow defeat this thing and get it out of my system. I've got to ask Scotty Bowman or Roger [Neilson], 'Can you leave it at the rink? Can you leave it alone?' I have to find out because I've dreamt that there's one more game in the Philadelphia series, and I have a chance to do something different I didn't do. I'm wondering if I'd put Danny Lacroix in at center, or if I'd change the system we were using. And then I wake up.

"Last year, I woke up two nights after the last Vancouver game, after Game 7, in a sweat. I was asleep on the couch and I grabbed the tape. I was looking for one more thing, even after we won. I've got to be aging at night, this year more than last year. I wake up in the morning with a body odor from sweating."

Campbell gained and kept the respect of his players. He forged a fine balance with Messier. He remained loyal to the Stanley Cup champions long after their defense of the Cup was tarnished by the seven-game losing streak—too loyal. He stood behind Richter long after it became evident that the goalie who stopped the world in 1994 couldn't do it again in 1995.

Campbell needed two pain-killing shots this season, one at the beginning of the year, one late in the year, for tendinitis in his right elbow. He got it from clasping his hands too tightly over his head when he slept.

"I don't know how you do this, but if I had to do it all over again: how do you turn your back on loyalty, on a guy who won you the Cup? We did it last year to the guys who took us to the Presidents' Trophy; on March 8, we took some of those guys and shipped them out, told them they couldn't win the Cup for us, so adios. How do Tony Amonte and Mike Gartner feel? But we felt we had to win.

"Maybe I should have been like Winston Churchill, when he was planning D-Day. He couldn't tell his people in a town in northern England to cover up and look out even though he knew the Germans were bombing them, because then the Germans would know the British had tapped into their communications system. Churchill had to let some of his people get killed. He had to lose the battle to win the war."

He never said he planned to define loyalty differently in 1995–96. He said he hoped to map out a season designed to ease the pain of the one he had just left.

"If there's anything good you can secure out of losing four straight, now we have a springboard to launch ourselves off of. Next year we have a mission again. We were embarrassed. I was embarrassed. We have to make sure we do react to this season. And that we don't overreact to this season."

A deal with the devilish coach for a season of personal hell and professional ecstasy . . . Tikkanen and Lidster for Nedved, which settled the sordid Keenan Affair but proved a disappointment . . . Gartner for Anderson, which left nothing a year later . . . Marchant for MacTavish, which left nothing as well . . . . Amonte for Matteau and Noonan, two forwards who had terrible years . . . A 22-23-3 season and a demoralizing four-game sweep in the second round . . .

Would he do it all again? It was a nasty question to be asking fewer than twelve hours after the Rangers' reign had ended, but Neil Smith didn't mind. He had already rehearsed the answer in April, when it looked as if the 1994 Stanley Cup champions wouldn't even get a chance to defend.

"When I got here in 1989, all I heard was, 'Please, please, Mr. Smith, end our misery.' I came in with the idea that it takes four or five or six years to build a Stanley Cup winner from scratch, and we had better than scratch when I got here. And then I get to New York and learn that it's not just about building for the future, but it's also about entertainment, and making sure you're the best at everything because New York always has to be the best at everything. And it was about making the fans a part of it, and letting them know we were doing it for them.

"And so we did it. We got the coach I knew was going to make everybody miserable because he gave us the best chance of delivering the miracle. And we won the Cup. We buried The Curse. And then it was 1995 and all of a sudden we had to do it again, although it was a short summer, we had a lockout, and the honeymoon would not end.

"Would I do it all again? Fuckin' right I would."

Epilogue

Campbell was encouraged by the Devils' Stanley Cup championship, and especially their grueling six-game semifinal triumph over the Flyers. That series proved that the Flyers' top-heavy roster could be beaten by a team with more depth, greater speed, and superior goaltending. It reaffirmed his belief that the two best teams in hockey were the ones who met in the epic 1994 semifinal series. After he divided his players into two categories, reliable and unreliable, the coach begged Smith to reduce the list of unreliables. One player in that group was Petr Nedved, who hadn't convinced Campbell he belonged.

Mike Keenan's St. Louis Blues made a first-round exit from the playoffs, which made Smith's summer more tolerable, but the job of retooling the roster for another serious run at the Cup in 1995–96 left him little time to relax.

- On July 19, he signed free-agent center Ray Ferraro to a three-year, $4.8 million contract. That gave the Rangers a bonafide number two scoring center, and Smith the flexibility to trade Nedved.
- On August 2, the GM signed free-agent right wing Wayne Presley for two years and $1.5 million to replace Brian Noonan, who in July had signed with St. Louis for two years and $1.8 million.

- On August 24, he signed free-agent defenseman Bruce Driver, the former Devil, for three years and $4.6 million. That move, signing a two-way defenseman who was proficient on the power play, enabled him to close a blockbuster deal he had been working on all summer.
- On August 31, the GM made Campbell a happy man. He dealt Nedved and Sergei Zubov to Pittsburgh for high-scoring left wing Luc Robitaille and defensive defenseman Ulf Samuelsson, one of the NHL's meanest players.

With two top lines like Graves-Messier-Verbeek and Robitaille-Ferraro-Kovalev, and two defense pairs like Leetch-Beukeboom and Driver-Samuelsson, Smith improved his lineup without opening any holes. Campbell began training camp on September 8 believing the Rangers had enough talent to reclaim the Cup.

"More so than the team we started last season with," he said. "I still think we have to make changes. I don't know when, and hopefully we won't. But jobs have to be done that didn't get done last year. We all had credit cards last year. They've all been recalled. Mine, too. This year there'll be no credit cards."

About the Author

Barry Meisel, thirty-seven, the *New York Daily News*'s award-winning investigative sports reporter, has also covered the Rangers, Islanders, Devils, and Giants for the *News*, where he has worked since 1985. He wrote his first book, *Boss: The Mike Bossy Story*, with the Hockey Hall of Famer in 1988. The Brooklyn, New York, native lives with his wife, Katy, son, David, and daughter, Jessica, in Warren, New Jersey.